Building Websites with VB.NET and DotNetNuke 4

A practical guide to creating and maintaining your own
DotNetNuke website, and developing new modules
and skins

Daniel N. Egan

Michael A. Washington

Steve Valenzuela

BIRMINGHAM - MUMBAI

Building Websites with VB.NET and DotNetNuke 4

First published: October 2006

First reprint: January 2007

Production Reference: 1100107

Published by Packt Publishing Ltd.
32 Lincoln Road
Olton
Birmingham, B27 6PA, UK.

ISBN 1-904811-99-X

www.packtpub.com

Cover Image by www.visionwt.com

Credits

Authors

Daniel N. Egan

Michael A. Washington

Steve Valenzuela

Additional Material

Charles Nurse

Reviewers

Jerry Spohn

Jim Wooley

Development Editor

Douglas Paterson

Technical Editors

Mithil Kulkarni

Bhushan Pangaonkar

Editorial Manager

Dipali Chittar

Indexer

Mithil Kulkarni

Proofreader

Chris Smith

Layouts and Illustrations

Shantanu Zagade

Cover Designer

Shantanu Zagade

About the Authors

Daniel Egan has held a variety of positions in the information technology and engineering fields over the last nine years. Currently, he is a System Development Specialist for Automated Data Processing's Southern California region, working extensively in database applications and web development. Daniel is an MCP and MCSD.

In addition to his development work, he teaches a VB.NET Certification course at California State University, Fullerton as well as serves on its .NET Advisory board. He is also the founder and chief author of Dot Net Doc (`www.DotNetDoc.com`), a .NET and DNN developer resource website built using the DotNetNuke framework. He has written numerous articles on DotNetNuke and the underlying DNN architecture. He is also the founder of the LA/Orange County DNN Usergroup and is currenly working on two DNN-related projects: DNNUsergroup Online (`www.DNNUGOnline.com`), a portal designed to allow usergroups to broadcast their meetings online, and DotNetNuke Radio, a live internet radio show about DotNetNuke.

Michael Washington is a website developer and an ASP.NET, C#, and Visual Basic programmer. He is a DotNetNuke Core member and has been involved with DotNetNuke for over three years. He is the author of numerous DotNetNuke modules and tutorials. He is one of the founding members of the Southern California DotNetNuke Users group (`www.socaldug.org`). He has a son, Zachary, and resides in Los Angeles with his wife Valerie.

Steve Valenzuela is the manager of the University Extended Education (UEE) IT Department at California State University, Fullerton, where he has worked for the last five years. Steve has worked specifically with DotNetNuke for over two years, in that time re-designing and delivering various Extended Education websites on the DotNetNuke portal framework as well as designing and delivering custom modules that support the function of University Extended Education.

Charles Nurse has been developing software for more than 25 years. He is owner of his own consulting business, Keydance Computer Services, and has been a DotNetNuke developer for over three years, the last two years as a Trustee. He was lead developer on the .NET 2 version of DotNetNuke (DNN 4.0).

A native of Bristol, England, he obtained a Bachelor of Arts in Chemistry from Oxford University. In 1978, he moved to Canada to continue his studies at the University of Bristish Columbia where he obtained a Ph.D. (also in Chemistry), and where he met his wife Eileen. More recently (2003) he completed a Post Baccalaureate Certificate in Object Technology Programming at Simon Fraser University.

He is in the process of developing his own DotNetNuke Developer Resource site (www.dnndevzone.com) where he will be providing articles for developing for and with DotNetNuke.

He lives in Langley, BC, Canada with his wife and two children, both students at Simon Fraser University.

About the Reviewers

Jerry Spohn has been working with computers since the age of 11, at which he first began learning programming on a Commodore VIC 20. Times have changed, and he moved through the interesting world of IBM mainframes into PCs. After taking numerous courses on database design, programming, and object-oriented methodologies, he moved into Visual Basic and other Microsoft languages.

Jerry currently works as a Development Manager for a medium-sized software company in Pennsylvania. He also manages over 25 different websites using DotNetNuke, and is the owner of Spohn Software LLC, which does custom development across the entire Microsoft development toolset.

Jim Wooley began working on portals by building his own engine base on XML and XSLT. Just as he was about to release it, the IBuySpy Portal was released.

Promptly dumping his custom solution, he has been working on extending and deploying a number of IBuySpy and DotNetNuke portals. He is always striving to stay at the forefront of technology and enjoys the thrill of a new challenge. In addition, he attempts to pass on the insights he has gained by being active in the community, including leading the Atlanta VB Study Group and serving as INETA NorAm Membership Manager for the Georgia region.

Table of Contents

Introduction

DotNetNuke is a free, open-source evolution of Microsoft's celebrated ASP.NET reference implementation, the IBuySpy portal solution kit. DotNetNuke began life as a framework for constructing data-driven intranet and Internet portal applications, and has now developed into an advanced **web content management system** with tools to manage a dynamic and interactive data-driven website. The DotNetNuke portal framework allows you to quickly create a fully featured community-driven website, complete with standard modules, user registration, and integrated security. This free open-source application puts a staggering range of functionality into your hands, and, either by using it as is or by customizing it to your requirements, you are giving your projects a great head start.

Supported and tested by thousands of developers in the DotNetNuke community across the world, the DotNetNuke framework, on one hand, offers you the luxury of a well-tested and proven architecture, and on the other, the ability to manage your site through an easy web-based administration system.

The book is structured to help you understand, implement, and extend the DotNetNuke framework; it will take you inside DotNetNuke, allowing you to harness its power for easily creating your own websites.

What This Book Covers

Chapter 1 introduces DotNetNuke (DNN) and discusses the meaning and purpose of web portals, and the common aspects of successful web portals. It looks at different types of open-source web portals, and discusses why we selected DotNetNuke for this book. We then meet our fictional client Coffee Connections and, using user stories, gather the requirements needed to build this client's site.

In *Chapter 2* we see how to install a local version of DotNetNuke with Microsoft SQL Server and SQL Server 2005 Express, and cover setting the required permissions on your machine to run DNN properly.

In *Chapter 3* we cover users, roles, and pages. Users are the individuals who visit or administer your portal, and their power depends on the roles that they have been assigned. We discuss how each page of your portal can be administered differently, laying the foundation for the rest of the book. From defining users, to registration, to security roles, this chapter will help you to begin administering a DNN portal.

In *Chapter 4* we cover the standard modules that come pre-packaged with DotNetNuke. We cover their basic uses as well as situations they may be used in. You will use these modules to build your portal's content.

Chapter 5 introduces the administrative functions available to the host and admin logins. These are special logins that have access to all areas of your portal, and are used to secure your site and make changes to its content. This chapter takes you through the tools to make sure you are comfortable with all that is available to you.

Understanding the core architecture of DNN is essential if you want to extend the system or even modify the existing code. In *Chapter 6* we learn how the DotNetNuke framework builds the pages, and the major classes that drive it.

In *Chapters 7* and *8* we take the knowledge we learned in the last chapter and use it to build a custom module. You will learn everything you need to know to start building your own modules so you can extend the capabilities of your portal. After creating your user controls, you will create your data access and business logic layers. In *Chapter 8* you will learn about the DotNetNuke **Data Access Layer** (**DAL**) and the **DAL+**, which take much of the routine work out creating custom modules. We finish our look at development by seeing how to package your module for distribution.

Chapter 9 talks about skins. A skin is the outer layer of your site, and defines the look and feel of the portal. In this chapter we design a custom skin for the Coffee Connections site. You will learn the skills needed to skin both your portal and your module containers.

When you finally have your portal the way you want it to look and function, you are ready to deploy it, and that is what *Chapter 10* shows you how to do. The chapter advises on what you should look for in a web host and helps to steer you clear of common deployment mistakes.

In *Chapter 11* we show you how to take advantage of one of the most exciting features of DotNetNuke: **multiple portals**. These are additional portals that use the same underlying database, but can contain different content. So instead of just having one website, you can create as many as you need using just one DotNetNuke installation. From parent portals to child portals, this chapter gives you the information necessary to create new portals from scratch or to use the new template structure built into the framework.

What You Need for Using This Book

This book has been written both for the beginner wanting to set up a website and also for ASP.NET developers with a grasp of VB.NET. No prior knowledge of DotNetNuke is assumed. To work with the DotNetNuke code, you will need access to Visual Studio .NET 2005 or Visual Web Developer 2005 Express.

This book uses the DotNetNuke open-source project available from `http://www.DotNetNuke.com`. To install and run DotNetNuke, you will need:

- The .NET Framework 2.0
- One of Windows Server 2003, Windows 2000, or Windows XP operating systems
- An installation of SQL Server 2005 or SQL Server 2005 Express Edition
- Visual Web Developer 2005 Express

You can download SQL Server 2005 Express Edition for free from `http://msdn.microsoft.com/vstudio/express/sql/download/`. Visual Web Developer 2005 Express can be downloaded for free from `http://msdn.microsoft.com/vstudio/express/vwd/download/`.

Conventions

In this book, you will find a number of styles of text that distinguish between different kinds of information. Here are some examples of these styles, and an explanation of their meaning.

There are three styles for code. Code words in text are shown as follows: "We then use the Add method of this object to add an item to the menu ".

A block of code will be set as follows:

```
Label1.Text = "Hello World!"
            Throw New Exception("Something didn't work right.")
        Catch exc As Exception
            Exceptions.ProcessModuleLoadException(Me, exc)
```

When we wish to draw your attention to a particular part of a code block, the relevant lines or items will be made bold:

```
Label1.Text = "Hello World!"
            Throw New Exception("Something didn't work right.")
        Catch exc As Exception
            Exceptions.ProcessModuleLoadException(Me, exc)
        End Try
```

New terms and **important words** are introduced in a bold-type font. Words that you see on the screen, in menus or dialog boxes for example, appear in our text like this: "clicking the **Next** button moves you to the next screen".

 Tips, suggestions, or important notes appear in a box like this.

Reader Feedback

Feedback from our readers is always welcome. Let us know what you think about this book, what you liked or may have disliked. Reader feedback is important for us to develop titles that you really get the most out of.

To send us general feedback, simply drop an email to feedback@packtpub.com, making sure to mention the book title in the subject of your message.

If there is a book that you need and would like to see us publish, please send us a note in the **SUGGEST A TITLE** form on www.packtpub.com or email suggest@packtpub.com.

If there is a topic that you have expertise in and you are interested in either writing or contributing to a book, see our author guide on www.packtpub.com/authors.

Customer Support

Now that you are the proud owner of a Packt book, we have a number of things to help you to get the most from your purchase.

Downloading the Example Code for the Book

Visit http://www.packtpub.com/support, and select this book from the list of titles to download any example code or extra resources for this book. The files available for download will then be displayed.

 The downloadable files contain instructions on how to use them.

Errata

Although we have taken every care to ensure the accuracy of our contents, mistakes do happen. If you find a mistake in one of our books—maybe a mistake in text or code—we would be grateful if you could report this to us. By doing this you can save other readers from frustration, and also help to improve subsequent versions of this book.

If you find any errata, report them by visiting http://www.packtpub.com/support, selecting your book, clicking on the **Submit Errata** link, and entering the details of your errata. Once your errata have been verified, your submission will be accepted and the errata added to the list of existing errata. The existing errata can be viewed by selecting your title from http://www.packtpub.com/support.

Questions

You can contact us at questions@packtpub.com if you are having a problem with some aspect of the book, and we will do our best to address it.

1

What is DotNetNuke?

From company intranets to mom and pop shops to local chapters of the 4H club, most organizations are looking to have a presence on the World Wide Web. Open-source web portals answer this demand by providing easy-to-install-and-use websites that are not only extremely functional but also free. Whether it is to sell services or to have a place to meet, web portals play an important part in communications on the Web.

In this chapter, we will first discuss what web portals are and what successful web portals have in common. We will explore different types of open-source web portals and discuss why we selected DotNetNuke for our project over other available portals. In addition, we will cover the benefits gained by using an established program as a framework and the benefits of DotNetNuke specifically. We will then introduce Coffee Connections, our fictional client. We will get a brief overview of Coffee Connections, determine the specific requirements for its website, and gather the requirements using user stories. This will give you a general overview of what to expect from this book and how to best use it depending on your role and experience with web portals and Visual Basic .NET.

Open-Source Web Portals

So what does it actually mean to have a web portal? We begin the chapter with an explanation of what a portal is, and then go on to the features of a web portal and reasons for selecting open-source web portals.

What is a Web Portal?

You have decided to start a portal and first need to find out what makes a web portal. Does throwing up a few web pages with links to different topics make it a web portal? A portal, in its most basic sense, aims to be an entry point to the World Wide Web. Portals will typically offer services such as search engines, links to useful pages, news, forums, and email, all in an effort to draw users to their site. In most cases, portals provide these services free in the hope that users will make the site their home page or at least come back often. Successful examples include Yahoo! and MSN. These sites are horizontal portals because they typically attract a wide audience and primarily exist to produce advertising income for their owners. Other web portals may focus on a specific group of users or be part of a corporate intranet. They will most often concentrate on one particular subject, like gardening or sports. This type of portal is a vertical portal because they focus inward and cater to a selected group of people.

The type of portal you create depends on the target audience you are trying to attract. You may discover that the portal you create is a combination of both horizontal and vertical portals in order to address specific needs, while simultaneously giving a broader range of services to your visitors. Whatever type of portal you decide on, horizontal or vertical, they both will share certain key characteristics and functionality that guarantee users will return to your site.

Common Portal Features

What makes a great portal? Is it a free prize giveaway, local weather forecasts, or sports scores for the teams you watch? While this package of extras might attract some users, you will certainly miss a large group of people who have no interest in these offerings. There are as many web portals to choose from as programming languages they are written in. However, one thing is for certain: there are particular services your portal should incorporate in order for it to be successful and attract a wide audience.

- **A Gateway to the World Wide Web**: Web portals are the way we start our day. Most of us have set up our home page to one web portal or another and whether you start at MSN, Yahoo!, or Apple, you will notice some common features. Local weather forecasts, movie reviews, or even maps of your community are a few features that make the web portal feel comfortable and tailored for you. Like reading the morning newspaper with a cup of coffee, it gives you a sense of home. Web portals attempt to be the place where all of your browsing starts.

- **Content Management**: Content management has come a long way from the days of paper memos and sticky notes. Computers have done away with the overflowing file cabinets holding copies of every document that crossed our desks. Little did we realize that even though we would be solving one problem, another one would rise in its place. How many times have you searched your computer wondering where you saved the document your boss needs right now? Then once you find it, you need to make sure that it is the correct version. Alternatively, if you run a Soccer Club, how do you ensure that all of your players can get a copy of the league rules? One of the commonest uses for a web portal is content management. It allows users to have one place to upload, download, and search for a file that is important to them or their company. It also alleviates the problem of having more than one copy of a document. If the document is stored only in one location, you will always have the current copy.

- **Community Interaction**: People have always found a place to meet. From the malt shop on Main Street to your local church, people like to find others who have the same interests. This is one of the main drawing powers of a web portal. Whether you are a Christian looking for other Christians (`http://www.christianwebsite.com/`) or someone who is interested in **Personal Digital Assistants (PDAs)** (`http://www.pdabuzz.com`) there is a web portal out there for you. Web portals offer different ways for users to communicate. Among these are discussion forums that allow you to either post a question or comment to a message board or comment on the posts of others. Chat rooms take this a step further with the ability to talk to one or more persons "live" and have your questions answered immediately.
  One of the most interesting ways to express your opinions or communicate your ideas to others on a web portal is to use a **blog**. A blog (also known as a weblog) is sort of like a diary on the Web, except you do not lock it when you are done writing in it. Instead, you make all your thoughts and observations available to the world. These blogs range in topic from personal and comical (`http://weblog.herald.com/column/davebarry/`) to technical (`http://weblogs.asp.net/scottgu`) and, in recent years, have exploded on the scene as the de facto way to communicate on the Internet. Most web portals will offer at least one of these ways to communicate.

- **Security & Administration**: Web portal security not only manages who can access particular sections of the site but also enables administrators to access, add, and change content on the site. Most web portals use a **WYSIWYG** (what you see is what you get) style editor that allows users to add and edit content without needing to know programming or HTML. It is as simple as adding content to a text file. Having users authenticate with the portal allows you to tailor the site to individuals so that they can customize their experience.

Why DotNetNuke?

When the time comes to decide how you want to build your portal, you will have to make many decisions: Do I create my portal from scratch? If not, which web portal framework should I use? What type of hardware and software do I have available to me? Moreover, what is my skill level in any particular platform? In this section, we will discuss some of the better-known portals that are available.

For our portal, we have decided that it would be counter-productive to start from scratch. Instead, we will be using an already developed framework in designing our portal. We will have many options from which to select. We will discuss a few of our options and determine why we believe DotNetNuke fits us best.

PHP-Nuke

Most likely the grandfather of DotNetNuke (in name at least) is PHP-Nuke (http://www.phpnuke.org). PHP-Nuke is a web portal that uses **PHP** (a recursive acronym for Hypertext Preprocessor) pages to create dynamic web pages. You can use it in a Windows environment but it is most comfortable in a Linux/Unix environment. PHP is an open-source, HTML-embedded scripting language, which is an alternative to Microsoft's **ASP** (**Active Server Pages**) the precursor to ASP.NET, which is the programming language used in DotNetNuke. PHP-Nuke, like DotNetNuke, is a modular system that comes with pre-built standard modules and allows you to enhance the portal by creating custom modules. Since we will be using a Windows platform, and are more comfortable using ASP.NET, this choice would not fit our needs.

Metadot

Metadot Portal Server is another open-source portal system available to those looking to create a web portal. Metadot states that "its user friendly environment" allows non-technical individuals to create powerful websites with just a "few clicks of the mouse". Like PHP-Nuke, Metadot runs primarily on the Linux operating system (although, it supports Windows as well), Apache web server, and a MySQL database. It uses Perl as its scripting language. For the same reasons as PHP-Nuke, this framework will not fit our needs.

Rainbow

Similar to DotNetNuke, the Rainbow project is an open-source initiative to build a CMS (content management system) based on the IBuySpy portal using Microsoft's ASP.NET. In contrast to DotNetNuke, the Rainbow Project used the C# implementation of IBuySpy as its starting point. It does run on Windows and uses ASP.NET, but our language of choice for this project is VB.NET so we will rule out Rainbow.

DotNetNuke

So why did we select DotNetNuke as the web portal of choice for this book? Well here are a few reasons for selecting DotNetNuke:

- **Open-source web portal written in VB.NET:** Since we wanted to focus on building our web portal using the new VB.NET language, this was an obvious choice. DotNetNuke was born out of a best-practice application called IBuySpy. This application, developed for Microsoft by Scott Stanfield and his associates at Vertigo Software, was created to highlight the many things that .NET was able to accomplish. It was supposed to be an application for developers to use and learn the world of .NET. IBuySpy was an application by the original author of DotNetNuke (formerly IBuySpy Workshop), Shaun Walker of Perpetual Motion Interactive Systems Inc. He originally released DotNetNuke 1.0 as an open-source project in December 2002. Since then DotNetNuke has evolved to version 4.x and the code base has grown from 10,000 to over 120,000 lines of managed code and contains many feature enhancements over the original IBuySpy Starter Kit.

- **Utilizes the new ASP.NET 2.0 Provider Model**: With the release of ASP.NET version 2.0, Microsoft debuted a new provider pattern model. This pattern gives the developer the ability to separate the data tier from the presentation tier and provide the ability to specify your choice of databases. The DotNetNuke framework comes pre-packaged with an SQL Data Provider (Microsoft's SQL Server, MSDE, or SQLExpress). You can also follow this model to create your own data provider or obtain one from a third-party vendor. In addition, the DotNetNuke framework also uses many of Microsoft's building-block services like the **Data Access Application Block** for .NET (http://www.microsoft.com/downloads/details.aspx?FamilyID=F63D1F0A-9877-4A7B-88EC-0426B48DF275&displaylang=en) introduced by Microsoft in its Patterns and Practices articles.

- **Contains key portal features expected from a web portal**: DotNetNuke comes pre-packaged with modules that cover discussions, events, links, news feeds, contact, FAQs, announcements, and more. This gives you the ability to spend your time working on specialized adaptations to your site. In addition to this, the DotNetNuke core team has created sub-teams to maintain and enhance these modules.

- **Separates page layout, page content, and the application logic**: This allows you to have a designer who can manage the "look and feel" of the site, an administrator with no programming experience who can manage and change the content of the site, and a developer who can create custom functionality for the site.

- **Ability to "skin" your site**: Separating the data tier from the presentation tier brings us to one of the most exciting advancements in recent versions of DotNetNuke, *skinning*. DotNetNuke employs an advanced skinning solution that allows you to change the look and feel of your site. In this book, we will show you how to create your own custom skin, but you will also find many custom skins free on websites like core team member Nina Meiers' eXtra Dimensions Design Group (`http://www.xd.com.au`), and Snowcovered (`http://www.snowcovered.com`). These give you the ability to change the look and feel of your site without having to know anything about design, HTML, or programming.

- **Supports multiple portals**: Another advantage of using DotNetNuke as your web portal of choice is the fact that you can run multiple portals using one code base and one database. This means you can have different portals for different groups on the same site but still have all of the information reside in one database. This gives you an advantage in the form of easy access to all portal information, and a central place to manage your hosting environment. The framework comes with numerous tools for banner advertising, site promotion, hosting, and affiliate management.

- **Designed with an extensible framework**: You can extend the framework in a number of ways. You can modify the core architecture of the framework to achieve your desired results (we will discuss the pratfalls of doing this in later chapters) and design custom modules that "plug in" to the existing framework. This would be in addition to the pre-built modules that come with DotNetNuke. These basic modules give you a great starting point and allow you to get your site up and running quickly.

- **Mature portal framework**: As of the writing of this book, DotNetNuke is on version 4.2. It means that you will be using an application that has gone through its paces. It has been extensively tested and is widely used as a web portal application by thousands of existing users. What this affords you is stability. You can be comfortable knowing that thousands of websites already use the DotNetNuke framework for their web portal needs.

- **Active and robust community**: Community involvement and continuing product evolution are very important parts of any open-source project and DotNetNuke has both of these. The DotNetNuke support forum is one of the most active and dynamic community forums on the ASP.NET website. There are currently over 280,000 users registered on the DotNetNuke website. At the time of writing, the much-anticipated DotNetNuke version 4.2 had just been released, and has brought about a significant number of improvements over its previous releases. The core team continues to move forward, always striving towards a better product for the community.

- **Recognized by the Microsoft team as a best-practices application**: In March 2004 at the VSLive conference in San Francisco, the premiere conference for Visual Studio .NET Developers, DotNetNuke 2.0 was officially released, and showcased for the public. This gave DotNetNuke a great leg up in the open-source portal market and solidified its position as a leader in the field.

Benefits of Using an Established Program

Whether you are building a website to gather information about your soccer club or putting up a department website on your company's intranet, one thing is certain — to write your web portal from the ground up, you should plan on "coding" for a long time. Just deciding on the structure, design, and security of your site will take you months. After all this is complete, you will still need to test and debug. At this point, you still have not even begun to build the basic functionality of your web portal.

So why start from scratch when you have the ability to build on an existing structure? Just as you would not want to build your own operating system before building a program to run on it, using an existing architecture allows you to concentrate on enhancing and customizing the portal for your specific needs. If you are like me and use Visual Studio to do your development, then you already adhere to this concept. There is no need for you to create the basic building blocks of your application (forms, buttons, textboxes, etc.); instead you take the building blocks already there for you and assemble (and sometimes enhance) them to suit your needs.

The DotNetNuke Community

The DotNetNuke community has one of the most active and dynamic support forums on the ASP.NET website and has over 280,000 users registered on the DotNetNuke website.

Core Team

The core team comprises individuals invited to join the team by Shaun Walker, whom they affectionately call the "Benevolent Dictator". Their invitations were based on their contributions and their never-ending support of others in the DotNetNuke forum. Each team member has a certain area of responsibility based on his or her abilities. From database functionality and module creation to skinning, they are the ones responsible for the continued advancement of the framework. However, not being a member of the core team does not mean that you cannot contribute to the project. There are many ways for you to help with the project. Many developers create custom modules they make freely available to the DotNetNuke community. Other developers create skins they freely distribute. Still others help answer the many questions in the DotNetNuke forum. You can also be a contributor to the core architecture. You are welcome to submit code improvements to extend, and/or expand the capabilities of DotNetNuke. These submissions will be evaluated by the core team and could possibly be added to the next version.

The DotNetNuke Discussion Forum

When the DotNetNuke project started, one of the things that helped to propel forward its popularity was the fact that its forums were housed on the ASP.NET forums website (`http://www.asp.net/forums/showforum.aspx?forumid=90`). With well over 200,000 individual posts in the main DotNetNuke forum alone, it was, and continues to be one of the most active and attentive forums on the ASP.NET forums website (`http://www.asp.net/forums/`). Beginning sometime after the version 3.x release, the DotNetNuke team puts its finishing touches on its own forum module. It now utilizes this module for most new DotNetNuke questions (`http://www.dotnetnuke.com/tabid/795/Default.aspx`). In both forums, you will find help for any issue you may be having in DotNetNuke.

The main forum is where you will find most of the action, but there are also sub-forums covering topics such as Core Framework, Resources, Getting Started, and Custom Modules. You can search and view posts in any of the forums but will need to register if you want to post your own questions or reply to other users' posts. The great thing about the forums is that you will find the core team hanging out there. Who better to answer questions about DotNetNuke than those who created it? However, do not be shy, if you know the answer to someone else's question feel free to post an answer. That is what the community is all about: people helping people through challenging situations.

The Bug Tracker

Like any application there are bound to be a few bugs that creep into the application now and then. To manage this occurrence, the DotNetNuke core team uses a third-party bug tracking system called *Gemini*, by CounterSoft. The bug tracker is not for general questions or setup and configuration errors; questions of that nature should be posted in the discussion forum. You can view the status of current bugs at the Gemini site (`http://support.dotnetnuke.com`), but will not be able to add new bugs to the system. Reporting a bug is currently done by posting to the DotNetNuke forum. Follow the guidelines currently posted there (`http://www.asp.net/forums/ShowPost.aspx?tabindex=1&PostID=752638`). To summarize: you need to first search the bug tracker to make sure that it has not already been reported. If you cannot find it in the system you will need to supply the forum with exactly what you did, what you expected to have happen, and what actually happened. Verified bugs will be assigned to core team members to track down and repair.

DotNetNuke Project Roadmap Team

If you want to find out what is in the works for future releases of DotNetNuke then you will want to check out the DotNetNuke Project Roadmap (`http://www.dotnetnuke.com/Development/Roadmap/tabid/616/Default.aspx`). The main purpose of this document is as a communication vehicle to inform users and stakeholders of the project's direction. The Roadmap accomplishes this by using User Stories. User Stories are closely related to Use Cases with the exception that they take the view of a fictitious customer requesting an enhancement. The priority of the enhancements depends on both the availability of resources (core team) and the perceived demand for the feature.

The License Agreement

The license type used by the DotNetNuke project is a modified version of the BSD (Berkeley Software Distribution) license. As opposed to the more restrictive GPL (GNU General Public License) used by many other open-source projects, the BSD license is very permissive and imposes very few conditions on what a user can do with the software; this includes charging clients for binary distributions, with no obligation to include source code. If you have further questions on the specifics of the license agreement, you can find it in the documents folder of the DotNetNuke application or on the DotNetNuke website.

Coffee Connections

Wherever your travels take you, from sunny Long Beach, California, to the cobblestone streets of Hamburg, Germany, chances are that there is a coffee shop nearby. Whether it is a Starbucks (located on just about every corner) or a local coffee shop tucked neatly in between all the antique stores on Main Street, they all have one thing in common, coffee, right? Well yes, they do have coffee in common, but more importantly, they are places for people with shared interests to gather, relax, and enjoy their coffee while taking in the environment around them. Coffee shops offer a wide variety of services in addition to coffee, from WiFi to poetry readings to local bands; they keep people coming back by offering them more than just a cup o' Joe.

But how do you find the coffee shops that have the type of atmosphere you are looking for? In addition, how do you locate them in your surrounding area? That's where Coffee Connections comes in; it is its desire to fill this void by creating a website where coffee lovers and coffee shop regulars can connect and search for coffee shops in their local area that cater to their specific needs. Coffee Connections has a vision to create a website that will bring this together and help promote coffee shops around the world. Users will be able to search for coffee shops by zip code, types of entertainment, amenities, or name. It will also allow its customers to purchase goods online and communicate with others through chat rooms and forums.

Determining Client Needs

In any project, it is important to determine the needs of the client before work begins on the project. When designing a business-driven solution for your client your options range from an extensive **Request for Proposal (RFP)** and case modeling, to user stories and **Microsoft Solutions Framework (MSF)**. To determine the needs and document the requirements of Coffee Connections we will use user stories.

We selected **User Stories** as our requirements collection method for two reasons. First, the DotNetNuke core team uses this method when building enhancements and upgrading the DotNetNuke framework. Thus using user stories will help to give you a better understanding of how the core team works, the processes team members follow, and how they accomplish these tasks in a short amount of time. Second, it is a very clean and concise way to determine the needs of your client. We will be able to determine the needs of Coffee Connections without the need for pages and pages of requirement documents.

What is a User Story?

User stories were originally introduced as part of **Extreme Programming**. Extreme Programming is a type of software development based on simplicity, communication, and customer feedback. It is primarily used within small teams when it is important to develop software quickly while the environment and requirements of the program rapidly change. This fits the DotNetNuke project and the DotNetNuke core team well.

User stories provide a framework for the completion of a project by giving a well-designed description of a system and its major processes.

The individual stories, written by customers, are features they wish the program to possess. Since the user stories are written by the customer, they are written in the customer's terminology and without much technical jargon. The user stories are usually written on index cards and are approximately three sentences long. The limited space for detail forces the writer to be concise and get to the heart of the requirement. When it is time to implement the user story, the developer will sit down with the customer—in what is referred to as an iteration meeting—to go over particular details of each user story. Thus, an overview of a project is quickly conceptualized without the developer or customer being bogged down in minor details.

User stories also help in the creation of **acceptance tests**. Acceptance tests are specified tests performed by the user of a system to determine if the system is functioning correctly according to specifications the user presented at the beginning of the development process. This assures that the product performs as expected.

Advantages of Using User Stories

There are many different methods of defining requirements when building an application, so why use user stories? User stories fit well into **Rapid Application Development (RAD)** programming. Software and the computer industry in general change on a daily basis. The environment is fast moving and in order to compete in the marketplace it is important to have quick turn around for your product. User stories help to accomplish this in the following ways:

- **Stressing the importance of communication**: One of the central ideas behind user stories is the ability to have the users write down what exactly is expected from the product. This helps to promote communication by keeping the client involved in the design process.

- **Being easily understandable**: Since user stories are written by the customer and not by the developer, the developer will not have the problem of "talking over the head" of the customer. User stories help customers know exactly what they are getting because they personally write down what they want in terms that they understand.

- **Allowing for deferred details**: User stories help the customer as well as the developer understand the complete scope of a project without being bogged down by the details.

- **Focusing on project goals**: The success of your project depends less on creative coding strategies and more on whether you were able to meet the customer's goals. It is not what you think it should do but what the customer thinks it should do.

Coffee Connections User Stories

Below you will find the user stories for Coffee Connections. From these stories, we will use DotNetNuke to build the customer's website. The title of the card is followed by a short description of what is needed. Throughout the book, we will refer back to these as we continue to accomplish the project goals for Coffee Connections.

Title	Description
Web Store	Users will be able to purchase coffee and coffee-shop-related merchandise through the website.
Coffee Shop Search	Users will be able to find coffee shops in their area by searching a combination of zip code, coffee shop name, amenities, or atmosphere and rating.
Coffee Finder Additions	Users will be able to post coffee shops they find and give a description of the coffee shop for other users to see.
Coffee Shop Reviews	Users will have the ability to rate the coffee shops that are listed on the website.
Site Updates	Administrators will have the ability to modify the site content easily using a web-based interface.
Coffee Chat	Users will be able to chat with people from other coffee shops on the site.
Coffee Forum	Users will be able to post questions and replies in a Coffee Shop Forum.

When referring back to the user stories later in the book, we will use a card to compare and determine if we have met the customer's needs.

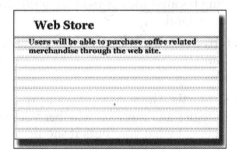

Summary

In this chapter, we have discussed the meaning and purpose of web portals, and what successful web portals have in common, looked at different types of open-source web portals, and discussed why we selected DotNetNuke. We then met our fictional client Coffee Connections, and using user stories, gathered the requirements to build its site.

The next chapter will cover the always-enlightening task of installing the software. We will cover what we need to run DotNetNuke and describe the process of installing the framework.

2
Installing DotNetNuke

In previous versions of DotNetNuke (version 3.0), whether you were a developer or just wanted to set up a quick and easy website, you needed to download the entire code base and install all of it up to your server. While the ability to download the code has not disappeared, the core team also allows you to download a slimmed-down version that only contains the files that are needed to upload and work with a basic DotNetNuke site.

In this chapter, we will cover the steps necessary to set up a non-developer version of the website on your local machine. We will show you how to set up the DotNetNuke portal and database by using Microsoft SQL Server 2005 Express Edition. Finally, we will log in as an administrator and change the default passwords.

Installing DotNetNuke (Local Version)

Before you begin installing DotNetNuke, you will need to determine if you have the .NET 2.0 Framework installed. The easiest way is to browse to the following location `C:\WINDOWS\Microsoft.Net\Framework` and look for a folder that starts with V2.0 (for example: v2.0.50727). If you do not see this folder, then you will have to download the 2.0 version of the .NET Framework. You can find the files at the .NET Framework home site (`http://msdn.microsoft.com/netframework/`). For our examples, we will be using Windows XP Professional, IIS 5.1, and version 2.0 of the .NET Framework.

In this section of the book, we will only be using the Install Package, which only contains the items that are needed to deploy to a web host: we will be using IIS to host our site. **IIS** stands for **Internet Information Services** and is the web server application that will run our web portal. If you have downloaded the Source Package and use Visual Studio 2005 then you do not need IIS to work with DotNetNuke. We will also be using SQL Server 2005 in this discussion. DotNetNuke will work easily with SQLExpress. We will discuss installing and working with the Source Package and SQLExpress when we discuss building custom modules. If you haven't installed IIS then make sure that it is installed prior to the .NET Framework.

Clean Installation

If this is the first time you are installing DotNetNuke, or you do not want to upgrade from a previous version, then you will want to perform a clean installation. This means that you will have to build your DotNetNuke instance from scratch. This chapter will walk you through all the steps necessary to accomplish this task. If you wish to upgrade DotNetNuke from a previous version, please refer to the *Upgrading* section towards the end of the chapter.

Downloading the Code

Before we start installing our web portal, we need to download the source code. Go to the DotNetNuke website `http://www.DotNetNuke.com`. You will be required to register before you can download the code. This step is simple, just click on the **Register** link in the upper right-hand corner, and fill in the required information. Provide a working email address, as the registration process will send an email that includes a verification code.

Once you receive the email you may continue to the DotNetNuke site, log in, and download the code. You will find the DotNetNuke source by clicking on the **Downloads icon**. If you want the documentation that comes with DotNetNuke, you will need to download both the Install Package and the Documentation Package. While the file is downloading, take time to explore what the DotNetNuke site has to offer. You will find information that will help you as you build your portal.

When you are downloading, you will also see a Starter Kit for DotNetNuke. The Starter Kit is used to help Visual Studio Developers work with DotNetNuke. We will discuss this download in the Module Development chapter.

Once you have the Install Package downloaded from the site, you can double-click on the ZIP file to extract its contents. Where you extract the file is entirely up to you. Most of the documentation you come across will assume that you extract it to C:\DotNetNuke so for consistency's sake we will do the same.

Setting Up a Virtual Directory

After you unzip the files, you will need to set up a virtual directory in IIS. If IIS is not already installed on your system, you can install it by going to **Control Panel | Add Remove Programs | Add Remove Windows Components.**

 For more information on installing and using IIS, http://www.IISFaq.com, (which utilizes the DotNetNuke framework for its portal) should suffice.

A virtual directory is a **friendly name**, also called an **alias**, that allows you to separate a physical folder from a web address and defines the application's boundaries. A virtual directory is needed if your files are not located in the home directory. The home directory for IIS is found at C:\Inetpub\wwwroot (if installed at the default location). The virtual directory, or alias name, is used by those accessing your website. It is the name they type in the browser to bring up your portal so select a simple name.

The following table shows examples of mapping between physical folders and virtual directories. As you can see, we will need to set up a virtual directory for DotNetNuke since its location is outside the home directory, in C:\DotNetNuke.

Physical Location	Alias	URL
C:\Inetpub\wwwroot	home directory (none)	http://localhost
\\AnotherServer\ SomeFolder	Customers	http://localhost/Customers
C:\DotNetNuke	DotNetNuke	http://localhost/DotNetNuke
C:\Inetpub\wwwroot\ My WebSite	None	http://localhost/MyWebSite

There are two different ways of setting up the virtual directory:

Using Windows Explorer (the Easy Way)

If you are using Windows XP then the easiest way for you to set up you virtual directory is to go to C:\DotNetNuke, right-click on the folder, and select **Sharing and Security**.

This will open up the **DotNetNuke Properties** dialog. Click on the **Web Sharing** tab and select **Share this folder**.

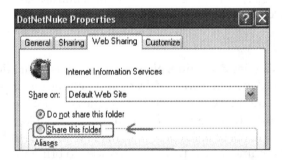

This will present you with the **Edit Alias** dialog box. The dialog box will default to the name of the folder it is in, so if you extracted your file to C:\DotNetNuke, then your virtual directory will be called DotNetNuke. Leave all the default permissions and click **OK** to save the settings.

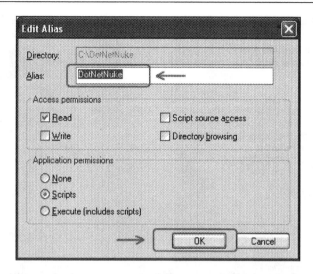

Using the Virtual Directory Creation Wizard

In this first step, you will set up your virtual directory using the **IIS Manager** and the **Virtual Directory Creation Wizard**. You will find the **IIS Manager** in the **Control Panel | Administrative Tools** section. Once you have IIS open, drill down until you see **Default Web Site**, right-click and select **New | Virtual Directory**.

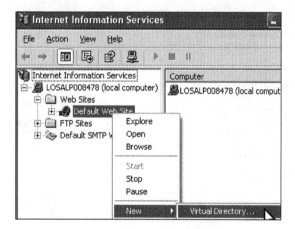

Click **Next** to begin the wizard. Then, enter an alias for your website. Type in **DotNetNuke** and then click **Next**.

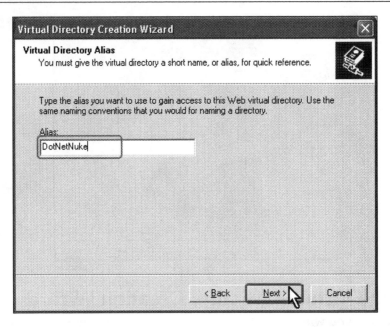

The next dialog box will ask you for the physical location of your DotNetNuke files. This is how IIS matches the virtual directory alias name to the web application files.

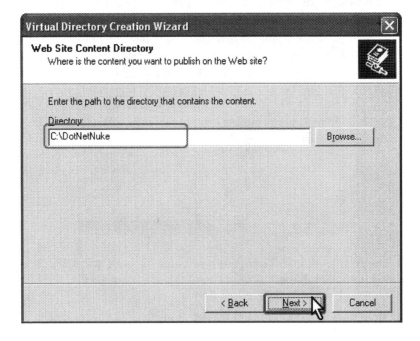

Type C:\DotNetNuke in the **Directory:** field and click **Next**. On the **Access**

Permissions page, leave all the default permissions and click **Next** to save the settings.

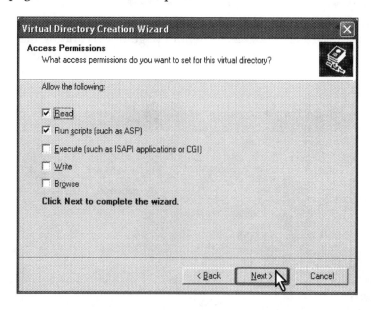

Click **Finish** to exit the wizard.

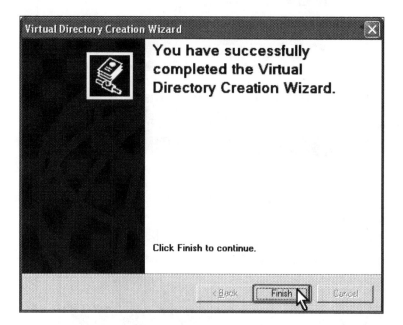

Verifying Default Documents

Default documents allow you to access a web page by typing in just the folder name. DotNetNuke uses `default.aspx` as its default page when running the portal. To ensure `default.aspx` is specified as a default document for your virtual directory, scroll down in IIS until you find the DotNetNuke Virtual Directory. Right-click and select **Properties**.

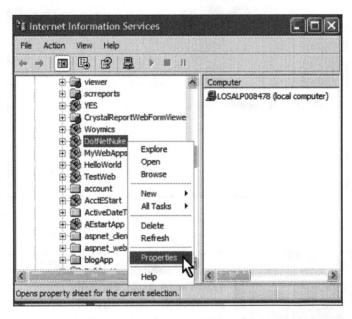

Select the **Documents** tab and confirm that you see `default.aspx` (in addition to `default.asp`) in the box. If you see it, click **OK** to close the properties box.

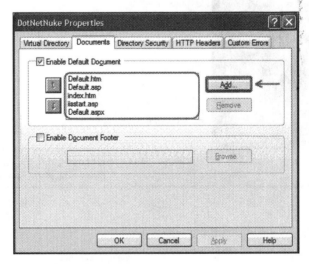

If `default.aspx` does not exist, click on the **Add** button to type it into the **Default Document Name** box and click **OK**. This will successfully complete the setup of the virtual directory for DotNetNuke.

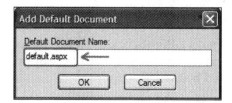

 If you have both versions of the .NET framework (1.x and 2.x) installed on your computer, you will need to tell IIS which framework to use with this website. On the ASP.NET tab you will need to change the ASP.NET version to the 2.x version of the framework as shown below.

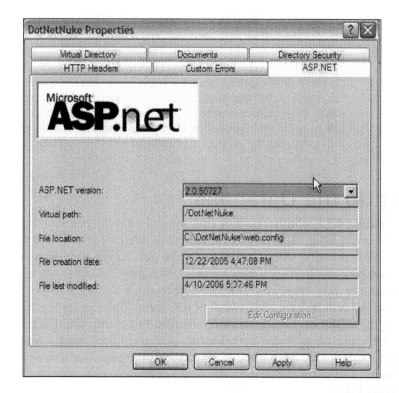

Setting Security Permissions

ASP.NET web applications will usually run using the built-in ASPNET account. To allow the extensive file uploading and skinning features in DotNetNuke, you will have to set some security permissions before they start working correctly. To change these permissions, open up Windows Explorer and browse to your DotNetNuke folder (usually C:\DotNetNuke). Right-click the folder, select **Sharing and Security** from the menu, and click on the **Security** tab. Add the appropriate user account and set permissions as discussed below.

If you are using Windows 2000 (IIS5) the account that needs permissions on the DotNetNuke folder is the {Server}\ASPNET user account, where {Server} is the name of your machine running the DotNetNuke installation. It must have read and write permissions for the DotNetNuke folder. If you are using Windows 2003 (IIS6), then instead of the ASPNET account you will need to give permissions to the NT AUTHORITY\NETWORK SERVICE user account. Again, it must have read and write permissions for the folder. Also, if you use Windows authentication, you need to give the full control permissions to the local user.

On an XP machine formatted to NTFS that is not part of a domain, the security tab may not be visible by default. To reveal the **Security** tab, open Windows Explorer, and choose **Folder Options** from the **Tools** menu. On the **View** tab, scroll to the bottom of the **Advanced Settings** and clear (click) the checkbox next to **Use Simple File Sharing**. Click **OK** to apply the change. You should now have a **Security** tab when viewing the properties of a file on an NTFS volume.

Setting up the Database

With DotNetNuke 4.3.3, you have a few options available to you when creating your database. If you are using SQL Server 2005 Express edition, you do not need to set up the database manually, since the DotNetNuke database will be attached during the installation process. In the *Custom Module Development* chapter we will be using SQLExpress as our datastore. To create the database for DotNetNuke to store data about our site, we will be using Microsoft SQL Server 2005 Express Edition. We will be using the **SQL Server Management Studio** to accomplish this task. For the Management Studio, click on the **Start** button, and go to **Programs | Microsoft SQL Server 2005 | SQL Server Management Studio**. Sign on to your server and drill down the (**local**) server by clicking on the plus (**+**) signs, right-click on **Databases,** and select **New Database**.

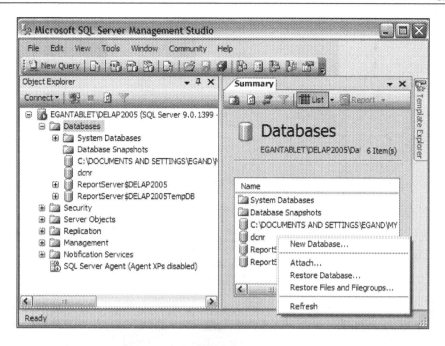

Type DotNetNuke into the **Database name** field and click **OK**.

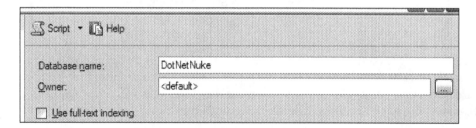

It will take a few moments for your database to be created. This will generate the system tables and stored procedures. The actual tables and procedures needed to run DotNetNuke will be created when you run the program for the first time. Once you create your database shell, you will need to rename and modify your web.config file to connect to SQL Server. Browse to C:\DotNetNuke and find a file named release.config. Select this file and rename it to web.config.

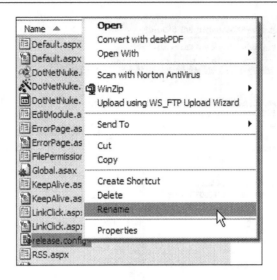

In earlier versions of DotNetNuke the `web.config`
file could be found in the main DotNetNuke folder
(`C:\DotNetNuke` in our setup) but to avoid the accidental
overwriting of this file when doing an upgrade, you
will find that the file will be given an initial filename of
`release.config`.

When renaming is complete, use Notepad to open up the `web.config` file. We will
explore this file in detail while discussing the DotNetNuke architecture; for now
we are only concerned with a few sections of the code. The `web.config` file is an
XML-based file so be careful while working with this file.

Within the `web.config` file, locate the `<connectionStrings>` section. In this section
you will notice that there are two `<add>` tags, which are both named SiteSqlServer.
The first one (the default) is for SQL Server Express. To use SQL Server Express, you
would need to comment out the second key. Commenting in the `web.config` file is
done using the opening tag <!-- and the closing tag -->. The example below shows
the original `<connectionStrings>` section in the `web.config`.

```
<connectionStrings>
  <!-- Connection String for SQL Server 2005 Express -->
  <add
    name="SiteSqlServer"
    connectionString="Data Source=.\SQLExpress;Integrated
    Security=True;User
    Instance=True;AttachDBFilename=|DataDirectory|Database.mdf;"
    providerName="System.Data.SqlClient" />
```

```
<!-- Connection String for SQL Server 2000/2005
<add
  name="SiteSqlServer"

  connectionString="Server=(local);Database=DotNetNuke;uid=;pwd=;"
  providerName="System.Data.SqlClient" />
-->
</connectionStrings>
```

We then need to enter the data for our SQL Server. Add the server name (Server=), database name (Database=), user ID (uid=), and the password (pwd=) so that our application knows how to connect to our server. This information will be based on how you have set up your SQL Server.

 For additional help, please refer to the following websites:
http://www.connectionstrings.com/
http://www.sqlstrings.com/
http://aspnet101.com/aspnet101/tutorials.
aspx?id=23

Next, we need to find the <appSettings> section and modify some more keys. The first thing you will notice is that the SiteSqlServer key is in this section as well. In order for our modules to connect to the database, you will need to fill out the information in these keys as well. For SQL Server Express 2005 you will again need to comment out the SQL Server 2005 version. Make sure you add the server name (Server=), database name (Database=), user ID (uid=), and the password (pwd=) so that our application knows how to connect to our server.

```
<appSettings>
    <!-- Connection String for SQL Server 2005 Express - kept for
backwards compatability - legacy modules    -->
    <add key="SiteSqlServer" value="Data Source=.\
SQLExpress;Integrated Security=True;User Instance=True;AttachDBFilenam
e=|DataDirectory|Database.mdf;"/>
    <!-- Connection String for SQL Server 2000/2005 - kept for
backwards compatability - legacy modules
    <add key="SiteSqlServer" value="Server=(local);Database=DotNetNuke
;uid=;pwd=;"/>
    -->
```

The next set of keys in the <appSettings> section is for the template that is used when setting up your site for the first time. A template is used to create the default look and feel of your site. By default, the base DotNetNuke template is used to create your site. If you would like to use any of the other templates, you will need to replace (comment/uncomment) the appropriate key.

```
<add key="InstallTemplate" value="DotNetNuke.install.config" />
<!--  Alternative Install Templates (included in package)
<add key="InstallTemplate" value="Club.install.config" />
<add key="InstallTemplate" value="Personal.install.config" />
<add key="InstallTemplate" value="SmallBusiness.install.config" />
-->
```

We will be using the default DotNetNuke template so we will not modify this section.

There are a few other optional settings that we may be concerned about at this time:

- **The** `AutoUpgrade` **key**: This is set to true by default and is used to determine if the upgrade/install process will run automatically.

- **The** `UseDNNConfig` **key**: This key is set to true by default and tells the installation if it should look in the database or the install file located in the install folder to determine if it should upgrade. This is implemented to reduce the number of calls to the database and improve performance.

- **The** `InstallMemberRole` **key**: This key is set to true by default and is used to determine whether or not to install the Membership Provider database tables for our installation. If you are sharing a database with another application that uses these tables then you would want to set this to false. We will leave it set to true for our installation.

There are many other settings located in the `web.config` file but for our basic implementation, we only need to be concerned with the items above. We will look at more of this information when we discuss the DotNetNuke architecture later in this book.

Once this is complete save the `web.config` file and you are ready to run DotNetNuke for the first time.

To do this, navigate to `http://localhost/DotNetNuke` in your browser. The first time you access your portal it might take a few moments to come up. This is because it is running the database scripts required to set up your SQL Server database.

While the install process is proceeding, you will see a step-by-step explanation of the process appear on your screen.

Installing DotNetNuke

Version: 04.03.04

Installation Status Report

00:00:00.046 - Installing Version: 3.1.0
00:00:00.234 - Installing Script: DotNetNuke.SetUp.SqlDataProvider
00:00:00.562 - Installing Script: DotNetNuke.Schema.SqlDataProvider
00:00:03.046 - Installing Script: DotNetNuke.Data.SqlDataProvider
00:00:04.921 - Installing MemberRole Provider:
00:00:04.921 - Executing InstallCommon.sql
00:00:09.187 - Executing InstallMembership.sql
00:00:10.109 - Executing InstallProfile.sql
00:00:10.406 - Executing InstallRoles.sql
00:00:11.468 - Upgrading to Version: 3.1.1
00:00:13.171 - Upgrading to Version: 3.2.0
00:00:13.265 - Upgrading to Version: 3.2.1

Once all the scripts have run, you will see the message below:

Installation Complete

Click Here To Access Your Portal

Once you click on the **Click Here To Access Your Portal** link you should finally see your DotNetNuke Portal.

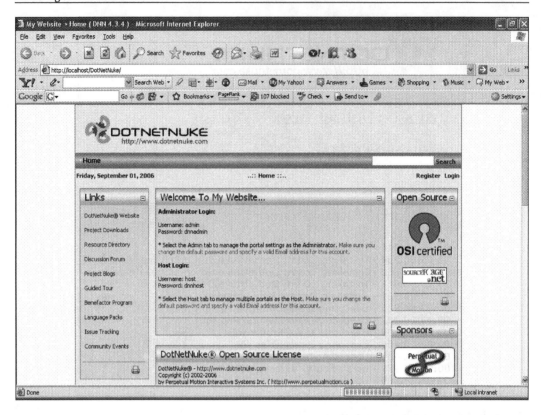

Upgrading

If you already have a DotNetNuke portal and would like to upgrade from version 3.x to version 4.x, a few steps are required. The amount of modification you have made to your installation will affect the amount of time required to complete your upgrade. Since there are distinct changes to the structure of the DotNetNuke files, the best resource for upgrading your site is the DotNetNuke *Installation Guide*, which can be found on the downloads page once you download the Documents Package. This will walk you through the steps necessary to upgrade your site.

Upgrade Checklist

While upgrading, there are a couple of things you will need to be aware of:

- **Do you have any custom modules, either built by you or purchased**? Since versions of DotNetNuke above version 4.0 employ a few changes to the module structure, some of these custom modules may no longer work. You will need to check to see if an updated version of the module is available and upgrade each module.

- **Have you made any modifications to the core architecture in the previous version**? Since we will be using the code from the new ZIP file, any changes you made to the old code will no longer be available. You will need to redo those changes in the updated framework after you update the files. For this reason, it is strongly recommended that you make no modifications to the core architecture itself.

- **Make sure you DO NOT overwrite your old web.config file!** One of the reasons that the `web.config` file is named `release.config` in the install package when it is downloaded is so that you do not accidentally overwrite your current `web.config` file. You will need to make sure that the MachineKeys in your new `web.config` file are exact copies of the MachineKeys in your old `web.config` file. If these are incorrect, your site will not work.

So if you have not done much to your site except use the standard modules then the steps to upgrade are fairly straightforward.

Back Up Your Database

1. For the Management Studio, click on the **Start** button, and go to **Programs | Microsoft SQL Server 2005 | SQL Server Management Studio**. Sign on to your server and drill down the (**local**) server by clicking on the plus (+) signs, right-click on **Databases**, look for **DotNetNuke**, and right-click on it to bring up the menu. Select **Tasks** and **Backup** to begin the backup procedure.

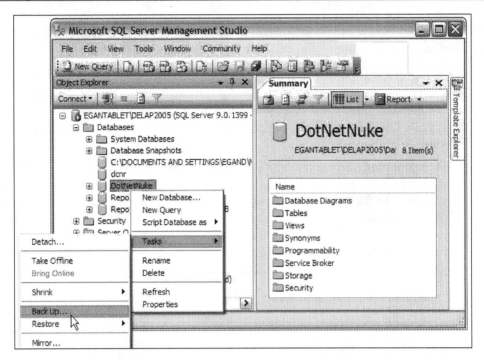

2. On the **General** tab, leave all the default settings and click on **Add**. In the **File Name** box, enter the location where you would like the backup saved and fill in a name for your backup.

3. It is common to put an extension of .bak at the end of the file name, but here it is not necessary. Click the **OK** button on the **Select Backup Destination** dialog and then click **OK** again on the **General** tab. You will receive a message box when the backup completes successfully.

Back up Your DotNetNuke files

Whenever you are about to make changes to your site it is always a good idea to back up the physical files located at C:\DotNetNuke. Make a copy of this folder and store it in a safe place. This will allow you to revert back to your old site if something goes wrong.

Logging In as Admin and Changing Passwords

There are two user accounts that allow you to maintain your portal. They are the admin account and host account. This makes changing the default passwords for the admin and host accounts one of the most important steps to take once you have your site up and running. The first page you see when you start up DotNetNuke gives you all the information you need to sign on.

First, we will log in as admin. For this, click on the **Login** icon in the upper right portion of the site. This will give you the **Account Login** screen. Enter **admin** for the username and **dnnadmin** as the password. When you do this, you will notice a few changes to the site.

There is now an admin tool pane, and most text has a pencil icon next to it. You will now be able to edit the site. All the options available to you as an admin or host user will be covered in Chapter 5; for now we only want to change the default password. In the upper right corner, just below where you clicked the login icon, you will see a link for **Administrator Account**. Click on this to bring up the **account** screen for the admin account.

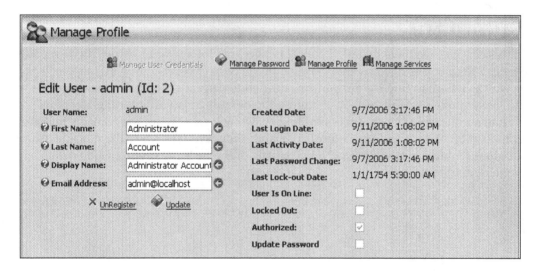

To change the password, click on the **Manage Password** link.

Fill out the **Current Password**, the **New Password**, the **Confirm New Password**, and all the other sections that are required (marked with an *). When finished filling out the information, click on the **Change Password** link to save your changes.

You may remove some of the required registration items by unchecking the boxes next to them. Note this means that these items will no longer be required for any user of your portal.

When you are finished, log out of the admin account by clicking on the **logout** icon in the right-hand corner of the page. You can then change the host password by signing in as **host**, and following the same steps we followed to change the admin password.

Summary

In this chapter, we have installed a local version of DotNetNuke using Microsoft SQL Server 2005 Express and covered how to set the correct permissions on our machine as well as where to find the procedures needed to upgrade from previous versions of DotNetNuke. We finished by changing the default passwords for the Host and Admin accounts. In the chapters that follow, we will explore all the features that are available to you as an admin or host user of the site. We will cover the modules and standard features that make DotNetNuke one of the fastest-growing web portals on the market today.

3

Users, Roles, and Pages

One of the most important and time-consuming aspects of running a DotNetNuke portal is trying to figure out how to administer the portal. From adding modules to working with users, it will take time before you start feeling comfortable with all the administration tasks associated with running a portal. The next few chapters are designed to give you a general understanding of how things work, and also to act as a reference for the tasks you have to perform only once or twice in a year. This chapter will familiarize you with managing users and pages within your portal. When you are done with this chapter you will possess a better understanding of the following areas:

- Creating and modifying user accounts
- How user accounts tie into the security of your site
- What DotNetNuke pages are and how to create and administer them
- How to structure your site using pages
- The new Membership Provider Model

User Accounts

If you are used to working within a network environment, or have worked with different portals in the past, then you are probably comfortable with the term "users", and how they interact with your portal. Everything that takes place on your portal revolves around users and user accounts. Whether users are required to register in order to use your services or you only need a few user accounts in order to manage the functionality and layout of your site, you will need to understand how to create and manage user accounts. Let's start with a general description of a user, and then you will see how to create and manage your users. In order to work through the examples, you will need to bring up your portal and sign in as **admin**.

What is a User?

The simplest definition of a user is an individual who consumes the services that your portal provides. However, a user can take on many different roles; from a visitor who is just browsing (unregistered user) or a person who registers to gain access to your services (registered user), to the facilitator (Administrator or Host) who is responsible for the content and design of your portal. Just about everything in DotNetNuke revolves around the user, so before we can do anything else, we need to learn a little about user accounts.

Creating User Accounts

Before you create the user accounts you must set how users will be able to register on the site. You have the choice of four different types of registrations: None, Private, Public (default), and Verified. To set the registration type for your portal go to the **Site Settings** link found on the **Admin** menu.

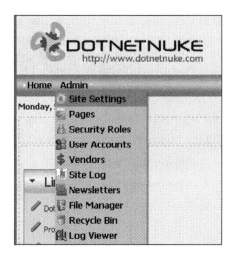

The **User Registration** section can be found under **Advanced Settings | Security Settings**:

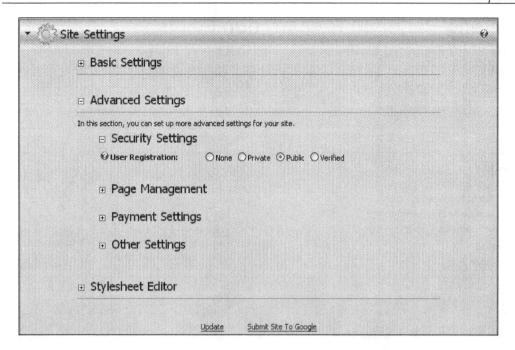

The type of registration you use depends on how you will be using your portal. What follows is a brief explanation of the different **User Registration** types.

Registration Setting	Description
None	Setting up user registration as None will remove the Register link from your portal. In this mode, users can only be added by the Admin or Host users. If you plan to have all sections of your site available to anyone then selecting none as your registration option is a good choice.
Private	If you select Private, the Register link will reappear. When users attempt to register, they will be informed that their request for registration will be reviewed by the administrator. The administrator will decide whom to give access to the site.
Public	Public is the default registration for a DotNetNuke portal. When this is selected, the users will be able to register for your site by entering the required information. Once the registration form is filled out, they will be given access to the site.
Verified	If you select Verified as your registration option, the users will be sent an e-mail with a verification code once they fill out the required information. This ensures that the e-mail address they enter in the registration process is valid. The first time they sign in, they will be prompted for the verification code. After they have been verified they will only need to type in their login name and password to gain access to the site.

Setting Required Registration Fields

The administrator has the ability to decide what information the user will be required to enter when registering. If you are logged in as an administrator, you can accomplish this through a combination of **User Settings** and **Profile Properties**.

To manage the **Profile Properties** for your site, select the **User Accounts** link on the **Admin** menu.

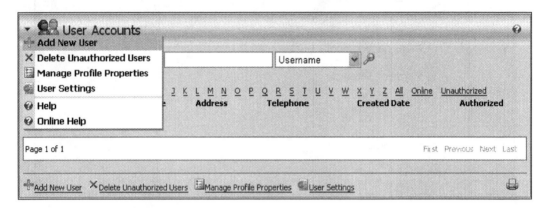

In this screen, select **Manage Profile Properties**, either by selecting the link at the bottom of the module container or by selecting the link in the **Action** menu. When you select this link you will be redirected to a screen that displays a list of the currently configured **Profile Properties**.

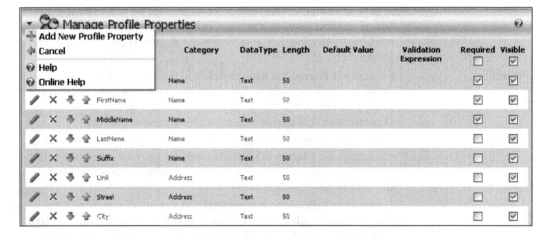

You can manage some attributes of the **Profile Properties** from within this screen. For instance you can delete a property by clicking on the **X** icon in the second column. Alternatively, you can change the display order of the properties by clicking on one of the Up or Down icons in the third and fourth columns. (If you do change the order this way, make sure you click the **Update** link at the bottom of the page to save any changes.)

If you want even more control you can edit a single property by clicking on the **Pencil** icon in the first column. You can also add a new property, by selecting the **Add New Profile Property** action from the **Action** menu. In either case you will be redirected to another page, where you can enter information about the property.

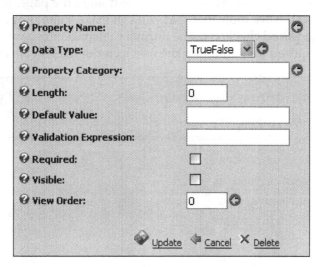

Note that if you are editing an existing property the first two fields cannot be changed, so make sure you get it right first time. Most of these fields are self-explanatory, but we will describe a couple of the fields.

The **Visible** checkbox controls whether the user can see the property. You can hide a property from the user by making sure that this checkbox is left unchecked — the important thing to remember is that the Administrator can still see this property. This feature allows the Administrator to record private confidential information about a user.

The **Required** checkbox controls whether the user is required to enter information for this property. If it is set the user will not be able to proceed without entering anything, although there are some settings that affect how this works in practice.

In addition to configuring the **Profile Properties** for the site there are some **User Settings** that control the Registration Process. In the **User Accounts** screen, you can access the **User Settings** by clicking on the link at the bottom of the pane or the link in the **Action** menu. This will bring you to the **User Settings** page.

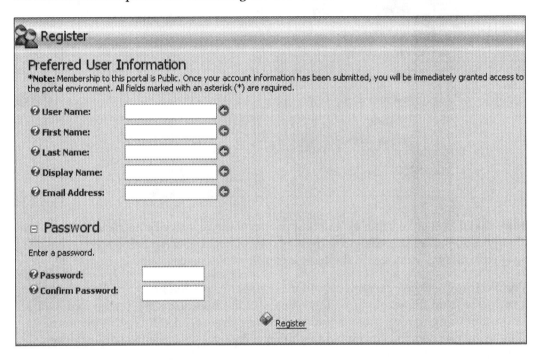

There are a lot of settings on this page. We will be focusing in this discussion on the settings that relate to Registration, towards the bottom of the page. In our discussion of the **Profile Properties** we indicated that you can make some properties required, by checking the **Required** checkbox. The normal registration behavior is that only the information required for validating the user's credentials is collected.

If the **Require a valid Profile for Registration** checkbox is checked then the registration page also contains the list of **Profile Properties** and the registration will not complete unless all the required properties have valid values.

Furthermore if the **Require a valid Profile for Login** checkbox is checked, a user will be required to update his or her profile on login if it is no longer valid. This can happen if an Administrator decides to make a profile property required after users have already registered, or if the Administrator decides to add a new required property.

Managing a Profile

When you log in as **Admin**, you will see the title **Administrator Account** in the upper right-hand corner of the current page (if you are using the default skin). Click this link to bring you to the **Manage Profile** page.

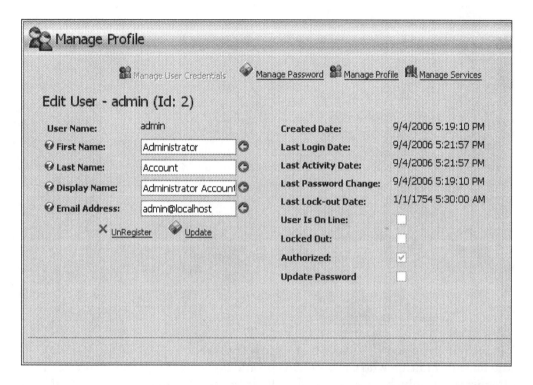

All users can access this screen in a similar way. There are four tabs (hyperlinks) at the top of this screen. A user can manage their own profile properties by clicking on the **Manage Profile** link.

⊟Name

❷ **Prefix:**	`mr` ◀	Visibilty: ◯ Public ◯ Members Only ◉ Admin Only
❷ **First Name:**	`Administrator`	Visibilty: ◯ Public ◯ Members Only ◉ Admin Only
❷ **Middle Name:**		Visibilty: ◯ Public ◯ Members Only ◉ Admin Only
❷ **Last Name:**	`Account`	Visibilty: ◯ Public ◯ Members Only ◉ Admin Only
❷ **Suffix:**		Visibilty: ◯ Public ◯ Members Only ◉ Admin Only

⊟Address

❷ **Unit:**		Visibilty: ◯ Public ◯ Members Only ◉ Admin Only
❷ **Street:**		Visibilty: ◯ Public ◯ Members Only ◉ Admin Only
❷ **City:**		Visibilty: ◯ Public ◯ Members Only ◉ Admin Only
❷ **Region:**		Visibilty: ◯ Public ◯ Members Only ◉ Admin Only
❷ **Country:**	▾	Visibilty: ◯ Public ◯ Members Only ◉ Admin Only
❷ **Postal Code:**		Visibilty: ◯ Public ◯ Members Only ◉ Admin Only

⊟Contact Info

❷ **Telephone:**		Visibilty: ◯ Public ◯ Members Only ◉ Admin Only
❷ **Cell/Mobile:**		Visibilty: ◯ Public ◯ Members Only ◉ Admin Only
❷ **Fax:**		Visibilty: ◯ Public ◯ Members Only ◉ Admin Only
❷ **Website:**		Visibilty: ◯ Public ◯ Members Only ◉ Admin Only
❷ **IM:**		Visibilty: ◯ Public ◯ Members Only ◉ Admin Only

Note the red arrow icon indicates that a property is required, while the visibility radio buttons indicate who can view this profile property. By default this is set to Administrators only, but users can allow their profile information to be available to other users (members) or all users including unauthorized users (public).

Registering a User Manually

As we discussed earlier, you can set your portal registration to **None**. This will remove the **Registration** link from your site. So the only way to add users to your portal is to register them manually. To do this, go to **Admin | User Accounts** on the main menu. This will bring you to the **Manage Users** screen. There are actually two ways to add a new user from this screen. You can select **Add New User** from the drop-down menu on the left of the module or click on the **Add New User** link at the bottom of the module.

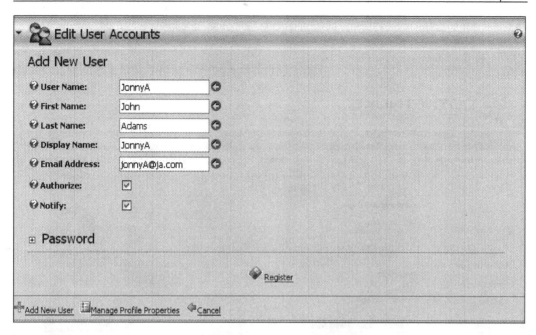

We will be setting up a user to help us administer the Coffee Connections site. We fill in the required information and click on the **Update** link.

When we are done, we will test the account we just created. To do this we need to log off as **admin** by clicking on the **Logout** link in the upper right-hand corner of the current page. Then click on the **Login** link. Enter in the **username** and **password** of the user we just created. You will notice that while you are logged in as this user you lose access to all the updating functionality that the administrator account possesses.

The ability to update the portal is not available to our new user because they do not have the authority to make the changes. Put another way, they do not belong to the right security role.

Understanding DotNetNuke Roles

We have just looked at how to add a user to your site, but are all users created equal? To understand how users are allowed to interact with the portal we will need to take a look at what a **Role** is and how it factors into the portal. There are plenty of real-world examples of roles we can look at. A Police station, for example, can have sergeants, patrol cops, and detectives and with each position come different responsibilities and privileges. In a police station there are multiple people filling those positions (roles) with each sharing the same set of responsibilities and privileges.

Roles in our portal work the same way. Roles are set up to divide the responsibilities needed to run your portal. If we refer to the user stories we created in Chapter 1, we will see that one of them falls into the area of users and roles.

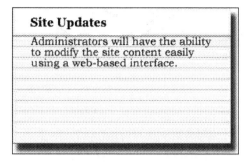

Site Updates

Administrators will have the ability
to modify the site content easily
using a web-based interface.

We want our portal to be easy for the administrators to manage. To do this we will need to settle on the different user roles needed for our site. To determine this we first need to decide on the different types of user that will access the portal. We will detail these user types below.

- **Administrator**: The Administrators will have very high security. They will be able to modify, delete, or move anything on the site. They will be able to add and delete users and control all security settings. (This role comes built into DotNetNuke.)

- **Home Page Admin**: The home page admins will have the ability to modify only the information on the home page. They will be responsible for changing what users see when they first access your site. (We will be adding this role.)

- **Forum Moderator**: The forum moderators will have the ability to monitor and modify posts in your forum. They will have the ability to approve or disapprove messages posted. (We will be adding this role.)

- **Registered User**: The registered users will be able to post messages in the forum and be able to access sections of the site set aside for registered users only. (This role comes built into DotNetNuke.)

- **Unauthenticated User**: The unauthenticated user is the most basic of the user types. Any person browsing your site will fall under this category. This user type will be able to browse certain sections of your portal but will be restricted from posting in the forum and will not be allowed in the **Registered Users Only** section. (This role comes built into DotNetNuke.)

Once you formulate the different user roles that will access the site, you will need to restrict users' access. For example; we only want the Home Page Admin to be able to edit items on the home page. To accomplish this DotNetNuke uses role-based security. Role-based security allows you to give access to portions of your website based on what role the user belongs to. The benefit of using a role-based security method is that you only have to define the access privileges for a role once. Then you just need to add users to that role and they will possess the privileges that the role defines. The diagram below gives you an idea of how this works.

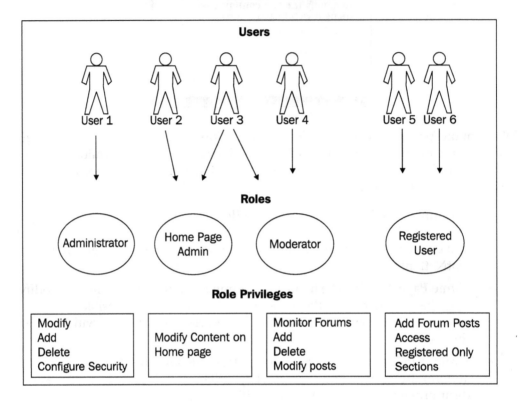

Looking at the diagram, we notice two things:

- Users can be assigned to more than one role.
- More than one user can be assigned to a single role.

This gives us great flexibility when deciding on the authorization that users will possess in our portal.

To create the roles we have detailed, sign in as **admin**, and select **Admin | Security Roles** on the main menu.

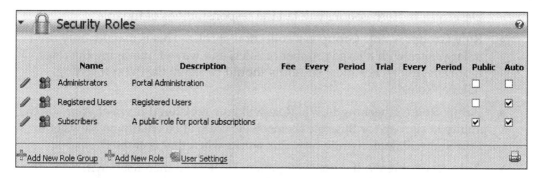

Notice that DotNetNuke comes with three roles already built into the system, the Administrators role (which we have been using), the Registered Users role, and the Subscribers role. We want to create an additional role for Home Page Admin. To do this you again have two choices. Either select **Add New Role** from the dropdown in the upper left or click on the **Add New Role** link. This will bring up **the Edit Security Roles** page. We will use this page to create the Home Page Admin role that we need.

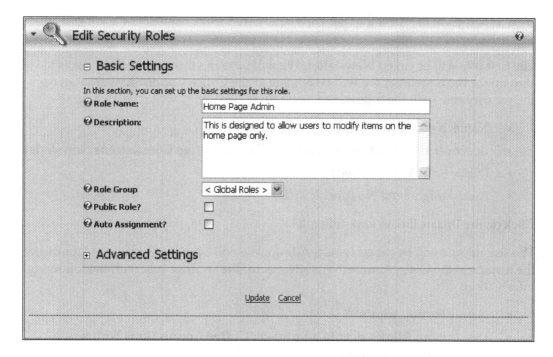

The basic settings shown in the screenshot are:

- **Role Name**: Make the name of your role short but descriptive. The name should attempt to convey its purpose.

- **Description**: Here you may detail the responsibilities of the role.
- **Role Group**: A Role Group is a collection of roles. This is usually only used in large sites with a large number of roles, as a way of managing the roles more effectively. For most sites this should be left at the default setting "Global Roles".
- **Public Role?**: Checking Public Role will give registered users of your site the ability to sign up for this role themselves. We will be creating a Newsletter Role and will demonstrate how this works when that is created.
- **Auto Assignment?**: If Auto Assignment is checked then users will automatically be assigned to this role as soon as they register for your portal.

Since we want to decide who will be the able to modify our home page we will leave both of these unchecked. To save settings click on the **Update** link.

The advanced settings section allows you to set up a fee for certain security roles. Depending on what you are offering on your portal, you can ask for a fee for a user to register for your portal or just to access particular sections.

Now to complete the roles that we will require for Coffee Connections, we will add two more security roles.

The first role will be called Newsletter. We will be using this role to allow users to sign up for the newsletter we will be hosting at the Coffee Connections site. Set up the security role with the following information:

- Name: **Newsletter**
- Description: **Allows users to register for the Coffee Connections Newsletter**
- Public Role: **Yes** (checked)
- Auto Assignment: **No** (unchecked)

Click on the **Update** link to save this role.

The second role will be called Forum Admin. We will be using this role to administer the forums at the Coffee Connections site. Set up the security role with the following information:

- Name: **Forum Admin**
- Description: **Allows user to administer Coffee Connections Forum**
- Public Role: **No** (unchecked)
- Auto Assignment: **No** (unchecked)

Click on the **Update** link to save this role.

The security roles, by themselves, do not determine the security on your portal. As the diagram showed, users and roles work together to form the basis of the security in your site.

Assigning Security Roles to Users

Security roles can be assigned to users by an administrator or, if **Public Role** is checked, can be assigned by the users themselves. To show you how users can sign up for security roles, log out as **admin** and log in as our sample user, **JonnyA**.

When signed on as **JonnyA**, in order to modify your user information, click on the user name in the upper right-hand corner of the portal. This will bring you to the **Manage Profile** screen shown below. This is the same as screen we looked at when signed on as the administrator previously.

Note that when logged in as a regular user there is no information on the right-hand side of the page. Only an Administrator can see this information. A user can change their password by clicking on the **Manage Password** tab, they can mange their profile by clicking on the **Manage Profile** tab, or they can unregister from the site by clicking on the **UnRegister** link.

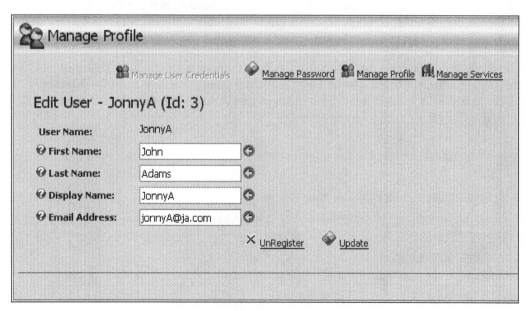

The **Manage Services** tab allows the user to manage the public security roles available to them. These are the roles for which we checked the **Public Role** checkbox. To subscribe to the role, click on the **Subscribe** link.

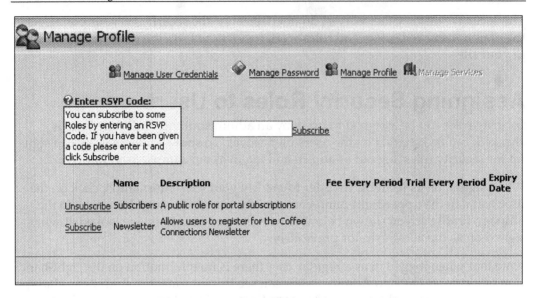

After you have subscribed to a service, you can unsubscribe by clicking on the **Unsubscribe** link. Since security roles such as Home Page Admin allow the user to modify the portal, they should not be assigned in this manner. As the administrator of the site, we want the ability to decide who is assigned to this role. To do this we will again need to sign off as **JonnyA** and sign back in as Admin.

Once logged in, select **Admin | Security Roles** on the main menu. Once there, click the pencil icon next to the **Home Page Admin** security role. Click on the **Manage Users** link that is located near the bottom of this screen. You will then be presented with the **User Roles** administration page.

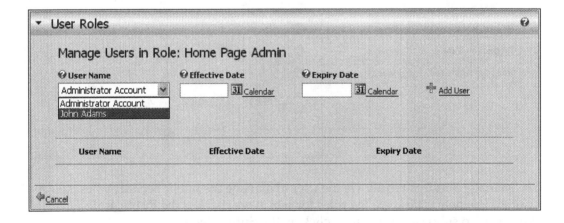

To add a user to a role, select them from the **User Name** dropdown. If you would like the role to expire after a specific date you may enter a date in the **Expiry Date** textbox or click on the **Calendar** link to select a date from a calendar. When you are done, click on the **Add Role** link to add the role to the user.

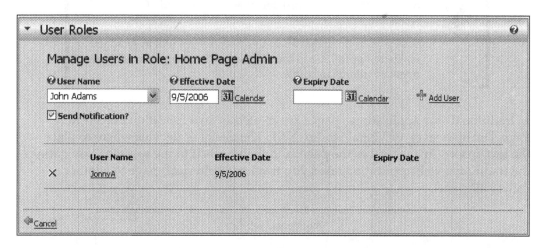

You can add as many users to the role as you wish. To remove a role from a user, click on the delete icon (⊠) next to the user's name. If the **Send Notification** checkbox is checked, the portal will send an e-mail notification to the users when they are added or removed from the role.

Up to this point, we have added security roles, and added users to roles both as an admin and by allowing users to add themselves through membership services. However, the security role authorizations still need to be set. To do this we will introduce you to the page architecture of DotNetNuke and in the process show you how to add security roles to sections of our portal.

Understanding DotNetNuke Pages and tabIDs

As we have been navigating through to different pages you may have noticed that the page name shown in your browser's address bar has not changed. Although the **tabID** portion of the address changes, every time you click on another item on the menu, it keeps showing Default.aspx. This is because DotNetNuke uses dynamic page generation to render the correct information for each page (e.g. http://localhost/DotNetNuke/tabid/39/Default.aspx).

You will see that some of the screenshots in this book as well as other pages you will find on your DotNetNuke portal refer to something called a **tab**. In previous versions of DotNetNuke the word 'tab' was used instead of the word 'page'.

I am sure in time, that all of these references will be changed inside the portal. Until then be aware that the words tab and page are interchangeable.

In traditional web applications, pages are created in an application like Front Page, Dreamweaver, or Visual Studio .NET. The designer decides where to place the text, inserts images, saves the page, and then posts it to the website. Navigating the traditional web application takes you from one "physical" page to another "physical" page.

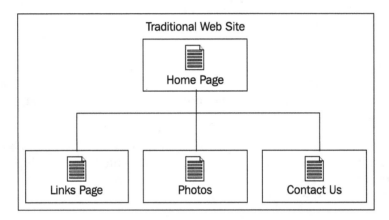

In DotNetNuke web portal, there is only one "physical" page used in the application. Instead of placing the information directly on the page, DotNetNuke holds the information for each page in the database. When a page is then requested on a DNN portal, the application looks in the database to determine what information should be on the page and displays it on `Default.aspx`. The database knows what information to pull from the database by looking at the tabID in the URL (e.g. `http://localhost/DotNetNuke/tabid/39/Default.aspx`).

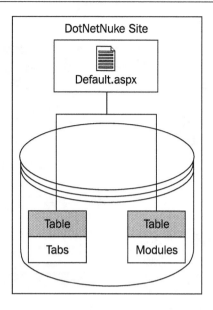

When users navigate to different items on the menu, they will see different information and will be presented with the illusion of multiple physical pages.

When you create new pages in DotNetNuke, you are not only creating the page information for the database but this same step will also build the navigation menu for your site.

To better understand the pages and menu structure we will create some new pages. To create a new page, we first need to log in as an admin. When you do you will see the **Page Functions** pane at the top of your portal.

To add a page, click on the **Add** link on the left side of the pane. We will be adding a page that will hold our Coffee House Search engine as well as a page that will eventually hold our forums. This **admin** screen is broken up into three different sections, **Basic Settings**, **Copy Page**, and **Advanced Settings**.

We will start with the **Basic Settings**:

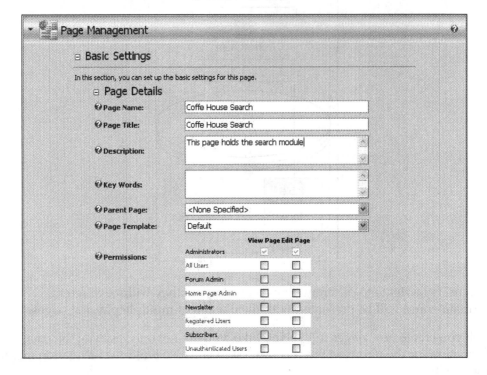

This is where we enter the following information to set up our page:

- **Page Name**: This is the name that will show up on the menu. You want to keep this name short in order to save space on the menu.

- **Title**: This is used to display the name of the page on the Internet Explorer title bar. This can be more descriptive than the page name.

- **Description**: Enter a short description of what the page will be used for.

- **Key Words**: This section is used to enter key words that will be picked up by search engines.

- **Parent Page**: As we discussed earlier, this information not only creates a page dynamically but is also used to create your site menu. If you would like this page to be positioned under another page in the menu select the parent page from the dropdown.

- **Permissions/View Page**: Roles that are selected in this column will have the ability to view the page. This means that only those roles checked will be able to see this page. If you are not in one of these roles you will not see the page. This can be used to restrict portions of your portal to certain groups of people.

- **Permissions/Edit Page**: Roles that are selected in this column will have the ability to administer this page. This means that a user who belongs to any of the roles checked will have the ability to edit, modify, and delete information on this page. Remember these privileges apply to this page only.

Under the **Copy Page** section you can select whether you would like to copy information from an existing page to create a new page.

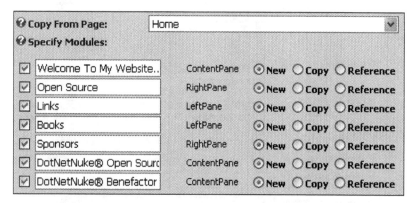

To copy a page, select the page you would like to copy from the dropdown. This then results in a list of the modules on that page. You can select whether to copy each module by checking the checkbox on the left of the list. You also have the ability to rename the module, or change its title, by changing the text in the text box. Finally, there are three options that relate to how the module is copied.

- **New** — An empty module of the same type is created on the new page.

- **Copy** — An exact duplicate of the module is created on the new page (with a new ID).

- **Reference** — A new instance of the module is created on the new page (with the same ID).

Initially there appears to be no difference between the last two options as the resulting modules look the same. However, a copied module is not related in any way to the original module, so modifying the contents of a copied module does not change the original module. A referenced module, on the other hand is the "same" content displayed on a different page. Changing the content in a referenced module will affect both pages.

The **Advanced Settings** section is broken up into three subsections, **Appearance**, **Security Settings**, and **Other Settings**.

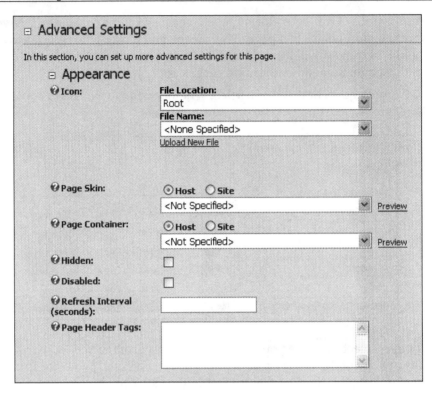

The **Icon** drop-down box allows you to add an icon next to the page name on the menu. You can see an example of this on the **Admin** menu.

In the **Admin** menu the Admin page is the parent for Security Roles, as well as the others in the list. As you can see, if you use an icon it will be placed on the left of the page name.

The next portion of the Page Management panel deals with skinning. For now we will leave <**Not Specified**> selected. We will cover how these items work when we discuss skinning in Chapter 9.

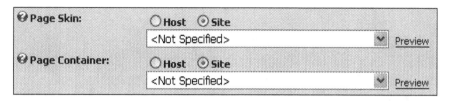

If you don't want the page to be displayed on the menu, check the **Hidden** checkbox. You can still access this page by creating a link to it in your portal. Administrators will be able to see and modify hidden pages using the page management section.

Checking the **Disabled** checkbox will allow a page to show up on the menu but will not allow the page to be shown. This is used to help with navigation for your site. The Admin page again is an example of this. It is used only as a parent page to allow you to navigate to the other pages beneath it. If you click on the admin menu item, no page will appear. If you check both hidden and disabled, you will only be able to access the page from **Admin | Pages** on the main menu. This can be useful if you would like to navigate to a page in a non-traditional way. For example, you can add a link to specific page using the links module that we will discuss in Chapter 4.

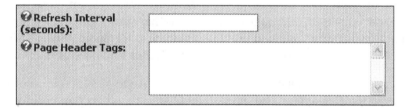

Finally, at the end of this section, you have the ability to add a **Refresh Interval** and **Page Header Tags**. The **Refresh Interval** will automatically refresh this page after the time (in seconds) that you specify. The **Page Header Tag** section allows you to interject Meta Tags into the header of this page. This is helpful because since DNN builds pages dynamicity, you can use this to modify the header. We will be leaving these sections blank.

```
⊟ Other Settings
  ❷ Start Date:        [_____]   Calendar
  ❷ End Date:          [_____]   Calendar
  ❷ Link Url:
                       Link Type:
                       ⦿ None
                       ○ URL ( A Link To An External Resource )
                       ○ Page ( A Page On Your Site )
                       ○ File ( A File On Your Site )
```

In the **Others Settings** section you can administer when your page appears and how its menu item is utilized.

- **Start Date**: This will determine the start date that your page will become visible to your users.

- **End Date**: This will determine the start date that your page will no longer be visible to your users.

- **Link Url**: If you would like a menu item to link to information that already exists on your site you can fill in the Link Url information. You can link to an external resource (a page or file on another site), a page on your site (an existing "physical" page on your website), or a file on your site. This can be used to incorporate existing ASP or HTML files you may already have.

To save your settings for this page, click on the **Update** link. When it is complete, you will see your new page on the menu bar. Therefore, when you build a page you are creating both a page to add content to and an item for your menu.

Administering Pages

You have now seen how you can create a page using the **Page Management Pane**. Next you will see how to work with all of your pages to build your menus in a straightforward manner. To get to the **Page Administration** section select **Admin | Pages** on the main menu.

By using the icons on the **Page Admin** pane you will be able to create a new page, edit or view an existing page, or modify where the link to the page appears on your menu. You will notice that neither the Host nor Admin menu items appear on this page. You are not able to modify those menus in this context. To test this, highlight the Coffee House Search menu item and click on the **View Selected Page** icon (magnifying glass). This will bring us right back to the page that we just created. Notice that the page is separated into three distinct panes. The **LeftPane**, **ContentPane**, and **RightPane** (you may need to click on the **Preview** icon in the **Page Functions** pane if the panes are not visible).

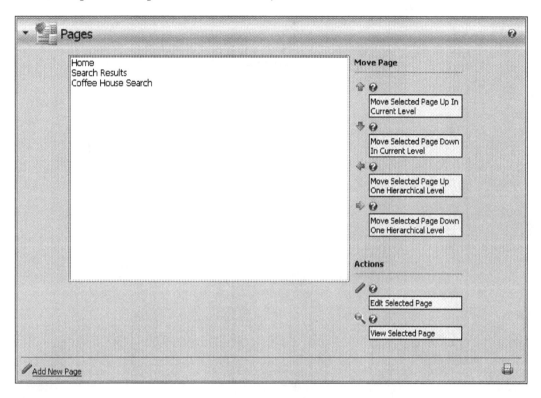

Take time to try out the functionality on this page and get comfortable with how you can edit, move, and modify your pages. Once we have created our page we will want to add information to it. To do this we need to add modules to our new page.

Summary

In this chapter, we covered the concepts of users, roles, and pages. This should lay a foundation for the rest of the information we will be covering in this book. Most of the concepts we will cover will deal with one or all of these items. In the next chapter we will introduce you to the concept of modules and discuss the sample modules that come prepackaged with DotNetNuke.

4
Standard DotNetNuke Modules

As we discovered in the last chapter, DotNetNuke dynamically builds its pages using the tabID to retrieve the information for each page from the database. This includes the modules that are located on each page as well as the content in those modules. In this chapter we will cover the following:

- The basic concepts of modules
- How to add and remove modules
- The standard modules that come prepackaged with DNN

We will discuss the modules, their practical purposes, and any administration or modification needed to work with each module.

DotNetNuke Modules

Adding content to DotNetNuke is done using modules. Modules are used as building blocks for your portal. Each module is designed to perform a given task. From providing links, to storing contacts, to adding a simple welcome message for your users, modules are what make your portal buzz.

Adding a Module

To begin, make sure you are logged in as **admin** and then navigate to the Coffee Connections **Search** tab we created earlier in the book. We will then turn our attention to the **Module Admin** pane at the top of the page. We will be using this pane to work with the modules on our page. To demonstrate the common module features we will be using the **Text/Html** module. Select **Text/Html** in the module drop-down.

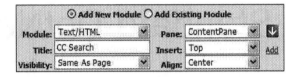

The **Pane** drop-down allows you to decide in which pane (or section) of the page you would like to place the module. Our choices for a default skin are **Left**, **Right**, **Content**, **Top**, or **Bottom**. These choices will vary depending on the skin you are using on your portal. We will be placing the Text/HTML module in the **ContentPane**. The **Align** drop-down allows you to left-, center-, or right-justify the module within the pane you select and the **Title** box allows you to create a title for the module. The **Visibility** drop-down allows you to decide on who is allowed to see the module (same as page or administrators) and the **Insert** drop-down allows you to tell it where to insert the module into the page (on top or below other modules).

To add the module to the tab, just click on the **Add** link located to the right of the **Align** drop-down. This will place the Text/HTML module into the content pane.

Module Settings

To access a module's settings you need to access the settings menu. To do this, use the drop-down icon in the right-hand corner of the module:

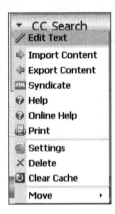

From this menu you will be able to do the following:

- Access the **Edit** page for the module
- **Import** or **Export** content
- **Syndicate** the information in the module using RSS
- Access online **Help** and documentation
- Change module **Settings**
- **Print** the contents of the module
- **Delete** the module
- **Move** the module

Editing a Module

The first item on the menu allows you to modify the content of the module. The **Edit** page as well as the name of the link may be different for each module depending on its functionality. The module developer can decide what shows up on the menu. We will cover how to use this option on each of the standard modules.

Importing and Exporting Content

DotNetNuke 4.0 allows you to export the content from one module and import it into another module. You can test this by going to the home page and using the export function on the **Welcome to DotNetNuke** Text\HTML box. If you then go to the Text/HTML box we placed on our Coffee House Search page, you can use the import function to import the information into this page.

Syndicate Information

You can also syndicate the information contained in your module allowing others to pull your information using RSS Readers. (We will discuss this further when we look at the News Feeds module.)

Online Help and Documentation

This item allows the developer of the module to have online help available to help users of the module.

Editing Module Functionality

The **Settings** menu item allows you to edit the basic functionality of each module. This will be the same for all modules. Let's take a look at this section. On the Text/HTML module, select **Settings** from the **Edit** menu.

This will bring up the **Module Settings** page. This section is divided up into three sections: general settings, security settings, and page settings.

When creating a module, you have the choice of adding custom settings to the **Settings** section. We will cover this when we learn how to develop custom modules later in this book.

Basic Settings

The first item on this page allows you to set a title to show at the top of your module. The title will default to the name of the module (in this case, Text.html). This is followed by the permissions for the module, which work in the same way as the role privileges on the page. Note that these permissions override the ones set on the page. So, you can, for example, keep a tab available to the **All Users** role but only allow users in the "registered users" role to see the modules on that tab. Keep in mind that the overriding only works one way. If you restrict the page to registered users and then try to give **All Users** access to the modules on the tab, they won't see the module because they will never see the page. The default permissions will be inherited from the page.

⊟ **Module Settings**

In this section, you can define the settings that relate to the Module content and permissions (ie. those settings that will be the same on all pages that the Module appears).

⊟ **Basic Settings**

Module Title:

CC Search

Permissions:

	View Module	Edit Module
Administrators	☐	☑
All Users	☐	☐
Forum Admin	☐	☐
Home Page Admin	☐	☐
Newsletter	☐	☐
Registered Users	☐	☐
Subscribers	☐	☐
Unauthenticated Users	☐	☐

☑ Inherit **View** permissions from **Page**

Advanced Settings

The **Header** and **Footer** sections allow you to enter information that will appear at the top and bottom of your module. Just as you did with the page, you can also decide on showing this module during a specific date range. In addition, you can also make a module show up on all the tabs (pages) that you create. You might want to do this if you have a set of links that you want on every tab.

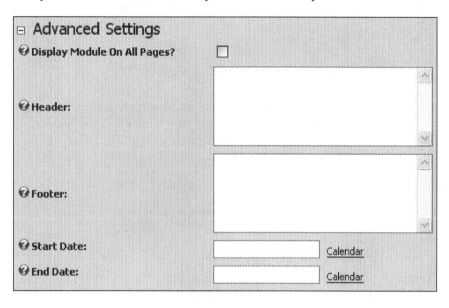

Page Settings

This final section deals mostly with the appearance of the module.

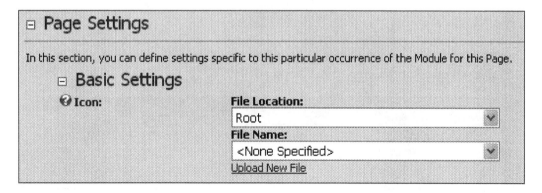

If you would like an icon to appear before the title, select one from the **File Name** drop-down or upload a new icon by clicking on the **Upload New File** link.

The next section allows you to modify the look and feel of your module. Although any formatting to the module should be done in the module skin, you can change the alignment of the text by selecting **Left**, **Right**, or **Center** from the list. Change the background color by entering a color code into the **Color** box, or add a border by entering a thickness in the **Border** box.

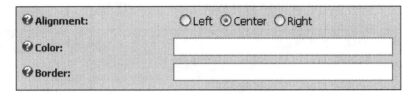

When you looked at the Text/HTML module, you may have noticed a small minus (-) sign in the upper left-hand corner next to the title. This gives the users of your site the ability to show or hide the content of each module.

You can set the default setting to **Minimized**, **Maximized**, or **None**, which will allow users to hide the content.

The next section allows you to determine whether you would like the title displayed on your module, whether you will allow users to print the contents, and if RSS syndication is allowed. Just check the boxes to enable these features.

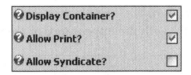

In addition, you may select a module container to skin your individual modules. Module containers are discussed in Chapter 9.

The **Cache Time** is used to speed up the rendering of your page. Caching stores a representation of the data contained in your module for the number of seconds that you place in this box. That means that subsequent attempts to access this page (even by other users) will show the same data. If the text in this module does not change very often then set this to a high number like 360. If this data is dynamic, or changes frequently, then set it to a low number or leave it at zero.

You can make the settings for this module the default settings and/or apply the settings to all modules in your site. The final option is to move your module to another page by selecting the page name from the drop-down. When you are finished with your modifications click the **Update** link to save your settings.

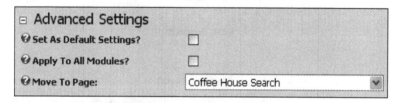

Standard Modules

The previous versions of DotNetNuke came prepackaged with nineteen standard modules for you to use on your portal. To further help the DotNetNuke core team focus on the core architecture, it was decided that the standard modules were to be broken out into separate sub-projects. Each of these sub-projects is managed by different team member. A list of the projects can be found on the DotNetNuke site by clicking on the **Projects** icon.

In this section, we will briefly go over each of the sub-project modules. As we cover each module, we will first give you the official description for the module as stated on the DotNetNuke main website. We will then discuss the modules in the following context:

- Practical purposes
- Administration and Modifications
- Special features

Account Login Module

The Account Login module permits users to log in to your portal. It features a **Register** button that a user can use to become a registered user of your portal, and a **Forgot Password?** link.

 There is a bug in the Account Login module, so that if you don't have the **Visibility** set to Maximized, the *Enter* key does not fire the **Login** button. It instead fires the Min/Max image.

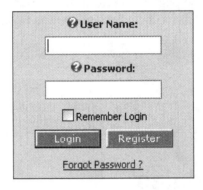

Practical Purposes

The Account Login module is a unique standard module. It is used to allow user login for your site. The site will come pre-loaded with this module already working on the site.

The default login will appear on a page all by itself. You may find that you want to add other modules or images when a user is logging into the portal. To accomplish this you will need to use the Account Login module.

Administration and Modification

To show you how this works we will need to add a new page to the site. Create a page with the following attributes:

- **Name: Login**
- **Title: Login Tab**
- **Hidden**: Checked
- **View Tab Roles: Administrators; Unauthenticated Users**

We do not want users to be able to navigate here so we make it a hidden page. We also want to make it available to unauthenticated and administrator roles. Since we are not able to navigate to this page, we will need to access it from the **Admin | Pages** menu.

Highlight the **Login** tab we just created and click on the viewing icon (magnifying glass). Once on the **Login** tab, select **Account Login** in the **Module** drop-down section of the Module pane and add it to the **ContentPane** by clicking on the **Add** icon. Your tab should look like the following screenshot:

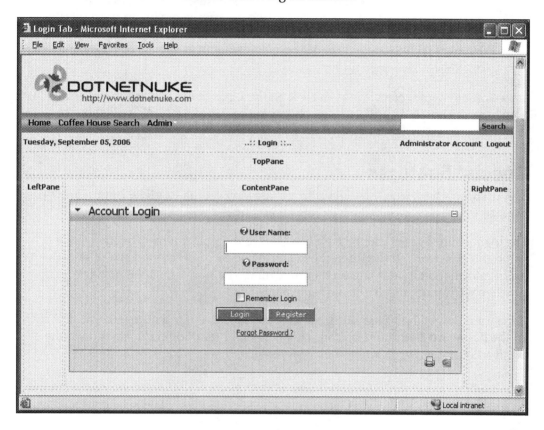

Next, we want to modify some settings on the Login module. Hover your mouse cursor over the **Edit** icon and select **Settings**. Modify the following properties:

- **Visibility**: **None**
- **Permissions (View)**: **Administrators**; **Unauthenticated Users**

We change the **Visibility** to **None** to avoid users inadvertently minimizing the module and not seeing it when they attempt to log in.

To use this tab for logging in instead of the default login we will need to go to the **Admin** | **Site** Settings tab. We will need to change two properties:

- **Login** page (Under **Advanced Settings | Page Management**): **Login**
  Setting this property to our login tab will tell DotNetNuke to use our new tab instead of the default tab. Just select our tab from the drop-down.

- **Home** page (Under **Advanced Settings | Page Management**): **Home**
  The default behavior of the login control is to stay on the current page once a user is authenticated. Since we have made this page available only to administrators and unauthenticated users, after users log in successfully, they will see an error on the page. To change this behavior we will set the **Home Tab Property** to our **Home** tab. This will direct users to the home page once they have been authenticated.

Once you have set these properties click on the **Update** link to save your settings. We now have the ability to add further content to the **Admin** tab. We will show you how this is done as we talk about other standard modules.

Special Features

Registration is built into the login control. Clicking on the **Register** button will bring the user to a registration page to create an account.

The login control gives users the ability to have the portal remember their login name and password. If the **Remember Login** checkbox is selected it will save the users' information in a cookie on their machine. The next time they navigate to the site they will automatically be authenticated.

If the users forget their password, they will be able to enter their username and click on the **Password Reminder** button. This will email their login information to the email account they used when they registered.

Announcements Module

The Announcements module produces a list of simple text announcements consisting of a title and brief description. Options include a **read more** link to a file, tab, or other site, announcement publish date, and expiration date.

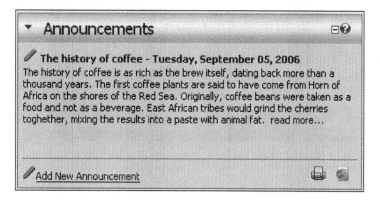

Practical Purposes

- **What's New Section**: This is a great use for the Announcements module. It is usually put on the home page of your site. It gives a headline with a short description of the content. It allows you to show a lot of information in a short amount of space by giving the users a **Read More** link for the items they want to read about more.

- **Article Listing**: The Announcements module allows you to link to pages internally and externally. This allows you to link to either articles you write or those that you have found on the Internet.

Administration and Modification

To create an announcement, click on the **Add New Announcement** link.

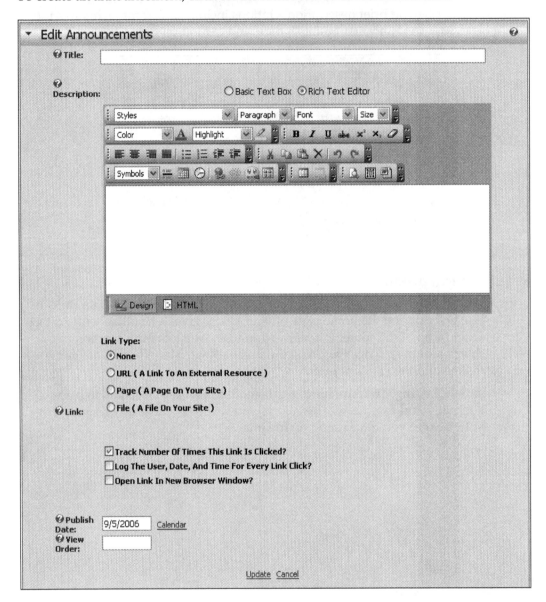

This will bring up the **Edit Announcements** page.

- **Title**: Type in a short title for the announcement; this will be displayed in bold at the top of the announcement.

- **Description**: The description is what allows you to give a short teaser of the full announcement. You can also use this to give a short announcement without giving a link to a larger article.

- **Link**: You have three choices as to where to link your announcement; you can link to any Internet URL, as we have done above, link to a tab on your site, or link to a file located in your folders. The last option allows you to link to any PDF, HTML, or Word document file located on your portal.

- **Track**: If this is checked, the module will track the number of times the link has been clicked.

- **Log**: If this is checked, the module will track who clicks on the **read more** link and when.

- **Open Link in a New Browser Window?**: As the title explains, this will cause a new browser window to open when a user clicks on the **read more** link.

- **Publish Date**: You can choose the publish date by clicking on the **Calendar** option; the date will be added to the title of the announcement.

- **View Order**: By default, announcements are ordered by the date that they are added or updated to the module. You can override this by placing a number in the view order box. The announcements will then be ordered numerically by the view order. If no number is entered, the order will be zero.

Special Features

Once you save your announcement, you will have the ability to track which announcements have the greatest interest to your users. To see this information, click on the pencil icon next to a particular announcement. (This option will be available only if the **Preview** option is unchecked.) At the bottom of the **Edit Announcement** page you can see how many times this announcement has been clicked and if the **Log** option is checked, then you can also see a log of who has clicked on it.

Banner Module

For a discussion on how to use the Banner module in conjunction with vendor advertising, see the *Vendors* sub-section under the *Host Tools* section in Chapter 5.

Blog Module

This module is a recent addition to the core distribution. It is actually a collection of related modules, which comprise all the working parts of a blog. When you add the Blog module to a page, you actually add all the working parts (which you can choose to delete or move). These presently include:

- **Menu**: List of blog-related actions that a user can take, based on permissions (e.g. changing settings, adding a post, etc.).
- **Search**: Utility for searching blog content.
- **Roll**: List of blogs on the site (or in some logical grouping).
- **Archive**: Calendar indicating dates when blogs have been posted.
- **Posts**: Display of the lists and content of the blogs.

In the example below, all five of the modules are shown. Menu (in the top of the left column), Roll (below the Menu in the left column), Posts (in the center column), Archive (in the right column), and Search (also in the right column).

The Roll module shows that there is already a blog on the site (**My Personal Blog**), which has two entries in the Posts module. If the current user does not have a blog, the Menu module indicates this displaying only one option—**Create My Blog**.

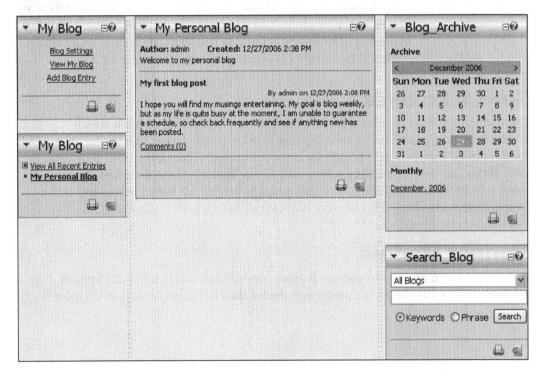

When the module is added to a page, all the individual modules are added automatically to the pane chosen by the user adding the module. Once the modules have been added they can be moved to provide the "traditional" blog view.

Practical Purposes

The term blog stands for WebLog. A WebLog is an online journal or diary. Users use blogs for a number of purposes:

- A personal diary, that may be of interest to friends and family
- A vacation journal
- A place to write editorial commentary

Administration and Modification

The Blog module is one of the newer modules available from the DotNetNuke website that has more advanced settings. These can be split into three categories:

- Settings that affect the Blog module as a whole
- Settings that relate to a single blog
- Settings that relate to a single blog post

A full description of all the administrative settings for this module is beyond the scope of this book. Let's look at the settings that relate to a single blog. To create a new blog click on the **Create My Blog** link in the blog menu.

Title:
This is the display title for your blog. It will display at the top of your entry list and in the blog directory.

Description:
This is a brief summary description of your blog. It's a good place to describe your intentions with your blog and what information readers can expect.

Blog Options:
These options control your blogs features.
☐ Make this blog public
☐ Allow users to post comments
☐ Approval for user comments required
☐ Allow anonymous users to post comments
☐ Approval for anonymous comments required
☐ Allow Trackback comments
☐ Approval for Trackback Comments required
☐ Trackback Auto Discovery (Client Mode)
☐ Send mail notification after comments and trackbacks are posted

When displaying your identity use:
◉ User Name ○ Full Name

The figure above shows the top half of the resulting page. It provides a number of properties that affect the new blog.

- **Title**: This is the title of the new blog. This will display in the blogroll.
- **Description**: This provides a description of the blog. This will display at the top of the Posts module when a user is viewing the new blog, and is a good place to provide information about your intentions for the blog.
- **Blog Options**: Next are a group of options that control how readers can interact with your blog. For the most part these options are self-explanatory.

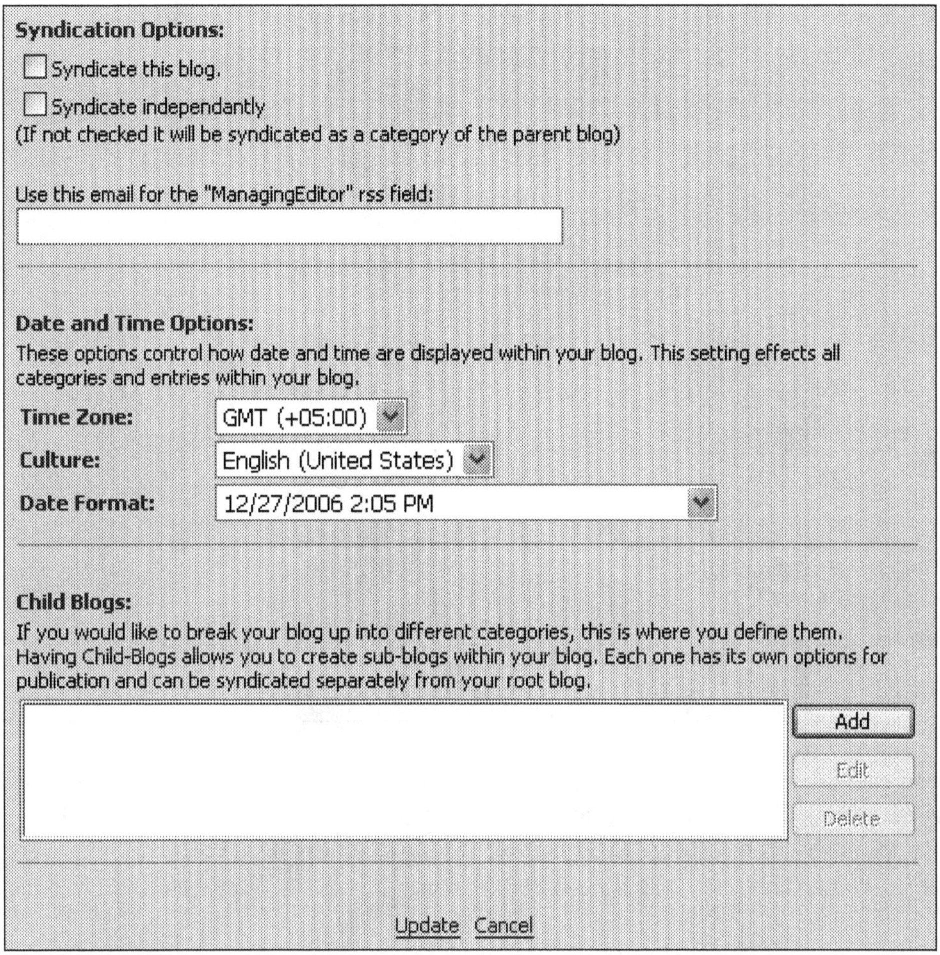

Syndication Options:

☐ Syndicate this blog.

☐ Syndicate independantly
(If not checked it will be syndicated as a category of the parent blog)

Use this email for the "ManagingEditor" rss field:

Date and Time Options:
These options control how date and time are displayed within your blog. This setting effects all categories and entries within your blog.

Time Zone: GMT (+05:00) ▾

Culture: English (United States) ▾

Date Format: 12/27/2006 2:05 PM ▾

Child Blogs:
If you would like to break your blog up into different categories, this is where you define them. Having Child-Blogs allows you to create sub-blogs within your blog. Each one has its own options for publication and can be syndicated separately from your root blog.

	Add
	Edit
	Delete

Update Cancel

- **Syndication Options**: These options control how you can syndicate your blog.
- **Date and Time Options**: The date and time options control how dates and times appear in your blog.

- **Child Blogs**: The Child Blogs area allows you to split up your blog into different categories, by creating sub-blogs of your blog.

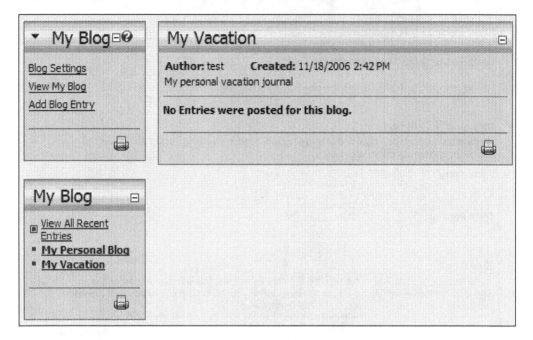

As you can see from the figure, once the blog is created it shows up in the blogroll (**My Vacation**). The Menu module provides a number of options, including the ability to modify the settings for this blog, and add a new blog entry.

To add a new blog entry click on the **Add Blog Entry** link.

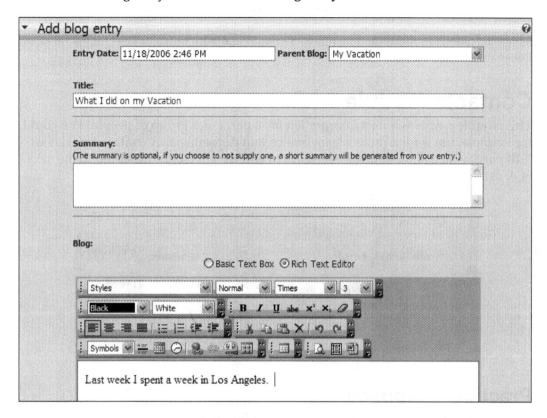

- **Entry Date**: The date for this blog entry.
- **Parent Blog**: Select the blog that this entry belongs to.
- **Summary**: A summary (or abstract) of the blog. If this is left empty, the first section of the blog itself will be displayed in the Posts module.
- **Blog**: The blog text itself.

Entry Options:

☑ Published (If not checked, only you will see this entry)
☑ Allow users to comment on this entry (overrides Blog Setting)
☐ Display Copyright notice at the bottom of your entry.

Trackback Url:

Update   Cancel

- **Entry Options**: At the bottom of the page is a group of options that apply to this blog entry. They are fairly self-explanatory.

Click on **Update** to create your blog. Clicking on **Cancel** would cancel all the entries made by you.

Contacts Module

This module renders contact information for a particular group of people. You could, for example, use it for a project team or a certain department. A contact includes an **Edit** page, which allows authorized users to edit the contacts data stored in the SQL database.

Practical Purposes

- Storing a list of contacts on your portal for all users.
- Storing internal company phonebook information protected by security roles.

Administration and Modification

To add a new contact, sign in as **admin**, hover the mouse cursor over the pencil icon by the **Contacts** title, and click on the **Add New Contact** link.

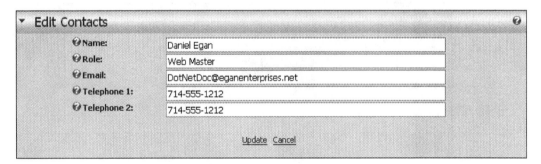

- **Name**: Enter a name for the contact.
- **Role**: Enter the role for this contact. This is not a security role, and should be the title of the contact (Manager, Owner, Partner, etc.).
- **Email**: Enter the email address for this contact.
- **Telephone 1**: Enter a primary phone number for this contact.
- **Telephone 2**: Enter a secondary phone number for this contact.

Click **Update** to save your settings.

Special Features

- **Mailto** hyperlink created by contact's email address is cloaked by creating a JavaScript function utilizing `String.fromCharCode` to keep spambots from harvesting email addresses.
- **Call** link available if page is browsed by a wireless telephone.

Documents Module

The Documents module provides a list of documents with links to view (depending on users' file associations) or download the document.

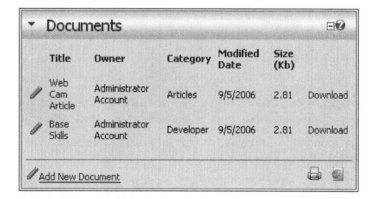

Practical Purposes

- Can be used as a document repository for Word, Excel, PDF, and so on.
- Can be used to give access to programs, modules, presentations, etc. contained inside a ZIP file.
- Can be used as a resource section by adding links to downloads on other sites.

Administration and Modification

To add a new document, sign in as **admin** and click on the **Add New Document** link.

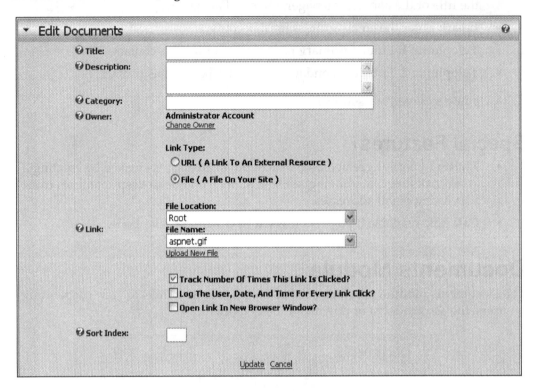

- **Title**: Fill in the title of the document.
- **Description**: Add a description of the document. This is for your own use in keeping track of the documents on the site. It is not displayed to the user.
- **Category**: Enter in a category for this download. The category is used to help organize the downloads.
- **Owner**: Shows the owner of the document. This defaults to the user that added the document, but if the **Change Owner** link is clicked the owner's name is changed to a drop-down list of users, allowing you to change the owner of the document.

- **Link**: Select a URL or file. Use a URL for content located on another site. Specify the file location for content located on this site. Either select the file from the drop-down or enter the URL for the download. You can use the upload link to upload new content to the portal.

- **Track** and **Log**: Check the **Track** and **Log** checkboxes if you would like this module to track downloads for this content. It will give you a detailed list at the bottom of the **Edit** screen showing you the date and time of each user downloading this item.

- **Sort Index**: You can control the order of the documents in the list by setting the **Sort Index** of the document.

Click on **Update** to save your settings.

Special Features and Additional Information

The owner of the download, as listed in the module, will be the user who adds the download to the module. Also, items will sort by when you added them to the module. There is no way to re-sort this information other than by removing and re-adding the items in the order that you would like them.

Events Module

The Events list/calendar module produces a display of up-coming events as a list in chronological order or in calendar format. Each event can be set to automatically expire on a particular date or to re-occur after a specified number of days, weeks, months, or years.

The original Events module has been replaced by a new Events module that is much more powerful. The new module adds the ability to allow viewers to register for events, and pay for the event registration through PayPal, as well as the ability to merge multiple calendars into a single display.

Practical Purposes

- Listing upcoming events for an organization.
- Keeping track of upcoming deadlines in a calendar format.
- Listing recurring appointments or reminders.

Administration and Modification

The Events module is the first standard module that we have discussed that utilizes the module-settings page for additional options. To see the custom options for this module, hover the mouse cursor over the **Edit** menu and click on the **Settings** menu item.

```
⊟ Event Module Settings

In this section, you can set up settings that are specific for this module.
❷ Help

      ⊞ General Settings
      _____

      ⊞ Event List Settings
      _____

      ⊞ Notification Settings
      _____

      ⊞ Enrollment Settings
      _____

      ⊞ Moderation Settings
      _____

      ⊞ Master Settings
      _____
```

Each of the sections has a number of settings that can control the behavior of the module. As an example, let's look at the **Enrollment Settings**.

```
⊟ Enrollment Settings

❷ Permit Event Enrollment (may be moderated - see        ☐
                                           below)

                ❷ PayPal Account (paid enrollments):  [            ]
```

This section allows you to determine whether event enrollment is permitted, and for paid enrollments, provides the ability to include the PayPal account that will be used for the payments.

To add a new event, sign in as **admin**, and click on the **Add Events** link.

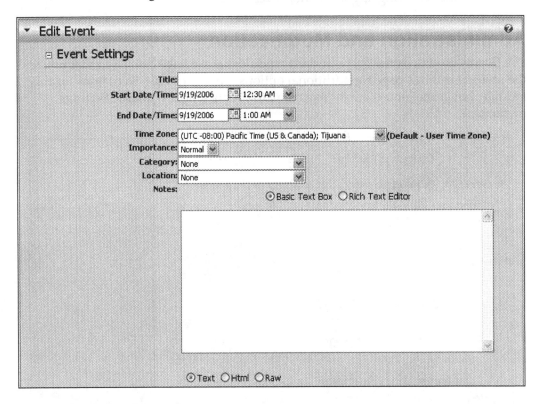

- **Title**: Enter a title for the event. This will be displayed in bold on the first line of the event for the list view or inside the cell for the calendar view.

- **Start Date/Time**: This is the date/time when the pattern will start if this is a recurring event. For a one-time event, this is the start date of the event.

- **End Date/Time**: This is the date/time for the end of the event.

- **TimeZone**: This is the time zone for the event. By default this is the same as the time zone for the site.

- **Importance/Category/Location**: These properties categorize the event and provide the location for the event.

- **Notes**: Enter a description for the event. This will be displayed in regular text in the detail view of the event.

You can expand the **Image Settings** section to set the properties for the image to associate with this event.

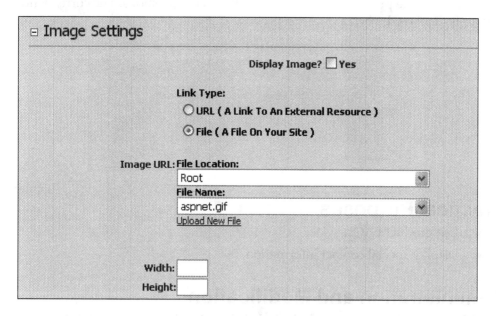

- **Display Image**: Select whether to display an image – the default is No.
- **Image URL**: Choose the URL of the image, which may be a file resource on the site or a link to an external or internal image URL.
- **Width**: Set the width of the image.
- **Height**: Set the height of the image.

Note that if both the width and height of the image are set, then they should be in the same ratio as the original image, or else the image will appear distorted.

Special Features and Additional Information

As mentioned above, the new Events module provides a lot of extra features and flexibility. These include:

- The ability to merge individual calendar modules into a single display.
- The ability to enroll for events, including the ability to use PayPal to collect any necessary payments.
- A more extensive control of the options for recurring events.

FAQs Module

The FAQs module produces a list of frequently asked questions. The corresponding answer is displayed when a question is clicked.

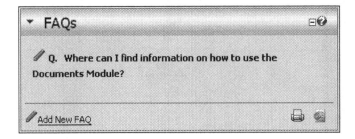

Practical Purposes

- List product FAQs.
- Display special contact information.

Administration and Modification

To add a new FAQ, sign in as **admin** and click on the **Add New FAQ** link.

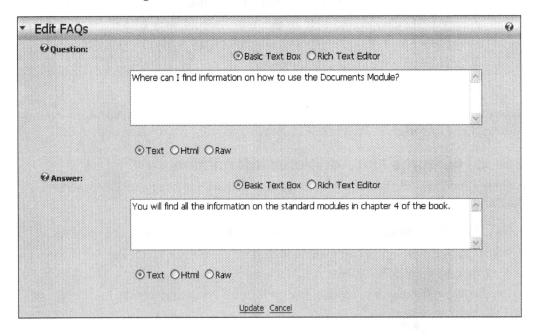

- **Question**: Enter the FAQ Question.
- **Answer**: Enter the FAQ Answer.

Click on **Update** to save your changes.

Special Features and Additional Information

The question is presented as a hyperlink. When the question is clicked, the answer will be shown. This helps to save space on your page by only showing the answers to the questions when they are requested.

Feedback Module

The Feedback module produces a form for visitors to send messages to a specific email address. If users are already logged in, their name and email address will be automatically placed into the form.

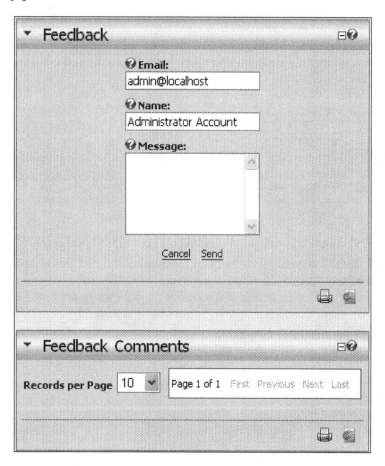

As we have already seen with the blog module. it comprises of two separate modules — the Main Feedback module, which is used to collect the feedback from the user, and the Feedback Comments module, which provides a listing of all the comments. In most scenarios this second module would only be made visible to administrators.

Practical Purposes

- Have users request content or changes on your portal.
- Use as a **Contact Us** section.
- Allow users to give general feedback about your portal.

Administration and Modification

The Feedback module is a simple but extensively used standard module.

By default, all Feedback modules send the email to the administrator of the site. If you would like to send the feedback to a specific email address, log in as **admin**, go to **Module Settings** on the **Module Edit** menu, and add the e-mail address into the **Send To** box found in the **Feedback Settings** section. Click on the **Update** link when finished.

⊟ **Feedback Settings**

In this section, you can set up settings that are specific for this module.

❷ **Help**

   ❷ **Send To:**

Special Features and Additional Information

When we discussed the general features of modules earlier in this chapter, we looked at an option that would put a module on every tab. The Feedback module would be a good candidate for this action. It fits nicely on either the left or the right pane, and allows your users to contact you with questions without having to go to any particular tab to use the module.

Forums Module

The Forums module is the single largest and most complicated module available in the DotNetNuke project. A full description of this module is way beyond the scope of this book—in fact this module is large enough to warrant its own book.

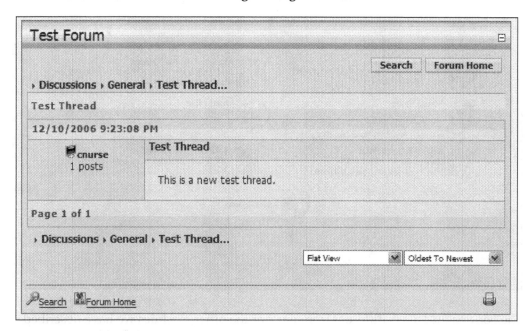

Practical Purposes

- Provide product support for an online store.
- Provide a discussion area for members of a club.

Administration and Modification

The Forums module has a complex set of Administration pages that are accessed through the **Forum Administration** menu item.

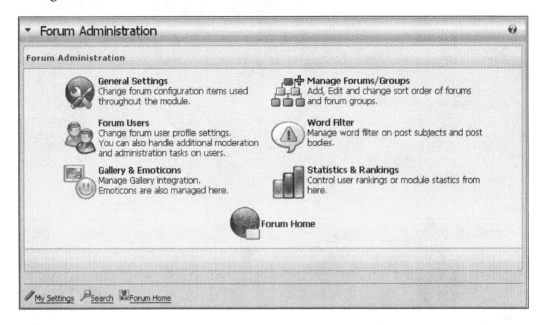

The Forums module is different from most of the other modules we have described so far, for the fact that it can be considered as an interactive module. Most other modules provide fairly static content that can be created and updated by an administrator. Typically, the Forums module is interactive for all users. We will therefore describe the interface that most users will use for creating a new thread—or for replying to an existing thread.

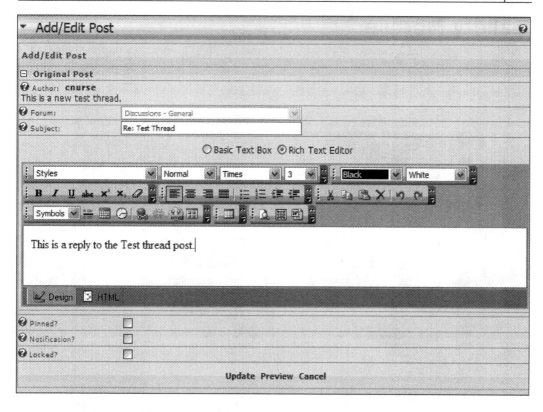

- **Author**: The first option displays the author. If the message being created is a reply to a previous post then the previous post is shown immediately below the author.

- **Forum**: This is a drop-down list of the forums on the site that are available to the user. This option is disabled if replying to an existing message.

- **Subject**: This is the subject of the post. In a reply the subject defaults to the same subject as the previous post preceded by **Re:**.

- **Message**: Next comes the message itself.

- **Pinned**: Some roles can pin the thread—make sure it remains at the top of a list of threads.

- **Notification**: If selected, and provided this is configured correctly in the Administration settings, a user can opt to receive an email whenever anybody replies to this post.

- **Locked**: An administrator can lock a thread (disable the ability to reply to the message).

Gallery Module

The gallery provides a central repository for media files. These files can be grouped into albums.

This module is also quite complex and a full description of this module is beyond the scope of this chapter.

Practical Purposes

- Provide an album of pictures from a vacation on a personal site.
- Provide an album of pictures from a club meeting on a club site.

Administration and Modification

The Gallery module has a complex set of Administration pages that are accessed through the **Gallery Configuration** menu item.

Most of the activities in this module are about uploading new media content to the modules. This is accomplished through a separate action menu that is part of the module.

Clicking on **Add File** brings up the **Edit Album** page, which allows you to edit and delete existing media in the gallery, as well as add new content.

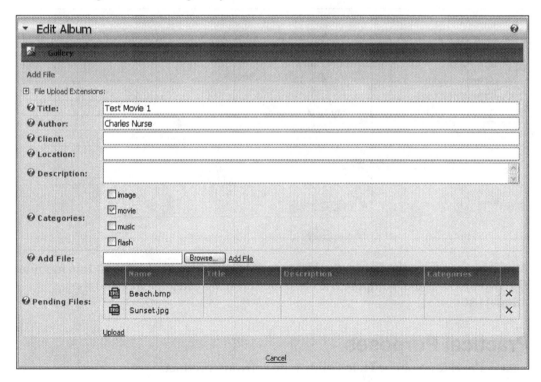

- **Title**: A title/name for the new media item.
- **Author**: The author of the media item.
- **Client/Location/Description**: These are extra fields that allow the user to categorize the media items being stored in this gallery.
- **Categories**: The type of the media item (currently image, movie, music, and flash are supported types).
- **Add File**: An upload file text box that allows the user to browse for the media file on their local computer and upload to the server.

At the bottom of this screen is a list of the current media files in this gallery.

Help Module

The Help module provides a list of articles or tutorials that can be assigned to one or more categories.

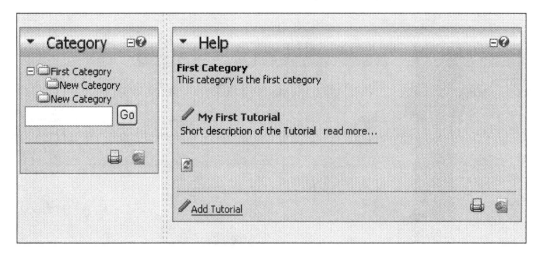

As can be seen from the figure, the Help module is another multiple-module module. The two modules that compose the Help module are a category tree and the tutorial list.

Practical Purposes

- Provide an online Help Guide for a software product.
- Provide a knowledge base of articles for a society.

Administration and Modification

Each of the two modules that compose the Help module has its own administration. Clicking **Manage Categories** on the category tree module will bring up the following page.

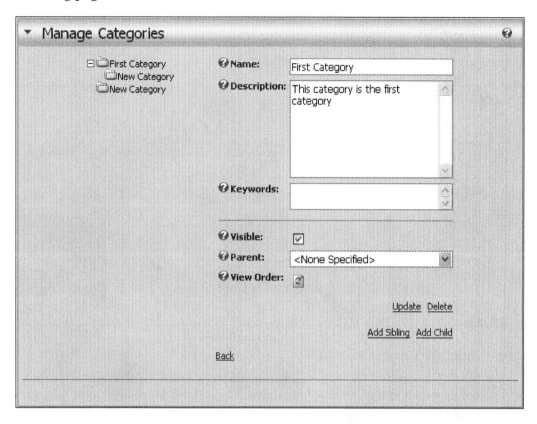

The **Manage Categories** edit page works somewhat similarly to the Lists Editor on the host menu. You first need to select an existing category in the tree. You can then edit that category by modifying the fields on the right-hand side of the screen, you can add a new category at the same depth in the hierarchy (**Add Sibling**), or you can add a child category of the current category (**Add Child**).

Adding a new category of either type immediately creates the new category and populates the fields on the right with default values, which you can then edit and update.

- **Name**: The name of the category.
- **Description**: A description of the category.

- **Keywords**: These keywords help in searching for tutorials in a large collection.

- **Visible**: Is this category visible to the user?

- **Parent**: This drop-down allows you to change the parent category of the current category in the category hierarchy.

Clicking the **Add Tutorial** menu option in the Tutorial List module brings up the following page that allows administrator users to create new tutorials.

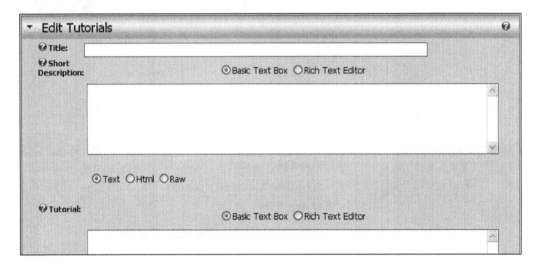

- **Title**: The name of the tutorial.

- **Short Description**: A short description of the tutorial (or abstract). This will be displayed in the Tutorial list followed by a **Read More** link that will take the reader to the complete tutorial.

- **Tutorial**: The complete text of the tutorial.

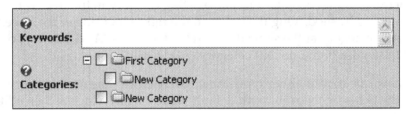

At the bottom of the edit page (after the Tutorial Editor), are two options that allow you to categorize the tutorial:

- **Keywords**: You can provide a list of keywords that assist in searching the list of tutorials for a specific tutorial.

- **Categories**: The tutorial can be assigned to one or more of the categories created in the **Manage Categories** module.

IFrame Module

IFrame is an Internet Explorer browser feature that allows you to display content from another website within a frame on your portal.

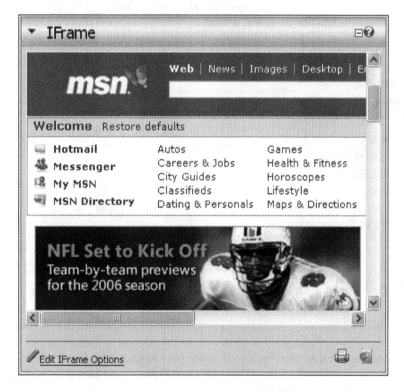

Practical Purposes

- Display dynamic content from another website.
- Keep users up to date on information on other sites.

Administration and Modification

To modify the IFrame module, sign in as **admin** and click on **Edit IFrame Options**.

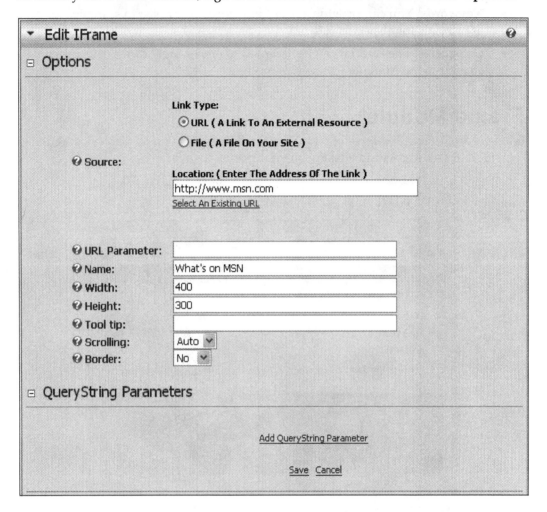

- **Source**: Select a source for the IFrame (the source is the web page you would like to be displayed in the IFrame). The IFrame captures a web page from another site like a mini browser.

- **Name**: Enter a name for this IFrame. This will not change the title of your module. To change the title of the module you will need to go to **Module Settings**.

- **Width**: Enter the width for the IFrame in pixels. This is how much of the page will show in your module.

- **Height**: Enter the height of the IFrame in pixels. This is how much of the page will show in your module.
- **Tooltip**: Text that displays in a tooltip when the user hovers the mouse cursor over the IFrame.
- **Scrolling**: Select a scrolling option. Since you are only showing a portion of the web page as determined in the **Width** and **Height** options, you will determine whether you would like to allow users to scroll the page for more information. Your options are **Auto** (Scrollbars will appear when needed), **Yes** (Scrollbars will be shown at all times), and **No** (Scrollbars will not be available).
- **Border**: Select whether you would like a border. **Yes** will display a border around your IFrame, while **No** will not.

Click **Update** to save your settings.

Special Features/Additional Information

Since the IFrame allows you to show content from other websites, you must make sure that you have permission to do this before setting up the IFrame. Contact the webmaster of the site to find out if this is allowed.

Image and Media Modules

The Image and Media modules are very similar. In fact, the Media module is an extension of the Image module and will probably replace the image module in future versions. Both modules display a single item of Media (Image is restricted to Image media types, while media can display other media types).

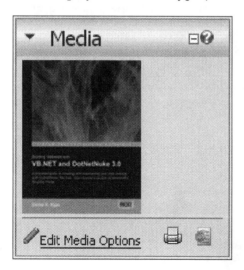

Practical Purpose

- Display a Video that users can watch.

Administration and Modification

To edit the options sign in as **admin** and click the **Edit Media/Image Options** link.

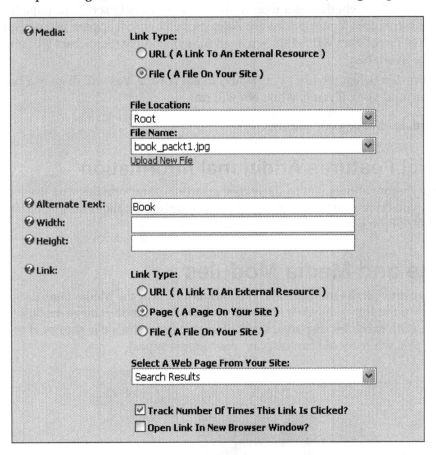

- **Media**: Select the source of the media. This can be a URL on an external site or a file on your own site.

- **Alternate Text**: The alternate text is displayed if the browser cannot display the media.

- **Width\Height**: You can specify the width and height is pixels. If the image is a different size the browser will scale the image accordingly.

- **Link**: You can turn the image into a hyperlink by providing a link here (this option is only available for the Media module).

Links Module

The Links module produces a list of hyperlinks to any tab, image, or file on the portal or to a web page, image, or file on the Web. The links can be set to display as a vertical or horizontal list, or as a drop-down box. The links appear alphabetically by default. An indexing field facilitates custom sorting. A supplemental description can be set to appear either on mouse rollover, or on the click of a dynamically generated link.

Practical Purposes

- Link to resources connected to your portal.
- Link to pages on your site.
- Link to internal site documents.

Administration and Modification

To add a new link to the Links module, sign in as **admin** and click the **Add Link** link.

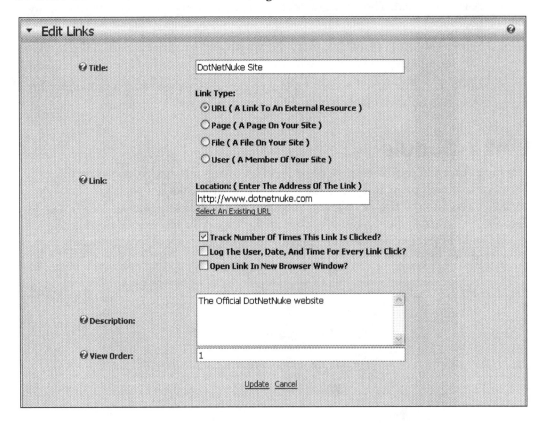

- **Title**: Enter the title for the link. The title is what the users see in the module and it is what they click on to open the link.

- **Link Type**: The Links module allows you to add links in three different ways:

  - **URL**: Allows you to link to an external web page (like Yahoo or MSN).

  - **Page**: Allows you to link to a page on your site. With this option you can create a **Quick Links** menu that allows users to quickly navigate to particular pages without having to navigate the main menu.

  - **File**: Acts as an option to the Documents module and allows you to give your users access to documents on your site.

- **Link**: Enter the destination of the link. Your options here will depend on what type of link you are using. If you are using **URL**, you can enter the address into the textbox. If using **Page option**, you will be presented with a drop-down of all your pages. If you are using **File**, you will be show a drop-down displaying the files on you portal.

- **Log** and **Track** boxes: Check these options. This will allow you to see how many users have used the links you provided.

- **Open Link In New Browser Window**: Check this box if you want your link to open in a new window (for example, when you link to another website or file).

- **Description**: The description section describes what the link is used for. You will be able to see this depending on the options you select.

- **View Order**: This will be used to sort your links numerically. If nothing is entered, this will default to zero and the links will be sorted by when they were added.

Special Features and Additional Features

The Links module gives you a choice of how you would like to view the content. To edit these options, sign in as **admin** and go to **Settings** on the **Module Edit** menu. You will find the settings under **Link Settings**.

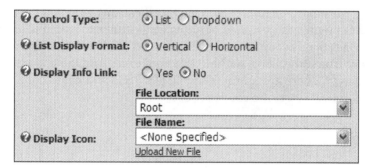

- **Control Type**: Select the control type you would like to use for your links. The default view for the Links module is to display them in a **List**, but you can choose to have them displayed in a **Dropdown**.

- **List Display Format**: Select the format in which you want to display your links—vertically or horizontally.

- **Display Info Link**: If **Yes** is selected, an ellipsis will be placed next to the link. When it is clicked it will show the description of the link that you entered when you created the link.

- **Display Icon**: You can select an icon to display with this link.

News Feed (RSS) Module

The News Feed module provides visitors with up-to-date and topical information on a wide range of topics (see `http://w.moreover.com/categories/category_list_rss.html` for one of the more comprehensive selections). Information includes a title linked to the source document, source, and publication date.

Practical Purposes

- Supply users with information updates on other sites.
- View favorite blogs directly on your portal.

Administration and Modification

RSS (**Rich Site Summary** or **Really Simple Syndication**) is an XML-based format for syndicated content. It is designed to allow individuals to distribute news or articles in a format that is easy for programs to read (XML). This allows you to gather relevant content from other sites without needing to rewrite the content or update articles on your site. There are many places to get RSS-syndicated content. One of the better known is `http://www.moreover.com`.

To add an RSS feed to your site, sign in as **admin** and click on the
Edit Newsfeed link.

- **News Feed Source**: You can select a news feed generated from your portal or from an external source. Type in the URL location for the news feed.

- **News Feed Style Sheet**: XSL style sheets allow you to determine how the data appears in your module. If nothing is selected it will use the default XSL RSS91.xsl, which is located in the DesktopModules/News folder. You can either leave the default, or link to an XSL style sheet on the Internet, or on your site.

- **Security Options (optional)**: Some news feeds are not free, and will require you to give a username, and password to use them.

Click **Update** to save your changes.

Special Features

RSS feeds are a great way for you to add important and relevant information to your site with very little effort.

Repository Module

The Repository module provides a centrally-categorized resource library. It can be used to store any kind of file, categorize it, and provide a description. The module's view control is templatable, enabling the module to provide a flexible look and feel.

In addition, the module provides "moderation". This feature allows unmoderated users to upload new files and create new entries in the repository, but these new files do not become "active" until approved by a moderator.

This module is another of the newer more complex module projects and a full description of the module is beyond the scope of this chapter.

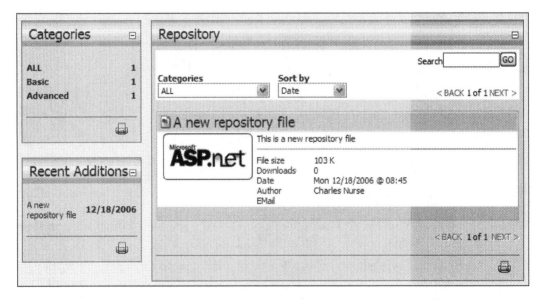

A separate Repository Dashboard module is also available. This module can be configured to provide multiple ways to access the resources. In the example above, there are two dashboard modules in the left column; the top one is configured to provide a list of categories, while the bottom is configured to provide a list of the most recent additions.

Practical Purposes

- A Membership Directory—each entry provides a link to a member's personal site.

- A catalog of downloadable tutorials in a Knowledge Base.

Administration and Modification

As mentioned above, a full description of the configuration of this module is beyond the scope of this article. We will focus on the process of adding a new entry (or editing an existing entry).

When logged in as a user with edit rights, an **Upload** button will appear at the top of the module's display area. (The actual location of the **Upload** button will depend on the template being used to display the module's content.) Click this button to add a new entry to the repository.

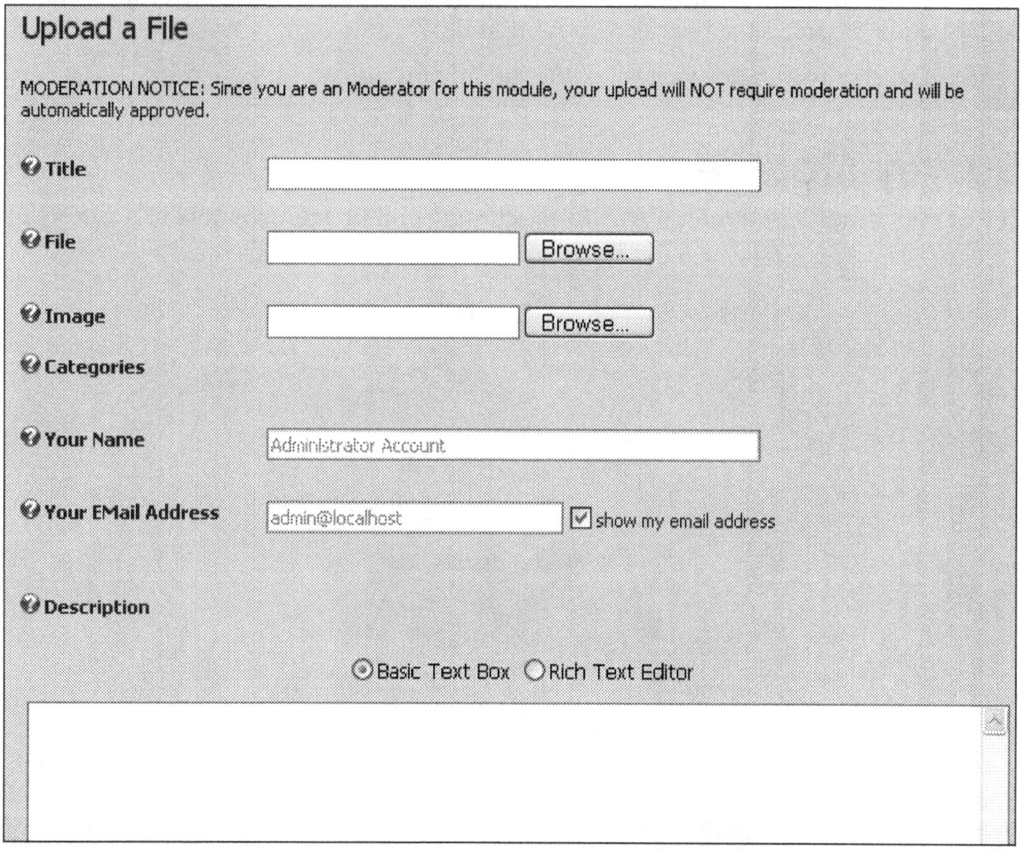

Upload a File

MODERATION NOTICE: Since you are an Moderator for this module, your upload will NOT require moderation and will be automatically approved.

Title

File   [Browse...]

Image   [Browse...]

Categories

Your Name   Administrator Account

Your EMail Address admin@localhost   ☑ show my email address

Description

⊙ Basic Text Box ○ Rich Text Editor

Note that at the top of the edit page is a **Moderation Notice**. This indicates to the user whether their upload will require approval. In this case, since the user is a moderator, the upload will be automatically approved.

- **Title**: A title (or name) for the repository entry.
- **File**: Here you select the file (on your local hard-drive) that you wish to add to the repository.
- **Image**: Here you can select an image to associate with the repository entry.
- **Categories**: You can identify the entry as belonging to one or more categories by checking the checkboxes in this row. (The categories are defined in the Module Settings for the module.)
- **Your Name**: Your name is displayed here.
- **Your Email Address**: Your email address is displayed here, together with a checkbox that allows you to control whether your email address is displayed in the repository listing. (Not all templates support the display of the email address, so this only affects those that do.)
- **Description**: A description of the item being uploaded.

Survey Module

The Survey module provides a way to solicit information from visitors to a site.

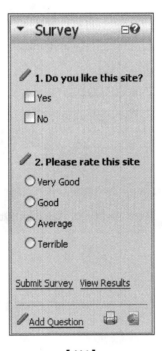

The figure on the page opposite shows the Survey module as it would appear to an administrator. It demonstrates the two primary types of survey questions—questions that can have multiple answers, indicated by the use of checkboxes, and questions that can only have one answer, indicated by the use of option buttons.

When a user has answered all the questions, they can view the results of the survey. This will look something like this:

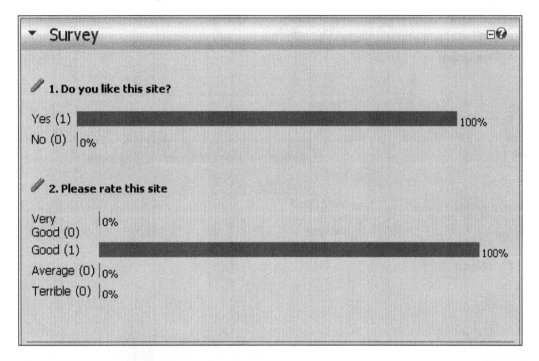

Administration and Modification

When logged in as a user with Edit rights a new survey question can be added by selecting the **Add Question** menu item.

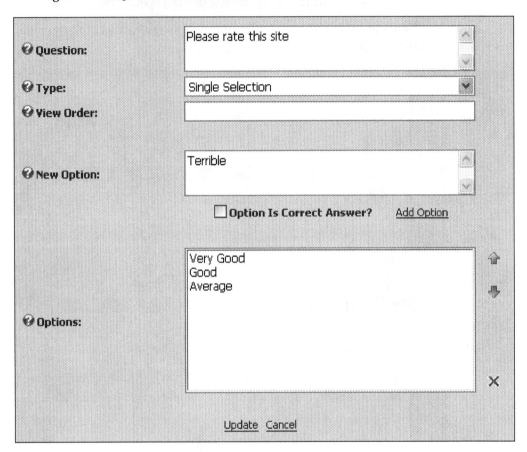

- **Question**: The survey question to display to the user.
- **Type**: The type of survey question (single selection vs. multiple selection).
- **View Order**: The order of the question in the list of questions.
- **New Option**: This field is used to add new options to the "Options" list. Add some text to this field and select **Add Option** to add a new option to display.

Text/HTML Module

The Text/HTML module provides for the input of simple or HTML-formatted text. Simple text is input in a standard textbox and a filter converts carriage returns (paragraph breaks) to HTML breaks. HTML-formatted text can be input directly, or generated by an alternative rich-text input utility that provides a number of advanced WYSIWYG features as well as a gallery of all uploaded images.

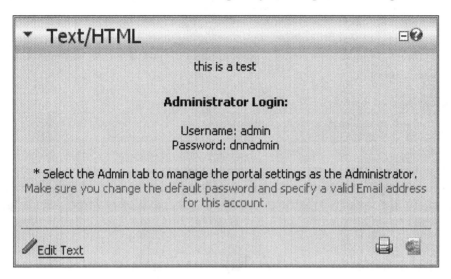

Practical Purposes

- Adding welcome information to your home page.
- Creating short tutorials with bolding, highlighting, and images.
- Building professional-looking ads to place on your site.

Administration and Modification

To edit the Text/HTML module, sign in as **admin** and select the module's **Edit** menu.

When adding content, you have two options: you can add text to the module using the basic textbox, or you can use the Rich Text Editor.

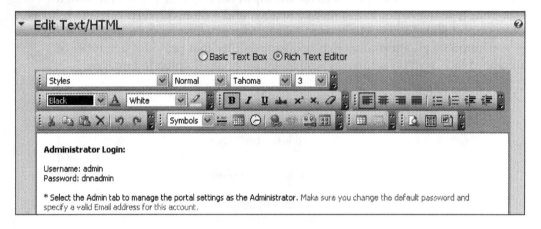

You are able to edit the text in many different ways. You can use tables to organize data, insert images, and modify the color, type, and size of the font. To accomplish this DotNetNuke uses FreeTextBox version 3.0. FreeTextBox is a freely-available control that can be used with ASP.NET. To save your data click on the **Update** link.

Special Features and Additional Information

Because of its versatility, the Text/HTML module is probably the most widely used module on a DotNetNuke site. Most tabs are filled with static data and this module fits the bill.

User Accounts Module

The User Account module permits registered users to add, edit, and update their user account details. Membership services are also managed here.

> If you use the Accounts Module for your user registration instead of the default you will need to create a page to hold the module and set the **User Tab** option in **Site Settings** in order for this to work. It is also important to note that if you set the **User Tab** option to a page that does not have a User Accounts module on it, you will be unable to sign into your portal.

Practical Purpose

- This module can be used to create a page that has many different user modules on it.

Administration and Modification

By default, the User Account module is found when users click on their respective names in the header. You are not allowed to modify this page. So, if you want to combine the User Accounts module with other modules, you can add it to any tab you would like.

Special Features and Additional Information

There are two sections to the User Account module. The first section is used to edit and update the user's information.

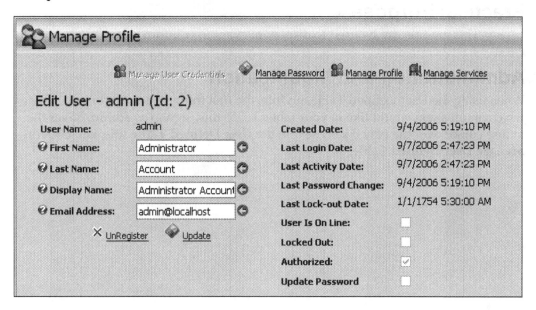

Here you are able to change your password and personal information, or unregister from the portal completely. The bottom section holds all the available member services. These services are set up by the admin while creating user roles. If the role is set up as a public role it will show up in this section.

User Defined Table Module

The User Defined Table module allows you to create a custom data table for managing tabular information.

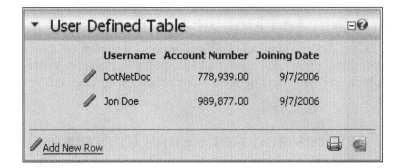

Practical Purpose

- This module can be used to display relevant user information.

Administration and Modification

When using the User Defined Table module, the first thing you must do is to decide what columns you would like in your table. To do this, sign in as **admin**, hover the mouse cursor over the pencil icon next to the **User Defined Table** title, and click on **Manage User Defined Table**.

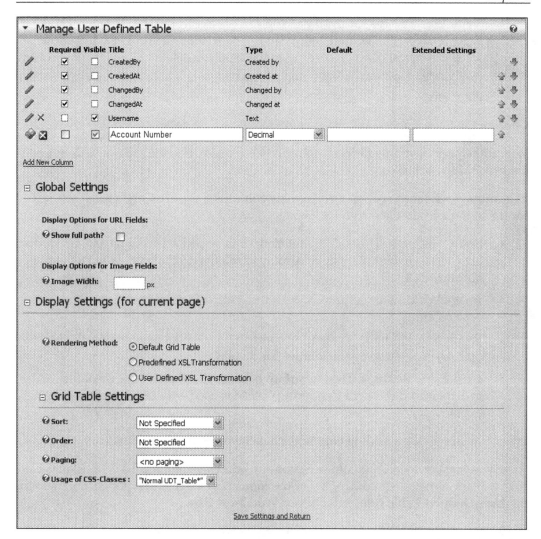

Click on **Add New Column**. This will present you with the dialog boxes necessary to create a new column for your table.

- **Required**: If this column is checked the column will be required i.e. when adding a new row this column cannot be empty.

- **Visible**: If you don't want the column to be visible to non-admin roles, uncheck the **Visible** checkbox.

- **Title**: Enter a title for the column.

- **Type**: Select a type for the data. You can choose from **Text, Integer, True/ False, Date**, and **Decimal**. Select the appropriate type from the drop-down. Data will be validated according to the type you select.

- **Default**: A default value to use if the user adding a new row does not enter anything.

Click on the **Save** icon to save the current column to the database.

Repeat the previous steps for each column you require. Use the arrows to determine the order of the columns.

In addition to the settings required for new columns there are some global settings for the module available through this page.

- **Show Full path**: This setting determines how URLs are displayed. URLs that are for the current site can be displayed relative to the root, or with the full absolute URL.

- **Image Width**: This setting controls the width of images in Image type columns.

- **Rendering Method**: This setting controls how the table is rendered. The XSL options provide more flexibilities for display.

- **Grid Table Settings**: The last group of settings controls how the table is displayed if the Grid Rendering option is used — these are fairly self-explanatory.

When you are finished adding columns, click **Save Settings and Return**.

After you have created your columns, you can add rows of data. To do this, make sure you are signed in as **admin**, hover the mouse cursor over the pencil icon next to the **User Defined Table** title, and click on **Add New Row**.

- Enter the data for the row. The data you enter will be validated from the type you selected when setting up the columns. If the data you enter is not valid, you will be shown an error message at the top of the page.

- Click on **Update** to save your row.
- Repeat these steps for additional rows.

Special Features and Additional Information

Since it is impossible to predict the different types of data that portal administrators may want on their site, the User Defined Table module gives you the ability to customize your site with data that is pertinent to you and your users.

XML/XSL Module

The XML/XSL module renders the result of an XML/XSL transform. The XML and XSL files are identified by their UNC paths in the `xmlsrc` and `xslsrc` properties of the module. The XML/XSL module includes an **Edit** page, which persists these settings to the SQL database.

Practical Purpose

- You can use this module for presenting XML data in a readable format.

Administration and Modification

News feeds are not the only application to use XML to deliver data. Whether you have a program on your local intranet or you are trying to access a web service, the XML/XSL module allows you to translate the XML data to a readable format fit for your web page.

Special Features and Additional Information

Like the User Defined Table module, the XML/XLS module gives you tremendous flexibility on the type of information you can present to your users. Using standard XML data, you can create different XLS style sheets to present the data differently for different users.

Summary

In this chapter, we covered the standard modules that come prepackaged with DotNetNuke. We covered their basic uses as well as situations they may be used in. You will use these modules to build the content of your portal. In the next chapter we will cover the administration options you have available to you as well as the differences between the admin and host login.

5
Host and Admin Tools

Running a DotNetNuke site requires someone to administer the site. There are two built-in roles for accomplishing the tasks associated with this. The host and admin roles are very similar in nature and ability, but possess some important differences. In this chapter, we will learn the following:

- The difference between host and admin
- How to access and use the admin tools
- How to access and use the host tools

The Difference between Host and Admin

There has always been a bit of confusion about what differentiates the admin and host roles. To understand the difference, you first have to look into how DotNetNuke works. An implementation of DotNetNuke is not restricted to one portal. DotNetNuke has the ability to run multiple portals from one database. This is where the difference between the roles comes in.

The host has the responsibility of, for lack of a better word, hosting the portals. The host will have access to any parent and/or child portals that are created, as well as all the administrative functions. This user is sometimes called a **superuser**. In previous versions of DotNetNuke, you were only allowed one superuser per installation. Starting with DotNetNuke 3.0, and continuing with DotNetNuke 4.0, you can add additional users with superuser abilities. This really helps to divide the tasks needed to run a portal.

The admin role on the other hand is responsible for only one portal. There can be more than one admin for every portal, but unlike the superusers, they only have the ability to access one portal. While the superuser has access to both host tools and the admin tools, the admin will only see the admin tools.

Admin Tools

When you sign on to your DotNetNuke portal using an admin login, you will see an admin menu item appear on the menu bar. In this section we will cover these menu items in detail.

The first admin menu item is **Site Settings**. The **Site Settings** cover a wide range of services for a site. Because of this, we cannot cover this in one section of the book. We will walk through each item on the **Site Settings** page and either describe its functionality or point you to where you can find the information in this book.

Site Settings

Like the other admin screens we have seen, the **Site Settings** page lays out several options that allow the administrator to customize the portal experience. These settings are divided into three sections: **Basic Settings**, **Advanced Settings**, and **StyleSheet Editor**. We will begin with the **Basic Settings** section.

Basic Settings

The **Site Details** are used to tailor your portal with the information that describes what your site is used for:

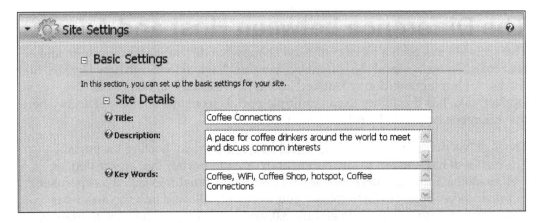

- **Title**: The title or name for your website. This will be displayed in the top bar of your browser along with the current tab information.

- **Description** and **Key Words**: Used by search engines when describing your site. The key words should be entered in a comma-separated format.

The **Appearance** section controls the basic look and feel of your site.

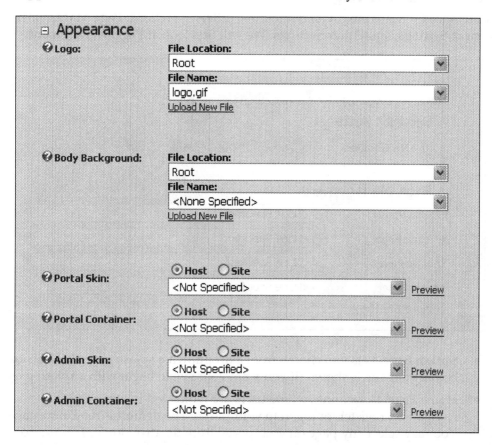

- **Logo**: If you are using the default look of DotNetNuke, you can change the logo from the DotNetNuke `logo.gif` to one of your choice.

- **Body Background**: As an alternative to skinning your site, you can choose to change the background of your site to any image you would like. To do this, select the image from the dropdown. You will need to upload the image to your site first. The ease of using skins makes this option almost obsolete.

- **Portal Skin**, **Portal Container**, **Admin Skin**, and **Admin Container**: This section allows you to select a skin for your portal. There are different sections for Admin and Portal skins because Admin sections of the site usually use only one frame and portal sections use three or more. You can find out more about skinning your portal in Chapter 9.

Advanced Settings

The advanced settings are divided into three different sections: **Page Management**, **Payment Settings**, and **Other Settings**. We will first look at **Page Management**.

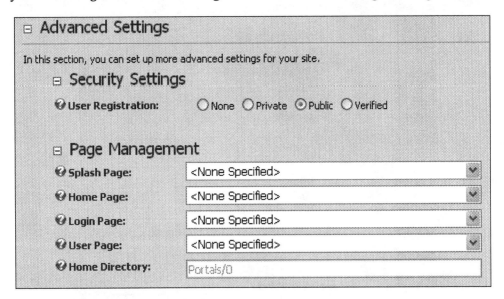

- **Splash Page**: Lets you choose from a dropdown a splash page that will load before your site is shown (if you want your site to begin with a splash page).

- **Home Page**: Determines where users are redirected to when they first navigate to, register, or log in to your portal. The default is the **Home** page. You may select any page on your portal from the dropdown. This is also the page where the user will be re-directed once they have completed the registration or the login process.

- **Login Page**: This is the page where the user will be directed to when they attempt to log in to the portal.

- **User Page**: By default, administrators can't edit the user account information page, but can place the User Accounts Module on a separate page along with other modules of their choosing. To change the default user accounts page to a different tab, you can select the page from the drop-down box. The user will be re-directed to this page if he or she is registering on the site.

- **Home Directory**: The physical path of your portal's location.

The **Payment Settings** section, as the name implies, allows you to add payment processing to your portal:

- **Currency**, **Payment Processor**, **Processor UserId**, and **Processor Password**: DotNetNuke gives you the ability to charge users for subscribing to a service on your site (see *Understanding DotNetNuke Roles* in Chapter 3). The only payment processor fully integrated into DotNetNuke at this time is PayPal.

The **Other Settings** section helps you customize your portal to fit the company's identity.

- **Copyright**: The copyright notice that appears on the footer of each page on the portal. Change this to reflect your portal name.

- **Banner Advertising**: Allows you to decide whether you want banner advertising to be on a single site or on all the sites under the host.

- **Administrator**: The default administrator for this site. You can select anyone who has been added to the administrator role.

- **Default Language**: Beginning with DotNetNuke 3.0, localization has been integrated into the DotNetNuke portal. At the time of writing, only English and German were available, but many more are on the way. You can set the default language of your portal by selecting it from the dropdown.

- **Portal Time Zone**: Allows you to localize your portal's time zone.

Stylesheet Editor

The **Stylesheet Editor** section is the final portion of the **Site Settings**.

- **Edit Style Sheet**: This will allow you to edit the CSS stylesheet for the DotNetNuke site. You can change the look and feel of the site by modifying the styles located in the stylesheet. This section has been made somewhat obsolete because of the new skinning solution for DotNetNuke.

```
/* ================================
   CSS STYLES FOR DotNetNuke
   ================================
*/


/* PAGE BACKGROUND */
/* background color for the header at the top of the page  */
.HeadBg {
}

/* background color for the content part of the pages */
Body
{
}

/* background/border colors for the selected tab */
.TabBg {
}
```

Pages Menu

You will find a discussion on pages under the *Understanding DotNetNuke Pages and tabIDs* section in Chapter 3.

Security Roles

You will find a discussion on Security roles under *Understanding DotNetNuke Roles* in Chapter 3.

User Accounts

You will find a discussion of user accounts under *User Accounts* in Chapter 3.

Vendors

You will find a discussion of vendors under the *Host Tools* section in this chapter.

Site Log

The site log gives you access to log files that keep track of most things that happen on your portal.

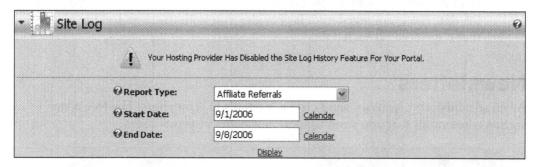

To use the site report, select one of the following options from the dropdown, select a **Start Date** and **End Date**, and click on the **Display** link.

- **Affiliate Referrals**: You can track when users enter your site from sites that are affiliated with you. To make this work, the link coming from the affiliate site must add a querystring to the URL. For example, instead of pointing the link to `http://www.CoffeeConnections.net`, you would point it to `http://www.CoffeeConnections.net?AffililiateID=108`. You would need to give different IDs to different affiliates. When someone logs in using one of those links, it is recorded into the database and you then have the ability to view reports of this data.

- **Detailed Site Log**: This report gives you the name of the user, the date and time they entered your site, the website they came from (referrer), the type of browser they are using (user agent), their IP address (UserHostAddress), and the name of the tab they entered on.

- **Page Popularity**: This report gives you the Page Name, number of times the page has been visited, and when the tab was last visited.

- **Page Views By Day**, **Week**, **Month**, **Hour**: The report gives you summarized views of how many visitors have been on your site.

- **Site Referrals**: This report gives you the website that referred users to the site (referrer), the number of times users came from the site, and the last time a user was referred by the site. Unlike the **Affiliate Referral**, this tracks users from any website, and not just those with which you have a relationship.

- **User Agents**: This report gives the types of browsers (user agents) used to browse your site as well as the number of times each browser was used.

- **User Frequency**: This report gives you the number of times each user has logged onto your site. It also displays the last time users logged on.

- **User Registration by Country**: This report details what country your users come from. The report depends entirely on the country the users select when registering on your portal.

- **User Registrations by Date**: This report sorts the registrations on your site by the date the users registered. It provides you with the date and the number that registered on each date.

Newsletters

As an administrator, you can send out bulk emails to your users. The **Newsletter** section contains all that you need to send newsletters to your users.

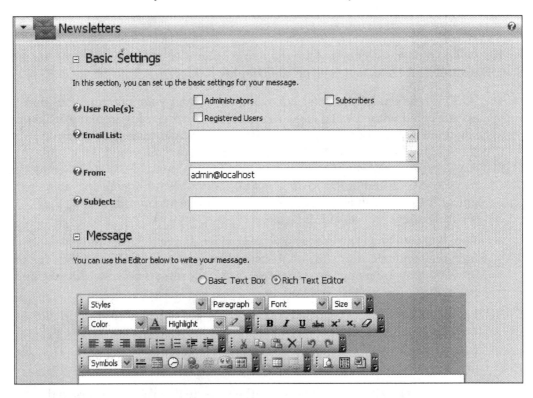

- **User Roles**: You can send an email to a select group of users based on the user roles you set up for your portal. (For more information on user roles, see *Understanding DotNetNuke Roles* in Chapter 3.)

- **Email List**: Optionally, you can send emails to email addresses in this email list. You will need to make sure that you separate each email address with a semi-colon.

- **Subject**: This will appear on the subject line when the email is received.

- **Message**: The body of the message that you want to send. You may use either a **Basic Text Box** or the **Rich Text Editor** (FreeTextBox).

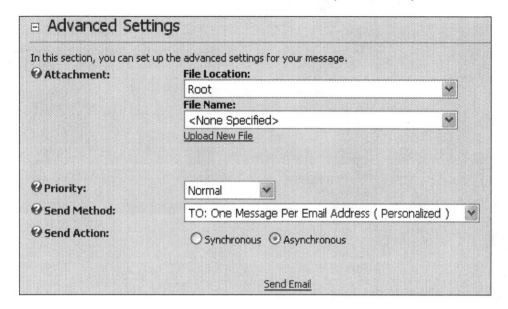

- **Attachment**: You can add an attachment to be sent out in the email. Select the attachment from the drop-down box or upload a new file. For more information on uploading files, see the *File Manager* section in this chapter.

- **Priority**: You can set the priority of your email to **Low**, **Normal**, or **High**.

- **Send Method**: You have two choices on how to send your message. The first method will send a separate email to each user that will be personalized with their user name. The second method will send one email with all the users entered into the BCC (Blind Carbon Copy) section of the email. The email will not be personalized, and all users will see the same message.

- **Send Action**: Selecting **Synchronous** will have your web page wait while the emails are sent. Selecting **Asynchronous** will send the emails on a new thread behind the scenes. Use this option when sending a personalized email.

- Click **Send Email** when your message is complete.

File Manager

The file manager allows the administrator to upload files to the portal. This control has been upgraded from previous versions. It gives the user much more flexibility for working with files.

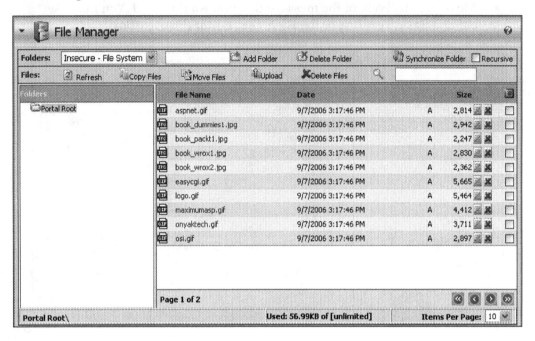

One of the nicer new features is the ability to upload files to folders other than the default **Portal Root** folder.

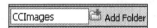

Version 4.3 of DotNetNuke introduced the concept of secure folders. Thus there are now three types of folder you can create.

- Standard or Insecure File System — this is the normal folder type. Files in this folder are accessible to anybody that knows the correct URL of the file.

- Secure File System — this folder type also exists on the server's file system but adds a level of security. This is achieved by renaming files that are uploaded to the folder, by adding a protected file extension. This file extension stops the server from serving the file to anybody who happens to know the correct URL. The file can still be processed through the DotNetNuke File Handler, thus achieving a level of security, in that only users with permissions to the file can access it. The only limitation in the use of this folder type is if a server administrator decides to change the protected file extension used to be an allowed file extension.

- Database — this option creates a Database Folder. Files in a database folder are actually stored in the database itself. This is the most secure type of storage, as it requires the file to be processed through the DotNetNuke File Handler.

To create a new folder, select the folder type from the drop-down list, type a name into the folder box and click on the Add Folder icon (the folder icon with a down arrow in the corner). This will then allow you to upload files to this folder. To upload a new file to the portal, from within the file manager, click on the Upload icon.

- Click on the **Browse** button to select the file to upload. This will open the **Choose File** dialog box. Navigate to the location of the file you would like to upload and select it. This will place the location of the file in the browse textbox.

- Select the folder where you would like to upload the file. Notice that the folder we created in the last exercise is now available to us.

- Click on the **Add** button to add the file to the list of files to be uploaded. The file must first be added to the list before it can be uploaded to the portal.

- **Decompress ZIP File**s: If you have selected a ZIP file to be uploaded to your portal, you can either have the files inside the ZIP file extracted (box is checked) or upload the ZIP file in its entirety (box is unchecked).

- Repeat these steps for all files to be uploaded.

- Click on **Upload New File** to finish the procedure.

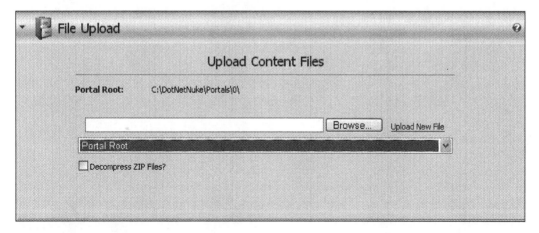

On the right of the Folders toolbar is a Synchronize Folder icon as well as a checkbox labeled **Recursive**. DotNetNuke stores information about each folder and file in the database, and throughout the application if a list of folders or files is required the list is generated from the information in the database, rather than the actual list of files on the server's file system. Clicking this button ensures that any files that may have been uploaded using an FTP (File Transfer Protocol) Client are added to the database. Checking the **Recursive** checkbox before clicking the Synchronize icon will cause any child folders of the current folder to also be synchronized.

On the bottom of the admin **File Manager** page are some options you can set to allow other users to upload files.

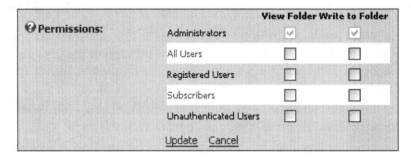

- Check the boxes next to the roles allowed to upload files.
- Click on **Update** to save your settings.

Recycle Bin

The **Recycle Bin** allows you to recover modules or tabs that you deleted.

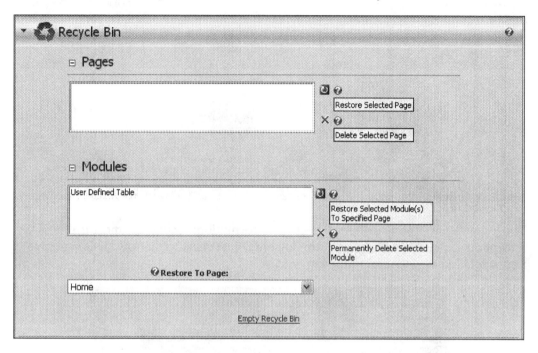

- To restore a page or module to its original location highlight it and click on the restore icon (). Note, a module cannot be restored if the page it was on has also been deleted. Restore the page before restoring the module.

- To delete a page or module permanently, highlight it and click on the delete icon (▧).

Log Viewer

The log viewer gives the administrator of the portal the ability monitor all transactions that occur on the portal.

> General Exception Errors will only show up in the log viewer when you are signed on as a superuser (host).

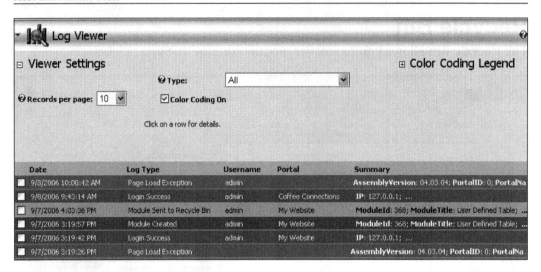

The log will track many different pieces of information; among the most useful is the Exception. To view the details for any log entry just click on the row. This will give you a detailed explanation of the log entry.

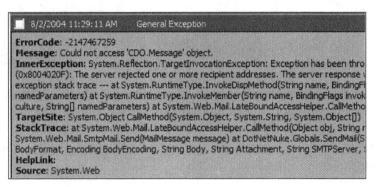

This information is very helpful when attempting to track down errors generated by your portal. To alert you to errors happening to other users, DotNetNuke gives you the ability to send error notices to any email address. To set this up, expand the **Send Exceptions** section at the bottom of the log viewer.

It is important to note that the emails will not be encrypted when sent. So be careful if sensitive data is involved.

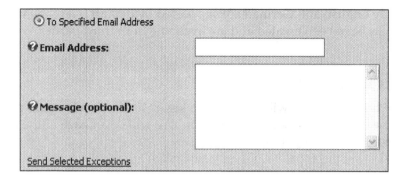

- **Email Address**: The email address of the person you would like the error notification to be sent to. This will send the addressee the detailed error message, including the stack trace. To send to more than one address, separate them with a semi-colon (;).
- **Message**: A message to accompany the exception.
- Click on **Send Selected Exceptions** link to save your settings.

Skins

This section allows you to browse through all of the skins and containers that have been uploaded to your portal. You can find a discussion on skins in Chapter 9.

Languages

Starting with DotNetNuke version 3.x you have the ability to localize your portal to the language of you choice. Clicking on the **Language Editor** link from the context menu or the bottom of the module will bring you to the following screen.

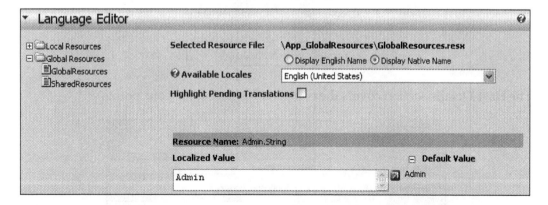

Currently only English and German are supported by default but many more language packs have been created and are available from third parties.

Host Tools

To access the host tools, you will first need to log on as the host for your portal. Once you have done this you will see the host menu. We will cover each of the tools that are available to you as a superuser.

Host Settings

The first menu item on the host menu is **Host Settings**. They are separated into **Basic Settings** and **Advanced Settings**. The host settings cover a very wide range of services for your portal. Because of this, we will walk through each item on the host settings page and either describe its functionality or point you to where you can find the information in this book.

Basic Settings

As we have seen when we looked at the admin **Site Settings**, the **Basic Settings** on the **Host Settings** page give you the ability to customize your hosting environment.

The **Site Configuration** section covers information about your current implementation of DotNetNuke, like the DNN Version Number, .NET Framework Version Number, Data Provider, Host Name, and so on.

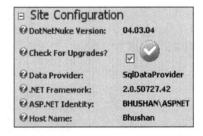

The **Host Details** section covers the contact information for your portal.

- **Host Portal**: The portal that serves as the host for all other parent or child portals that you create.

- **Host Title**: The text for the hyperlink that is displayed. The **Host Title** is located on the footer of every tab in your portal.

- **Host URL**: The location to which the user will be taken to when the **Host Title** hyperlink is clicked.

- **Host Email**: The email address used when sending out certain administration emails.

The **Appearance** section controls the basic look and feel of the site:

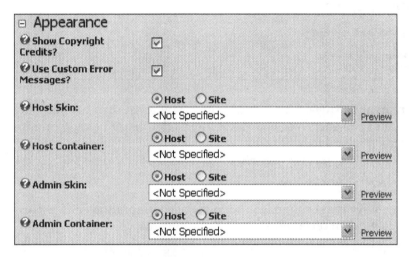

- **Show Copyright Credits**: Unchecking this box will remove the DotNetNuke copyright from the footer and the (DNN 4.X) from the IE header.

- **Use Custom Error Message**: DotNetNuke uses a custom provider for its error handling. If you would like to turn this feature off and use the default ASP.NET error handling, uncheck this box.

- **Host Skin, Host Container, Admin Skin**, and **Admin Container**: This section allows you to select a skin for your portal. There are different sections for admin and portal skins, because admin sections of the site usually use only one frame and portal sections utilize three or more. You can find out more about skinning your portal in the Chapter 9.

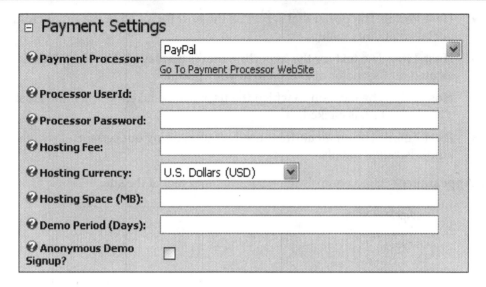

- **Payment Settings**: This section allows you to set up a payment processor for your site and gives you the ability to charge for hosting multiple DotNetNuke sites.

Advanced Settings

The **Advanced Settings** section is used to make configuration changes to your portal to enable it to work in certain restricted environments.

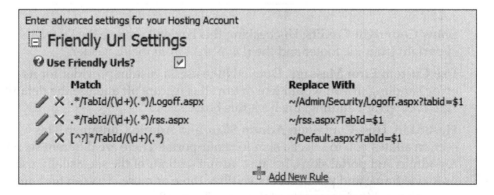

Checking the **Use Friendly Urls** box (default) will create URLs that are search-engine friendly. Search engines, for the most part, prefer URLs without query strings. This option will create the URL in a friendlier version, allowing your site to perform better on search sites.

The screenshot above displays a list of Registered Expressions that are used to configure how to rewrite the Urls. A discussion of Regular Expressions is beyond the scope of this book, but if you do know how to write regular expressions then you can provide very precise control over how this feature works.

Some intranet or Internet configurations need to use a proxy server to allow modules to make web requests to the Internet. An example of this is the RSS NewsFeed module, which requests data from a news feed source on the Internet. This next section allows you to configure DotNetNuke to use a proxy server:

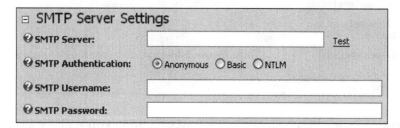

- **Proxy Server**: The IP address of the proxy server
- **Proxy Port**: The port that the proxy server uses to fulfill web requests
- **Proxy Username**: The username needed to connect through the proxy server
- **Proxy Password**: The password needed to connect through the proxy server
- **Web Request Timeout**: The time, in seconds, for which DotNetNuke will attempt to fulfill a web request

For the email functionality to work on your portal, you will need to configure your SMTP (Simple Mail Transfer Protocol) server. Once the correct information has been entered, you can click on the **Test** link to determine whether it is working. If the test succeeds, you will receive a message that says **Email Sent Successfully**. If there is an error, it will say **Could not access 'CDO.Message' object**. This is a generic error message; look in the log viewer for specific details.

- **SMTP Server**: The address of your mail server. This can be obtained from your ISP. It is usually your domain name with `mail` replacing the `www`.

- **SMTP Authentication**: The type of authentication to use for your site. Starting with version 4.0 you now have the ability to use Active Directory to manage your users.

- **SMTP Username**: The username for your SMTP server, if required.

- **SMTP Password**: The password for your SMTP server if required.

The **Other Settings** section is set up to hold all the information that does not fit into any particular group.

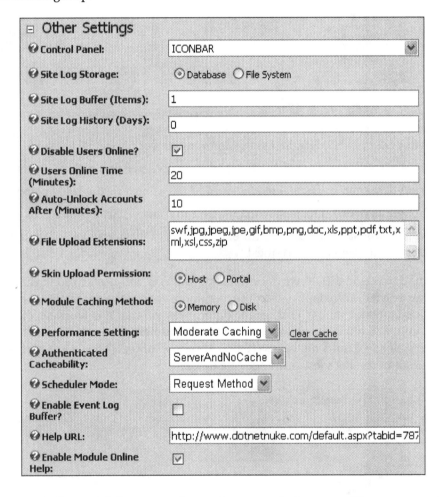

- **Control Panel**: When signed on as host or admin, you will see a control panel at the top of the screen. If you prefer a slimline version of the control panel, you can choose the Classic option.

- **Site Log Storage**: You can select whether you would like the site logs to be stored in your database or in the file system.

- **Site Log Buffer (Items)**: The site log buffer is a setting for the number of Sitelog records that have to be reached before DotNetNuke writes them to the database. They are held in memory before they are written to the database. This can help to speed things up on a busy site. Be careful when increasing this number, because if the application is reset you will loose the records in the buffer. Setting the number to 1 before you reset the application will prevent this from happening.

- **Site Log History (Days)**: This tells the system how many days of history to keep for your site log. The default is **60** days.

- **Disable Users Online** and **Users Online Time (Minutes)**: This setting allows the administrator to disable users and show the time period for which users have been online (in minutes) respectively.

- **Auto-Unlock Accounts After (Minutes)**: If a user is locked out because of successive unsuccessful logins, they will have to wait X number of minutes until they can attempt again.

- **File Upload Extensions**: This setting restricts the files that users are able to upload to your site. This is done for security purposes so that users are not able to upload malicious script files to the server. Separate file extensions (without a period) by using a comma.

- **Skin Upload Permissions**: This setting determines who has the authority to upload new skins to the site. Setting it to **Portal** allows portal administrators to upload skins.

- **Module Caching Method**: This setting allows you to decide weather to use memory caching or disk caching for your portal.

- **Performance Settings**: The performance settings are used to speed up the rendering of your portal. Caching stores a representation of the data contained in your page. This means that subsequent attempts to access this page (even by other users) will show the same data. Setting this to **Heavy Caching** will keep the cached data the longest. To clear the cache click on the **Clear** link.

- **Authenticated Cacheability**: This setting controls how the output content is cached. Caching can improve performance as either the client or the server retains a copy of the content in its buffer. For the most part this setting should be left at its default value. Only host users with considerable experience configuring web-servers should modify this setting. The settings available include:

    ° **NoCache** — no client-side caching – the browser should fetch a new copy each request.

- ° **Public** — allows the output to be cached by both the client and server (including proxy Servers).
- ° **Private** — allows the output to be cached on both the client and server (but not Proxy Servers).
- ° **Server** — the output is only cached on the server.
- ° **ServerAndNoCache (default)** — a comination of the Server and NoCache settings.
- ° **SerberAndPrivate** — a combination of the Server and private settings.

- **Scheduler Mode**: This setting is used to let you set how the scheduler is activated and used. You can choose between **Timer Method**, **Request Method**, and **Disabled**.

- **Enable Event Log Buffer**: This setting allows you to decide if you want the event log to be stored in memory or to be stored to disk.

- **Help URL**: The URL used for online help your site will provide. By default it is set to the DotNetNuke online help.

- **Enable Module Online Help**: This option allows you to decide if you would like to use the DotNetNuke online help for your module help. Otherwise you will have to provide this in each module setting section.

The last item on the **Host Settings** tab is the **Upgrade Log For Version** section. When you upgrade DotNetNuke from one version to the next, it keeps a log file. To view the log files for a particular version, select the version from the dropdown and click on **Go**.

Portals

For a discussion on running multiple portals, please refer to Chapter 11 on *Creating Multiple Portals*.

Module Definitions

For a discussion of modules and module definitions, please see Chapter 7 *Custom Module Development*.

File Manager

The file manager under the host settings functions just like the file manager under the Admin menu (see the *Admin Tools* section in this chapter). The only difference is that the host, by default, is able to upload not only content files, skin packages, and container packages, but also custom modules.

Vendors

DotNetNuke comes equipped with vendor and banner advertising integration. To set up a new vendor for your site, click on the **Add New Vendor** link at the bottom of the page:

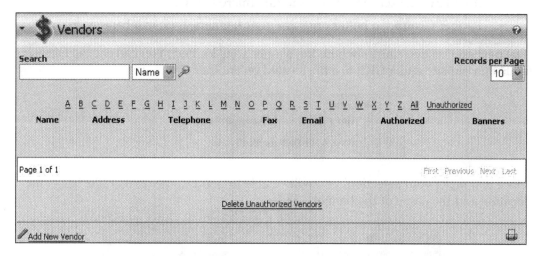

Fill out the vendor information and click on **Update** to save the vendor. Once you have saved the vendor information, you can add banners to this vendor by editing the vendor record.

To add a banner to a vendor, edit the vendor, open the **Banner Advertising** section, and click on **Add New Banner**:

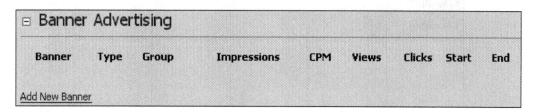

This allows you to add the specifications necessary to associate banner ads with your vendors.

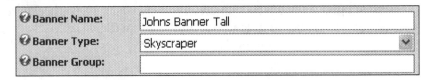

- **Banner Name**: Enter the name of the banner. This can be anything you want. Make it descriptive to help organize your banners.
- **Banner Type**: This refers to the size of the banner. Banners can be anything from large skyscraper banners to tiny micro banners.
- **Banner Group**: To better organize your banners, type in a banner group.

The next section determines where the banner ad is located. You can choose between a file on your site and a URL to a file located on another site.

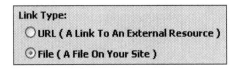

Once you make your selection, you will be able to point to the correct file. Select the location and the name of the banner ad file:

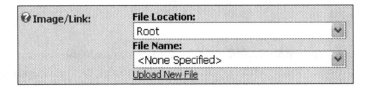

You can set the **Width** and **Height** of the banner in this section.

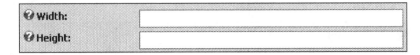

If you selected **URL**, you would need to enter the URL of the file.

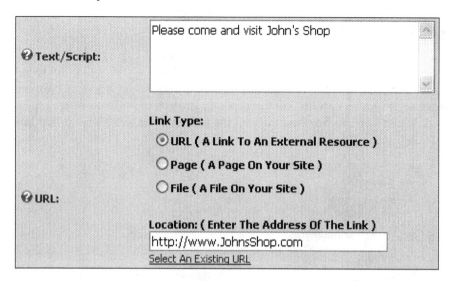

Next you will want to determine what happens when the user clicks on a banner.

- **Text/Script**: The alternative text to be displayed with the banner.
- **URL**: The URL that users will be redirected to when they click on a banner ad. If no URL is listed here, the URL in the vendor setup will be used.

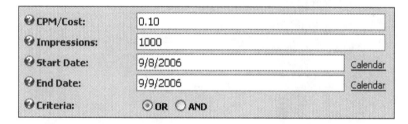

- **CPM/Cost**: The amount you will charge for every 1000 impressions. An impression is how many times the banner is displayed on the site.
- **Impressions**: The number of impressions the vendor has paid for.
- **Start Date** and **End Date**: Start and end dates for the ad campaign.
- **Criteria**: Used to determine whether to stop the ads after the date has expired or the number of impressions has been reached.

When you are done adding the banner details, click on the **Update** link to save your data.

To view your banners on the portal, you will need to add a banner module to one of your pages. Once you have added a banner module, select **Banner Options** from the module drop-down menu.

To edit the banner, enter the **Banner Source** and **Banner Type** to display your banner. Since the vendor was created from the Host tools, you will need to select **Host** for the source. By using the information you used to set up your banner in the vendor section, you can decide the types or groups of banners you would like displayed. When you are finished adding the information, click on the **Update** link to save your settings.

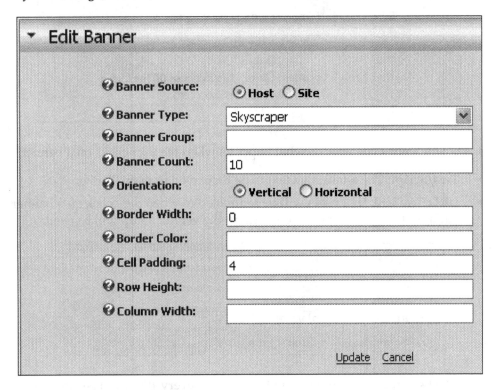

SQL

Use the **SQL** host option to run simple SQL queries against the DotNetNuke database.

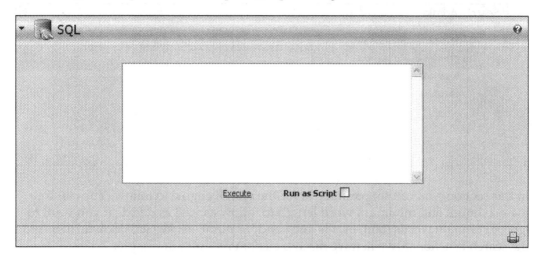

Simply type in your SQL statement and click on the **Execute** link. You will then be presented with a simple tabular representation of your data. Since this is part of the DotNetNuke framework, you can also run scripts that use the `<objectQualifier>` and `<databaseOwner>` tags by checking the **Run As Script** checkbox.

Schedule

With the addition of users online and site log in DotNetNuke 2.0, there arose a need to schedule recurring tasks. To address this, the core team developed the **scheduler**. The scheduler allows you to perform recurring actions on the portal.

Languages

Starting with DotNetNuke version 3.x, and continuing in version 4.x, you can localize your portal to the language of you choice. Currently only English and German are supported, but many more are on the way.

Search Admin

You may have noticed in the upper right-hand corner of your screen, a box with a **Search** button.

DotNetNuke gives the portal visitors the ability to search the portal for relevant information. The administration for the functionality is found on the Host menu.

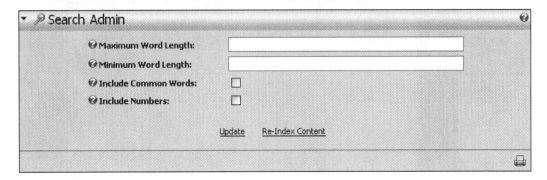

In this section, you can set parameters for the search engine to follow. You can set the maximum and minimum word length to follow as well as decide if you want to ignore common words (and, or, the, etc.) and/or numbers. We will look further into the search functionality when we discuss custom modules in Chapter 7.

Lists

Many of the controls in DotNetNuke use lists to populate the information need to fulfill a task. A good example of this is the user account registration control.

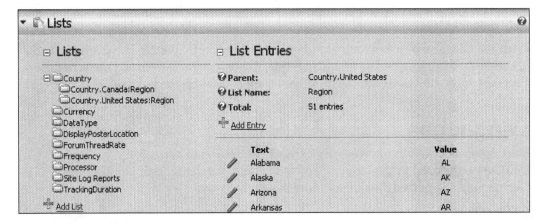

When users register for your site, they are presented with drop-down lists that allow them to select their country and region/state. This section allows the Host to add items or remove items from the list. This allows you to customize the items show in the list.

Superuser Accounts

In previous versions of DotNetNuke, only one Host (superuser) account was available. This restriction was eliminated version 3.0 onwards with the addition of the SuperUser section. From here, you can create additional user accounts that will have the same abilities as the host.

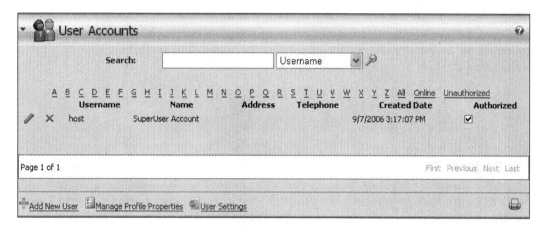

Remember that these users will have the freedom to control access to every part of your portal, from creating portals to deleting users, so be careful when issuing these sign-ons.

Extra Options on the Admin Menu

When you are signed on as a superuser, you may notice a few extra items on the Admin menu. If you look at the **Site Settings**, you will see an extra section called **Host Settings** that allows a superuser to control certain aspects of the portal. In addition, if you view the **Log Viewer** on the Admin menu when signed on as a superuser, you will see exceptions generated by the portal. These exceptions are logged here by the framework, but are only available to the superuser. Finally, at the bottom of the **Site Settings** pane, you will see an extra section for **Portal Aliases**.

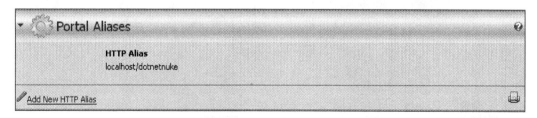

The portal alias of the site must be located in this section. When you first set up your site on a local machine, it will be added for you, but when you upload your site to a remote server, you will need to add the URL of your site to this section. We will cover deploying to a remote server in Chapter 10.

Common Tasks

So far we have used the icon bar at the top of the portal to work with pages and to install modules. The last section of the icon bar is used to perform common administrative tasks.

These are shortcuts to common tasks that you can find on the administrative menus and are meant to help you be more productive. The only item on the **Common Tasks** bar that we have not yet talked about is the **Wizard**. We will discuss this in more detail in Chapter 11 on running multiple portals.

Summary

This chapter has covered a variety of information. It should have given you, as the administrator of a DotNetNuke portal, the skills needed to maintain your website. In the next chapter, we will delve deep into the core of the DotNetNuke architecture and find out what really makes our portal run.

6

Understanding the DotNetNuke Core Architecture

In this chapter, we will be exploring the core functionality of the DotNetNuke architecture. We will be using the source code version of DotNetNuke 4.3.3 that can be downloaded from the DotNetNuke website. We will start with an overview of the architecture, touching on key concepts employed by DotNetNuke. After this, we will examine some of the major sections that make up the framework. Finally, after we learn about the objects that make up the core, we will follow a request for a page through this process to find out how each page is dynamically created.

Architecture Overview

As opposed to traditional web applications that may rely on a multitude of web pages to deliver content, DotNetNuke uses a single main page called `Default.aspx`. The content for this page is presented dynamically by using a tabID value to retrieve from the DotNetNuke database the skins and modules needed to build the page requested. Before we move on, we should discuss what is meant by a **tab** and a **page**. As you read this chapter, you will notice the word tab is sometimes used when referring to pages in your DotNetNuke portal. In the original **IBuySpy** application, pages were referred to as tabs because they resembled tabs when added to the page.

This continued in the original versions of the DotNetNuke project. Starting with version 3.0, and continuing with version 4.3.3, an effort has begun to rename most of these instances to reflect what they really are: pages. Most references to "tabs" have been changed to "pages", but the conversion is not complete. For this reason, you will see both—tabs and pages—in the database, in the project files, and in this text. We will use these terms interchangeably throughout this text as we look into the core architecture of DNN.

We will begin with a general overview of what happens when a user requests a page on your DotNetNuke portal. The process for rendering a page in DotNetNuke works like this: a user selects a menu item; this calls the `Default.aspx` page, passing the `tabid` parameter in the querystring to let the application identify the page being requested. The example `http://www.dotnetnuke.com/Default.aspx?tabid=476` demonstrates this.

> DotNetNuke 3.2 introduced something called URL Rewriting. This takes the querystring shown above and rewrites it so that it is in a format that helps increase search-engine hits. We will cover the HTTP Module that is responsible for this later in this chapter. The rewritten URL would resemble `http://localhost/DotNetNuke/tabid/476/Default.aspx`.
>
> While referring to URLs in this chapter we will be using the non-rewritten version of the URL. URL Rewriting can be turned off at the **Host Settings** page.

The querystring value (`?tabid=476`) is sent to the database, where the information required for the page is retrieved.

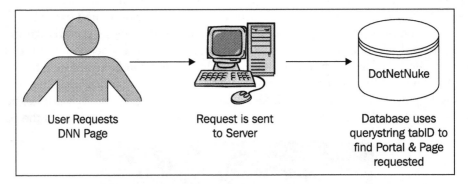

| User Requests DNN Page | Request is sent to Server | Database uses querystring tabID to find Portal & Page requested |

The portal that the user is accessing can be determined in a number of ways, but as you can see from the `Tabs` table, each page/tab contains a reference to the portal it belongs to in the `PortalID` field. Once the server has a reference to the page that the user requested (using the tabID), it can determine what modules belong on that page.

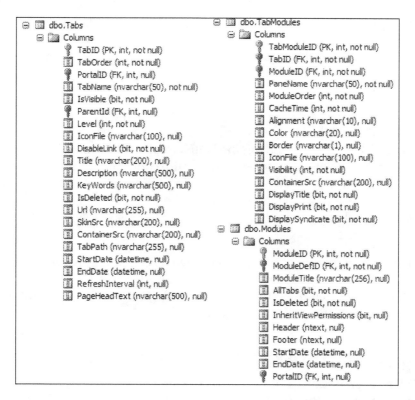

Although there are many more tables involved in this process, you can see that *these* tables hold not only the page and modules needed to generate the page, but also what pane to place them on (`PaneName`) and what container skin to apply (`ContainerSrc`).

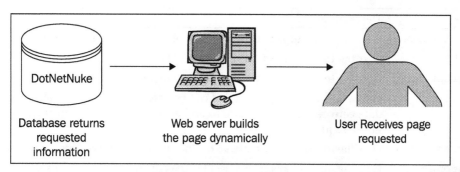

All of this information is returned to the web server, and the `Default.aspx` page is constructed with it and returned to the user who requested it along with the required modules and skins.

Now, this is of course a very general overview of the process, but as we work through this chapter, we will delve deeper into the code that makes this process work, and in the end show a request work its way through the framework to deliver a page to a user.

Diving into the Core

There are over 80,000 lines of code in the DotNetNuke application. There is no practical (or even possible) way to cover the entire code base. In this section, we will go in depth into what I believe are the main portions of the code base: the `PortalSettings` as well as the `companion` classes found in the `portals` folder; the `Web.Config` file including the HTTP Modules and `Providers`; and the `Global.aspx` and `Globals.vb` files.

We will start our discussion of the core with two objects that play an integral part in the construction of the architecture. The `Context` object and the `PortalSettings` class will both be referred to quite often in the code, and so it is important that you have a good understanding of what they do.

Using the Context Object in Your Application

ASP.NET has taken intrinsic objects like the `Request` and the `Application` objects and wrapped them together with other relevant items into an intrinsic object called `Context`.

The `Context` object (`HttpContext`) can be found in the `System.Web` namespace. Below you will find some of the objects that make up the `HttpContext` object.

Title	Description
Application	Gets the `HttpApplicationState` object for the current HTTP request.
Cache	Gets the `Cache` object for the current HTTP request.
Current	Gets the `HttpContext` object for the current HTTP request.
Items	Gets a key-value collection that can be used to organize and share data between an `IHttpModule` and an `IHttpHandler` during an HTTP request.
Request	Gets the `HttpRequest` object for the current HTTP request.
Response	Gets the `HttpResponse` object for the current HTTP response.

Title	Description
Server	Gets the `HttpServerUtility` object that provides methods used in processing web requests.
Session	Gets the `HttpSessionState` instance for the current HTTP request.
User	Gets or sets security information for the current HTTP request.

Notice that most of the descriptions talk about the "current" request object, or the "current" response object. The `Global.aspx` file, which we will look at soon, reacts on every single request made to your application, and so it is only concerned with whoever is "currently" accessing a resource.

The `HttpContext` object contains all HTTP-specific information about an individual HTTP request. The `HttpContext.Current` property in particular can give you the context for the current request from *anywhere* in the application domain. The DotNetNuke core relies on the `HTTPContext.Current` property to hold everything from the Application Name to the Portal Settings and through this makes it available to you.

The PortalSettings Class

The portal settings play a major role in the dynamic generation of your pages and as such will be referred to quite often in the other portions of the code. The portal settings are represented by the `PortalSettings` class, which you will find in the `Components\Portal\PortalSettings.vb` file. As you can see from the private variables in this class, most of what goes on in your portal will at some point need to access this object. This object will hold everything from the ID of the portal to the default language, and as we will see later, is responsible for determining the skins and modules needed for each page.

```
Private _PortalId As Integer
Private _PortalName As String
Private _HomeDirectory As String
Private _LogoFile As String
Private _FooterText As String
Private _ExpiryDate As Date
Private _UserRegistration As Integer
Private _BannerAdvertising As Integer
Private _Currency As String
Private _AdministratorId As Integer
Private _Email As String
Private _HostFee As Single
Private _HostSpace As Integer
Private _AdministratorRoleId As Integer
```

```
Private _AdministratorRoleName As String
Private _RegisteredRoleId As Integer
Private _RegisteredRoleName As String
Private _Description As String
Private _KeyWords As String
Private _BackgroundFile As String
Private _SiteLogHistory As Integer
Private _AdminTabId As Integer
Private _SuperTabId As Integer
Private _SplashTabId As Integer
Private _HomeTabId As Integer
Private _LoginTabId As Integer
Private _UserTabId As Integer
Private _DefaultLanguage As String
Private _TimeZoneOffset As Integer
Private _Version As String
Private _DesktopTabs As ArrayList
Private _ActiveTab As TabInfo
Private _PortalAlias As PortalAliasInfo
```

The `Portal` class itself is simple. It is filled by using the only instance method of the class, the `GetPortalSettings` method. The method is passed a tabID and a `PortalAliasInfo` object. You already know that the tabID represents the ID of the page being requested, but the `PortalAliasInfo` is something new. This class can be found in the same folder as the `PortalSettings` class and contains the following information:

- `PortalID`: This is the ID the portal is assigned in the database.
- `PortalAliasID`: Since each portal can have more that one alias, this ID references the specific alias used for the portal.
- `HTTPAlias`: This is the actual alias used to access the portal (`www.MyPortal.com`, `localhost/dotnetnuke`, etc.).

From this object, we can retrieve all the information associated with the portal. If you look past the initial declarations, you can see that the portal settings are saved in cache for the time that is specified in on the Host Settings page.

A drop-down box on the Host Settings page (`admin\host\hostsettings.ascx`) is used to set the cache.

- No Caching: **0**
- Light Caching: **1**
- Moderate Caching: **3**
- Heavy Caching: **6**

The value in this dropdown ranges from **0** to **6**; the code above takes the value set in the dropdown and multiplies it by 20 to determine the cache duration. Once the cache time is set, the method checks if the portal settings object already resides there. Retrieving these settings from the database for every request would cause your site to run slowly, so placing them in a cache for the duration you select helps increase the speed of your site.

```
PortalId = objPortalAliasInfo.PortalID
' get portal settings
objPortal = CType(DataCache.GetPersistentCacheItem _
            ("GetPortalSettings & PortalId.ToString, _
            GetType(PortalInfor)), PortalInfo)
```

If the object is not already cached, it will use the `PortalId` passed to the `GetPortal` method to retrieve the portal settings from the database. This method is located in the `PortalController` class (`components\Portal\PortalController.vb`) and is responsible for retrieving the portal information from the database.

```
If objPortal Is Nothing Then
      ' get portal settings
      objPortal = objPortals.GetPortal(PortalId)
```

This will fill a `PortalInfo` object (`components\Portal\PortalInfo.vb`), which, as the name suggests, holds the portal information. This object in turn is used to create the `PortalSettings` object. In this section (code not shown) some custom properties are set, the application version is determined, and the administrator email address is discovered. Once this is complete, the object is then cached.

```
' cache object
If intCacheTimeout <> 0 Then
    DataCache.SetCache("GetPortalSettings" & PortalId.ToString, _
    objPortal, TimeSpan.FromMinutes(intCacheTimeout), True)
End If
```

After the portal settings are saved, the tabs are retrieved. Like the portal settings themselves, the tabs are saved in cache to save resources. In the `get portal tabs` section, the code will loop through all of the non-host tabs on the site.

```
' get portal tabs
    arrTabs = CType(DataCache.GetCache("GetTabs" & _
                                    Me.PortalId.ToString),
ArrayList)
            If arrTabs Is Nothing Then
                arrTabs = objTabs.GetTabs(Me.PortalId)
                If Not arrTabs Is Nothing Then
```

After all the portal tabs are iterated through and added to an `ArrayList`, the host tabs are collected. Again, you can change the default behavior of the host tabs in this section.

```
' host tab
    objTab = objTabs.GetTab(Me.SuperTabId)
        If Not objTab Is Nothing Then
          ' set custom properties
            objTab.StartDate = Date.MinValue
            objTab.EndDate = Date.MaxValue
            objTab.Url = NavigateURL(objTab.TabID, Null.NullString, _
                            "portalid=" & objTab.PortalID.ToString)
            arrTabs.Add(objTab)
        End If

' host child tabs
  Dim arrHostTabs As ArrayList = _
                            objTabs.GetTabsByParentId
                            (Me.SuperTabId)

  If Not arrHostTabs Is Nothing Then
        For Each objTab In arrHostTabs
          ' set custom properties
            objTab.StartDate = Date.MinValue
            objTab.EndDate = Date.MaxValue
            objTab.Url = NavigateURL _
              (objTab.TabID, Null.NullString, "portalid=" & _
                objTab.PortalID.ToString)
            arrTabs.Add(objTab)
        Next
  End If
```

The method ends by taking the lists of tabs that were just created and uses them to call the `GetSkin` and `GetPortalTabModules`, which will apply both the skins and modules that are associated with each tab. You will see the `PortalSettings` class referenced many times as we work through the rest of the code, so gaining a good understanding of how this class works will help you as you move along.

Working with the Configuration Files

Next, we will continue our exploration of the DotNetNuke architecture by looking at a couple of files in the main DotNetNuke folder. The DotNetNuke source code version download is broken up into many different projects. This has been done so that you can open up only the files that you are concerned with. In this section, we will work with the website project along with the `Providers` used by the core. If you open up the solution file in the source code download, you will find that the website project will start with `http://localhost/DotNetNuke`.

Expand the website project to expose two very important files, the `web.config` file, and the `Global.aspx` file. You will need to rename the `release.config` file to `web.config` before we begin.

> If this is the first time you have worked with the download, you will notice that there is no `web.config` file. The `web.config` file will originally be called `release.config`. This has been done to help ensure that during an upgrade you don't overlay the original `web.config`. Since DotNetNuke uses encryption keys to store user passwords in the database, if you overlay this file your users will not be able to log in.

The web.config File

The `web.config` file is an XML-based file that contains configuration information specific to your web application. At run time, ASP.NET stores this configuration information in cache so that it can be easily retrieved by your application. If changes are made to this file, ASP.NET will detect the changes and automatically apply the new configuration. The `web.config` file is very extensible: it allows you to define new configurations and write handlers to process them. DotNetNuke takes full advantage of this ability, as we will discover as we move through this file.

We will only touch on the areas of the `web.config` file that are specifically used in DotNetNuke. In the `DotNetNuke` project, open up the `web.config` file. The first section in the file is the local configuration settings. Here we find the settings for our provider models. For our providers to work, we need a configuration section and configuration section handler.

Configuring the Providers Used in DotNetNuke

`<configSections>` is broken into two separate groups. The first group, `<dotnetnuke>`, describes the providers that are available to the application.

```
<sectionGroup name="dotnetnuke">
    <section name="data" requirePermission="false" type="DotNetNuke.
Framework.Providers.ProviderConfigurationHandler,DotNetNuke"/>
    <section name="logging" requirePermission="false"
type="DotNetNuke.Framework.Providers.ProviderConfigurationHandler,
DotNetNuke"/>
```

```
        <section name="scheduling" requirePermission="false"
type="DotNetNuke.Framework.Providers.ProviderConfigurationHandler,
DotNetNuke"/>
        <section name="htmlEditor" requirePermission="false"
type="DotNetNuke.Framework.Providers.ProviderConfigurationHandler,
DotNetNuke"/>
        <section name="navigationControl" requirePermission="false"
type="DotNetNuke.Framework.Providers.ProviderConfigurationHandler,
DotNetNuke"/>
        <section name="searchIndex" requirePermission="false"
type="DotNetNuke.Framework.Providers.ProviderConfigurationHandler,
DotNetNuke"/>
        <section name="searchDataStore" requirePermission="false"
type="DotNetNuke.Framework.Providers.ProviderConfigurationHandler,
DotNetNuke"/>
        <section name="friendlyUrl" requirePermission="false"
type="DotNetNuke.Framework.Providers.ProviderConfigurationHandler,
DotNetNuke"/>
        <section name="caching" requirePermission="false"
type="DotNetNuke.Framework.Providers.ProviderConfigurationHandler,
DotNetNuke"/>
        <section name="authentication" requirePermission="false"
type="DotNetNuke.Framework.Providers.ProviderConfigurationHandler,
DotNetNuke"/>
        <section name="members" requirePermission="false"
type="DotNetNuke.Framework.Providers.ProviderConfigurationHandler,
DotNetNuke"/>
        <section name="roles" requirePermission="false"
type="DotNetNuke.Framework.Providers.ProviderConfigurationHandler,
DotNetNuke"/>
        <section name="profiles" requirePermission="false"
type="DotNetNuke.Framework.Providers.ProviderConfigurationHandler,
DotNetNuke"/>
</sectionGroup>
```

This custom configuration section handles the different providers integrated into the framework. Providers give the developer the ability to have a pluggable architecture. The data provider, for example, lets us decide which data store to use (Access or SQL Server), while the logging provider allows us to decide what logger we would like to use for our web application. The framework separates the act of logging from the type of logger being used. To change the logging, or any of the other providers, you would need to write your own provider to handle the functions as you see fit.

The first declaration states the name that you will use when you refer to this section in your configuration file. In other words, this is the tag you need to look for in your `web.config` file in order to see the providers that will handle this functionality:

```
name="data"
```

It also includes the type, which is the configuration section handler. This should include the Global Assembly Cache location information for the class.

```
type="DotNetNuke.Framework.Providers.ProviderConfigurationHandler,
    DotNetNuke"
```

The `type` declaration follows the following configuration.

```
type="configuration section handler class, assembly"
```

The providers serve some of the following functions:

- The `data` Provider: Gives the ability to decide which datastore type you would like to use. The DotNetNuke framework is prepackaged with SQL Server and Access (default), but there are others, such as MySQL and Oracle, which are in development by third-party providers.

- The `logging` Provider: Used for all logging associated with the core framework. This handles, among other things, exception handling.

- The `scheduling` Provider: One of the newer features, along with the logging, this provider helps to facilitate reoccurring functionality.

- The `htmlEditor` Provider: The default HTML WYSIWYG editor is the FreeTextBox. This configuration setting allows you to substitute other rich textbox components for the FreeTextBox.

- The `searchIndex` Provider: The default provides, if implemented, the ability to search the content of the modules located on your portal.

- The `searchDataStore` Provider: The default provides the ability to search for information inside the datastore you have selected as your data provider.

- The `friendlyUrl` Provider: The default provides the ability to rewrite the URL in a manner that is friendly to search engines.

Handling the Providers

The configuration section only tells the application where each provider will be handled. The configuration section has a companion section in the `web.config` file. This defines the configuration section handlers. You will find two handler sections in the `web.config` file, one for each group we described above. The first handler section we will look at is the `<dotnetnuke>` section. This corresponds to the `sectionGroup` name in the configuration section.

The <dotnetnuke> Group

Within the `<dotnetnuke>` section, we see the handlers for our individual providers, beginning with the HTML provider. The first node in this section defines the default provider. The `defaultProvider` attribute is advised, but is optional. If it's left out, the first provider in the list will serve as the default. The default as well as the *only* provider for the `htmlEditor` is the `Ftb3HtmlEditorProvider`.

The next node starts the provider section; it is followed by a `<clear/>` node. This node is used to clear out the providers from the configuration settings that may have been added in the `machine.config` file. The final node is the `<add/>` node. This node is used to add our provider to the list of available providers. This list is used by the DotNetNuke core to tell it what is handling each section that uses a provider. Inside this node, we need to define a few attributes:

- `name`: This is the friendly name of our provider. This will be the name of the class you create to handle this functionality.
- `Type`: This again follows the `[namespace.class]`, `[assembly name]` format.
- `providerPath`: This attribute points to where the provider class can be found within the application structure.

After the end of the `<add/>` node, the structure is completed with the closing tags for `add`, `providers`, and `htmlEditor`.

```
<dotnetnuke>
  <htmlEditor defaultProvider="FtbHtmlEditorProvider">
    <providers>
       <clear/>
       <add name="Ftb3HtmlEditorProvider"
        type="DotNetNuke.HtmlEditor.Ftb3HtmlEditorProvider,
        DotNetNuke.Ftb3HtmlEditorProvider"
        providerPath="~\Providers\HtmlEditorProviders\
        Ftb3HtmlEditorProvider\" toolbarStyle="Office2003"
          enableProFeatures="false" spellCheck=""/>
    </providers>
  </htmlEditor>
```

This is followed by the `<navigationControl>` handler. This allows you to decide what control you would like to use for your menu navigation. The default is SolpartMenu.

The next two configuration handlers are for the search facility built into the DotNetNuke framework. The `searchIndex` and `searchDataStore` follow the same configuration as the `htmlEditor`. We will look further into these providers when we create a custom module in Chapter 7.

This is followed by the `data` provider.

```
<data defaultProvider="SqlDataProvider">
  <providers>
```

```
        <clear/>
        <add name="SqlDataProvider" _
            type="DotNetNuke.Data.SqlDataProvider, _
                    DotNetNuke.SqlDataProvider"
            connectionStringName="SiteSqlServer"
            upgradeConnectionString=""
            providerPath="~\Providers\DataProviders\SqlDataProvider\"
            objectQualifier=""
            databaseOwner="dbo"/>
    </providers>
</data>
```

The `data` provider has some additional attributes we did not see in the HTML provider.

- `connectionStringName`: This provides the name of the connection string you will use for your portal. This string can be found in the `<appSettings>` section of the `web.config` file.

- `upgradeConnectionString`: This connection string is used for installation and updates. It is only used to run the upgrade scripts. This can be used to run the updates using a database user with more privileges.

- `objectQualifier`: The `objectQualifier` is used to allow multiple installations to run inside the same database. If for example you added CC1 in the object qualifier before you installed DotNetNuke, all the tables and stored procedures would be prefixed with CC1. This would allow you to run another DotNetNuke implementation inside the same database by setting the object qualifier in the second one to CC2. Inside the database, you would have two of every stored procedure and table. Each pair would be named according to the pattern CC1_users, CC2_users, which would keep them separate.

- `databaseOwner`: The `databaseOwner` is set to `dbo`. This is the default database owner in SQL Server. Some hosting companies will require you to change this to reflect your user.

The next configuration handler is for the `logging` provider. The `logging` provider handles all logging, including errors, associated with the portal.

```
<logging defaultProvider="DBLoggingProvider">
  <providers>
   <clear/>
    <add name="XMLLoggingProvider"
            type="DotNetNuke.Services.Log.
            EventLog.XMLLoggingProvider,
            DotNetNuke.XMLLoggingProvider"
            configfilename="LogConfig.xml.resources"
```

```
                    providerPath="~\Providers\LoggingProviders\
       XMLLoggingProvider\"/>
         <add name="DBLoggingProvider"
                 type="DotNetNuke.Services.Log.
                 EventLog.DBLoggingProvider.DBLoggingProvider,
                 DotNetNuke.Provider.DBLoggingProvider"
                 providerPath="~\Providers\LoggingProviders\
                 Provider.DBLoggingProvider\"/>
         </providers>
       </logging>
```

This is followed by the handler for the DNNScheduler:

```
       <scheduling defaultProvider="DNNScheduler">
          <providers>
            <clear/>
            <add name = "DNNScheduler"
               type = "DotNetNuke.Scheduling.DNNScheduler,
                           DotNetNuke.DNNScheduler"
               providerPath = "~\Providers\SchedulingProviders\
                           DNNScheduler\"
               debug="false"
               maxThreads="-1"
               />
          </providers>
       </scheduling>
    </dotnetnuke>
```

The scheduler has a few additional attributes we have not seen so far.

- debug: When this is set to true, it will add additional log entries to aid in debugging scheduler problems.

- maxThreads: This sets the maximum number of thread-pool threads to be used by the scheduler (1-10). Setting it to -1 tells the scheduler to determine this on its own.

The next handler for this section is for handling friendly URLs. We will be looking further into this functionality when we discover the HTTP Modules that DotNetNuke employs later in this chapter.

```
       <friendlyUrl defaultProvider="DNNFriendlyUrl">
          <providers>
            <clear/>
            <add name="DNNFriendlyUrl" type="DotNetNuke.Services.Url.
              FriendlyUrl.DNNFriendlyUrlProvider,
              DotNetNuke.HttpModules.UrlRewrite"
```

```
    includePageName="true"
    regexMatch="[^a-zA-Z0-9 _-]"/>
    </providers>
</friendlyUrl>
```

The final handler for this section is for handling authentication. We will also be looking further into this functionality later in this chapter.

The <system.web> Group

The `<system.web>` section of the `web.config` file is where most of the configuration of your ASP.NET web application is placed. We will be discussing most of the information contained in this section (including the HTTP Modules) but for now, we'll concentrate on the providers that are defined in this section. As we saw in the `<dotnetnuke>` section earlier, here we see the information needed to handle our provider. The first provider we find in the `<system.web>` section is the `AspNetSqlMembership` Provider. The setup is similar to those we have already seen with the exception of the additional attributes.

You will also find the `members`, `roles`, and `profile`, providers in the `<system.web>` section of the `web.config`. They all follow the same pattern as the `Membership` provider, inheriting the `Microsoft` provider and overriding the `ApplicationName` property.

HTTP Modules

Located at the beginning of the `<system.web>` section is the `HTTPModule` section.

HTTP Modules give you the ability to intercept the request for a page and modify the request in some way. In DotNetNuke, they have been added to abstract some of the code that used to reside inside the `Global.asax.vb` file. This gives a greater degree of modularity and allows developers to change behavior without affecting the core architecture. An HTTP Module is a class that implements the `IHTTPModule` interface. This interface has two methods you need to implement.

- `Init`: This method allows an HTTP Module to register its event handlers to the events in the `HttpApplication` object.

- `Dispose`: This method gives the HTTP Module an opportunity to perform any cleanup before the object gets garbage-collected.

These methods are called when they are hooked into the **HTTP Pipeline**. The HTTP Pipeline refers to the path followed by each request made to your application. The following diagram shows the path a typical request takes through the pipeline.

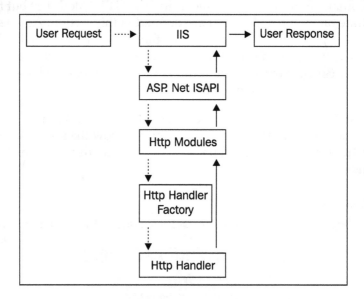

 For more information on how HTTP Modules work within the HTTP Pipeline, check out this great MSDN article by George Sheperd at `http://msdn.microsoft.com/msdnmag/issues/02/05/asp/`.

HTTP Modules plug themselves into the ASP.NET request process by adding entries into the `web.config` file. This allows them to intercept the request before it is returned in order to modify the request to perform certain actions. DotNetNuke uses this process for a number of things.

To see an example of this we will look at the `Exception` module. It is first declared in the `web.config` file.

```
<add name="Exception"
  type="DotNetNuke.HttpModules.ExceptionModule,
      DotNetNuke.HttpModules.Exception"/>
```

This will place the `ExceptionModule` in the HTTP Pipeline, allowing it to intercept each request. Let's take a look at the `ExeptionModule` class found in the `HttpModule.Exception` project. As we learned earlier, the `Init` method is called when the module is hooked into the pipeline with a declaration in the `web.config` file. In this method, we add an event handler to the `application.Error` event that is thrown whenever an error happens in your application:

```
Public Class ExceptionModule

    Implements IHttpModule
    Public ReadOnly Property ModuleName() As String
        Get
            Return "ExceptionModule"
        End Get
    End Property

    Public Sub Init(ByVal application As HttpApplication) _
                            Implements IHttpModule.Init
        AddHandler application.Error, AddressOf Me.OnErrorRequest
    End Sub
```

The `OnErrorRequest` method is then called and the error is passed to the `Error` provider designated in the `web.config` file. The actual logging of the error is done by the logging provider. The default implementation of DotNetNuke comes with a both a `XMLLoggingProvider`, and a `DBLoggingProvider`, but you may write your own provider to fit your needs.

```
Public Sub OnErrorRequest(ByVal s As Object, ByVal e As EventArgs)

        Dim Context As HttpContext = HttpContext.Current
        Dim Server As HttpServerUtility = Context.Server

        Dim lex As New Exception("Unhandled Error: ",
        Server.GetLastError)
        Dim objExceptionLog As New _
        Services.Log.EventLog.ExceptionLogController
        objExceptionLog.AddLog(lex)

End Sub
    Public Sub Dispose() Implements IHttpModule.Dispose
    End Sub

End Class
```

As opposed to the first two HTTP Modules you have seen, the `UrlRewrite` module is quite extensive. Just like the others, the first thing that is needed is a designation in the `HTTPModules` section of the `web.config` file.

```
<add name="UrlRewrite"
     type="DotNetNuke.HttpModules.UrlRewriteModule,
     DotNetNuke.HttpModules.UrlRewrite"/>
```

You can view the `UrlRewrite` HTTPModule by looking in the `HTTPModule.UrlRewrite` project. This class is responsible for taking a querystring that looks like this:

```
http://www.dotnetnuke.com/Default.aspx?tabid=476
```

and converting it to look like this:

```
http://localhost/DotNetNuke/tabid/476/Default.aspx
```

There are a few reasons why you would want to rewrite your URLs; among them are a cleaner appearance or hiding the physical page names, but probably the most important reason for DotNetNuke is to increase traffic to your site. Search engines crawl your site with bots that look to catalog your pages. Search bots prefer non-dynamic web pages. By using URL rewriting, you can increase the popularity of your links on the major search engines.

As you look at this module, you can see that although the code that does the URL rewriting is extensive, it is hooked into the pipeline in the same fashion as the other modules. The `Init` method is used to add an event handler to `Application.BeginRequest`, which fires every time a user requests a page on your site, so that on every request to your site the `OnBeginRequest` method is called and the URL is rewritten before it is sent on its way.

```
Public Sub Init(ByVal application As HttpApplication) _
               Implements IHttpModule.Init

    AddHandler application.BeginRequest, _
    AddressOf Me.OnBeginRequest

End Sub
```

The rest of the HTTP Modules follow this same pattern, and although they differ in complexity, they all accomplish their task by intercepting the request. We will visit a few of these again when we develop a custom module in the next chapter.

Application Settings

Let's look at one of the remaining sections of `web.config`. Below `<configSettings>` you will find a section called `<appSettings>`. This section holds three items that are of interest to us: `SiteSqlServer`, `InstallProcedure`, and `InstallTemplate`:

```
<appSettings>
    <add key="SiteSqlServer"
        value=" Data Source=.\SQLExpress;Integrated Security=True;User
Instance=True;AttachDBFilename=|DataDirectory|Database.mdf;"/>

    <add key="InstallTemplate" value="DotNetNuke.install.config"/>
    <add key="AutoUpgrade" value="true"/>
    <add key="InstallMemberRole" value="true"/>
    <add key="ShowMissingKeys" value="false"/>
    <add key="EnableWebFarmSupport" value="false"/>
    <add key="EnableCachePersistence" value="false"/>
    <!-- Host Header to remove from URL so
      "www.mydomain.com/johndoe/Default.aspx" is treated as
      "www.mydomain.com/Default.aspx" -->
    <add key="RemoveAngleBrackets" value="false"/>
    <!--optionally strip angle brackets on public login and
      registration screens-->
    <add key="InstallationDate" value="7/22/2006"/>
</appSettings>
```

The `SiteSqlServer` is used for backwards compatibility for older modues. It holds the connection string for your datastore. In .NET 2.0 these setting are now held in the `<connectionStrings>` section. The next few keys help you decide how your portal is installed. `IntallTemplate` allows you to set which template to use when your portal is created.

The `AutoUpgrade` key allows you to determine if the application will automaticly upgrade your portal if the database version is different than your file version. If this is set to false, it will only alert you that an upgrade is needed but will not do the upgrade.

So if the hosting environment will not allow you to run the scripts necessary to install the membership provider on your own, you can use this key to turn this off so that the scripts can be run by your hosting provider manually.

The rest of the keys allow you to customize your portal to work in special environments.

The Global Files

The `Global.aspx.vb` and `Globals.vb` files share similar names but the parts they play in DotNetNuke are vastly different. The `Global.aspx.vb` is used by DotNetNuke to handle application-level events raised by the ASP.NET runtime. The `Globals.vb` file, on the other hand, is a public module that contains global utility functions. Before we take a look at these files, we first want to look at what object is being passed around in these transactions.

Global.aspx.vb

Much of the logic that used to reside in the `Global.aspx.vb` file has now been abstracted to the HTTP Modules. We will look into the code that remains.

Application Start

When the first request is made to your application (when the first user accesses the portal), a pool of `HttpApplication` instances are created and the `Application_Start` event is fired. If you have a very busy site, this will (theoretically) fire just once and on the first `HttpApplication` object in the pool. When there is inactivity on your portal for a certain amount of time the application (or worker process `aspnet_wp.exe`) will be recycled. When this happens, your application will restart (and this event will fire again) when the next request is made for your application.

> Since the new version of DotNetNuke uses the .NET website structure, you will find the `Global.asax.vb` file in the `App_Code` folder.

In the `Application_Start`, we are using the `Context` object and the `System.Reflection` namespace to initialize some global variables. As we will see shortly, the global variables reside in the `Globals.vb` file. In addition to this, we use the `AutoUpgrade` method to determine if an upgrade is needed for the site as well as to start the scheduler. These are performed in the `Application_Start` because we want them to be called only once.

```
Private Sub Application_Start(ByVal Sender As Object, _
                              ByVal E As EventArgs)

    Dim Server As HttpServerUtility = _
                                HttpContext.Current.Server
    'global variable initialization
    ServerName = Server.MachineName
```

```
    If HttpContext.Current.Request.ApplicationPath = "/" Then
        ApplicationPath = ""
    Else
        ApplicationPath = HttpContext.Current.Request.ApplicationPath
    End If
    ApplicationMapPath =
    System.AppDomain.CurrentDomain.BaseDirectory.Substring(0,
    System.AppDomain.CurrentDomain.BaseDirectory.Length - 1)
    ApplicationMapPath = ApplicationMapPath.Replace("/", "\")

    HostPath = ApplicationPath & "/Portals/_default/"
    HostMapPath = Server.MapPath(HostPath)

    AssemblyPath = ApplicationMapPath & "\bin\dotnetnuke.dll"

    'Check whether the current App Version is the same as the DB
    'Version
    CheckVersion()

    'Cache Mapped Directory(s)
    CacheMappedDirectory()

    'log APPLICATION_START event
      LogStart()

     'Start Scheduler
     StartScheduler()

      'Process any messages in the EventQueue for the
      'Application_Start event
      Dim oEventController As New EventQueue.EventQueueController
          oEventController.ProcessMessages("Application_Start")

      End Sub
```

Examining Application_BeginRequest

The Application_BeginRequest is called for each request made to your application.
In other words, this will fire every time a page (tab) is accessed in your portal.
This section is used to implement the scheduler built into DotNetNuke. Starting in
version 2.0, two items, "users online" and "site log", require recurring operations. You
can find out more about the scheduler by looking at the DotNetNuke Scheduler.doc
document found in the C:\DotNetNuke\Documentation\Public folder. (only if you
download the documentation pack).

```
    Private Sub Application_BeginRequest(ByVal sender As Object, ByVal e
                              As EventArgs)
```

```vb
'First check if we are upgrading/installing
If Request.Url.LocalPath.EndsWith("Install.aspx") Then
    Exit Sub
End If

  Try

  If Services.Scheduling.SchedulingProvider.SchedulerMode = _
     Scheduling.SchedulerMode.REQUEST_METHOD _
     AndAlso
     Services.Scheduling.SchedulingProvider.ReadyForPoll Then

    Dim scheduler As Scheduling.SchedulingProvider = _
                    Scheduling.SchedulingProvider.Instance
    Dim RequestScheduleThread As Threading.Thread
        RequestScheduleThread = New
          Threading.Thread(AddressOf scheduler.ExecuteTasks)
        RequestScheduleThread.IsBackground = True
        RequestScheduleThread.Start()
          Services.Scheduling.SchedulingProvider.
          ScheduleLastPolled _
          = Now

  End If

  Catch exc As Exception
            LogException(exc)
  End Try

End Sub
```

The Globals.vb File

As part of the namespace-reorganization effort associated with DotNetNuke version
3.0, general utility functions, constants, and enumerations have all been placed in a
public module named Globals. Since items in a .NET module are inherently shared,
you do not need to instantiate an object in order to use the functions found here. In
this module, you will find not only global constants:

```vb
Public Const glbAppVersion As String = "04.00.03"
Public Const glbAppTitle As String = "DotNetNuke"
Public Const glbAppDescription As String =
                            "DotNetNuke Web Application Framework"
Public Const glbAppCompany As String =
                            "Perpetual Motion Interactive Systems Inc."
Public Const glbAppUrl As String = "http://www.dotnetnuke.com"
Public Const glbLegalCopyright As String = "DotNetNuke® is copyright
          2002-YYYY by Perpetual Motion Interactive Systems Inc."
```

```
Public Const glbTrademark As String = "DotNetNuke"
Public Const glbHelpUrl As String = "http://www.dotnetnuke.com/
                                    default.aspx?tabid=787"

Public Const glbRoleAllUsers As String = "-1"
Public Const glbRoleSuperUser As String = "-2"
Public Const glbRoleUnauthUser As String = "-3"

Public Const glbRoleAllUsersName As String = "All Users"
Public Const glbRoleSuperUserName As String = "Superuser"
Public Const glbRoleUnauthUserName As String = "Unauthenticated Users"

Public Const glbDefaultPage As String = "Default.aspx"
Public Const glbHostSkinFolder As String = "_default"
Public Const glbDefaultSkinFolder As String = "/DNN-Blue/"
Public Const glbDefaultSkin As String =
                            "Horizontal Menu - Fixed Width.ascx"
Public Const glbDefaultAdminSkin As String =
                            "Horizontal Menu - Fixed Width.ascx"
Public Const glbDefaultContainerFolder As String = "/DNN-Blue/"
Public Const glbDefaultContainer As String =
                            "Image Header - Color Background.ascx"
Public Const glbDefaultAdminContainer As String =
                            "Image Header - Color Background.ascx"
Public Const glbDefaultControlPanel As String =
                            "Admin/ControlPanel/IconBar.ascx"
Public Const glbDefaultPane As String = "ContentPane"
Public Const glbImageFileTypes As String =
                                "jpg,jpeg,jpe,gif,bmp,png,swf"
Public Const glbConfigFolder As String = "\Config\"
Public Const glbConfigFile As String = "\Install\dnn.config"
Public Const glbAboutPage As String = "about.htm"

Public Const glbSuperUserAppName As Integer = -1
```

but a tremendous number of public functions to help you do everything, from retrieving the domain name:

```
Public Function GetDomainName(ByVal Request As HttpRequest) As String
```

to setting the focus on a page:

```
Public Sub SetFormFocus(ByVal control As Control)
```

This one file contains a wealth of information for the developer. Since there are more than 1600 lines in this file and the methods are fairly straightforward, we will not be stepping through this code.

The `Globals.vb` file can now be found in the `DotNetNuke.Library` project in the `\Components\Shared` folder.

Putting It All Together

We have spent some time looking at some of the major pieces that make up the core architecture. You might be asking yourself how all this works together. In this section, we will walk you through an overview version of what happens when a user requests a page on your portal.

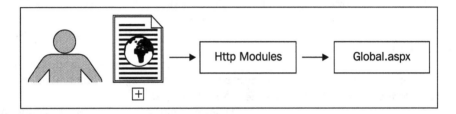

When a user requests any page on your portal, the HTTP Modules that have been declared in the `web.config` file are hooked into the pipeline. Some of the modules, like the `LoggingModule`, run their code when the `Init` method is called. Others such as the `UrlRewriteModule` use the `Init` method to attach event handlers to application events.

The request then goes through the `Global.aspx` page. As just mentioned, some of the events fired here will be intercepted and processed by the HTTP Modules, but the authentication of the user will be done in this file.

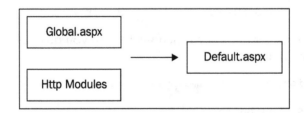

Next, the page that was requested, `Default.aspx`, will be processed. As we stated at the beginning of this chapter, all requests are sent to the `Default.aspx` page and all the controls and skins needed for the page are created dynamically by reading the tabID from the querysting. So let's begin by looking at the HTML for this page.

The HTML of the page is pretty simple and straightforward. The attributes at the top of the page tell us that the HTML page inherits from the `DotNetNuke.Framework.` `CDefault` class, which is found in the `Default.aspx.vb` code-behind page. We will be examining this class soon.

```
<%@ Page Language="vb" AutoEventWireup="false" Explicit="True"
Inherits="DotNetNuke.Framework.DefaultPage" CodeFile=
                                        "Default.aspx.vb" %>
<%@ Register TagPrefix="dnn" Namespace="DotNetNuke.Common.
                        Controls" Assembly="DotNetNuke" %>
<!DOCTYPE HTML PUBLIC "-//W3C//DTD HTML 4.0 Transitional//EN">
```

The title and meta-tags are populated with variables we will find in the code-behind file:

```
<HTML>
  <HEAD id="Head">
    <META NAME="DESCRIPTION" CONTENT="<%= Description %>">
    <META NAME="KEYWORDS" CONTENT="<%= KeyWords %>">
    <META NAME="COPYRIGHT" CONTENT="<%= Copyright %>">
    <META NAME="GENERATOR" CONTENT="<%= Generator %>">
    <META NAME="AUTHOR" CONTENT="<%= Author %>">
    <META NAME="RESOURCE-TYPE" CONTENT="DOCUMENT">
    <META NAME="DISTRIBUTION" CONTENT="GLOBAL">
    <META NAME="ROBOTS" CONTENT="INDEX, FOLLOW">
    <META NAME="REVISIT-AFTER" CONTENT="1 DAYS">
    <META NAME="RATING" CONTENT="GENERAL">
```

After the meta-tags, placeholders are set to hold CSS and Favicons. These are declared in this manner so that the actual files can be determined by the skin being used on the site. This is followed by a script declaration for the file; this declaration is responsible for the module drag-and-drop capability of DotNetNuke 3.0.

```
<style id="StylePlaceholder" runat="server"></style>
<asp:placeholder id="CSS" runat="server"></asp:placeholder>
</HEAD>
```

The body of the HTML is relatively bare. The important code in this section is the `SkinPlaceholder`, used to inject the selected skin into the body of the page.

```
<BODY ID="Body" runat="server" BOTTOMMARGIN="0" LEFTMARGIN="0"
    TOPMARGIN="0" RIGHTMARGIN="0" MARGINWIDTH="0" MARGINHEIGHT="0">
<noscript></noscript>
<dnn:Form id="Form" runat="server" ENCTYPE="multipart/form-data"
            style="height:100%;>
   <asp:Label ID="SkinError" Runat="server" CssClass="NormalRed"
                            Visible="False"></asp:Label>
```

```
        <asp:placeholder id="SkinPlaceHolder" runat="server" />
        <input id="ScrollTop" runat="server" name="ScrollTop"
            type="hidden">
        <input id="__dnnVariable" runat="server"
            name="__dnnVariable" type="hidden">
    </dnn:Form>
  </BODY>
</HTML>
```

Now we will venture into the code-behind class for this file. If you look past the `Imports` statements, you will see that this class is declared `MustInherit` and itself inherits from the `DotNetNuke.Framework.PageBase` class.

```
Partial Class DefaultPage
        Inherits DotNetNuke.Framework.CDefault
```

Its base class handles the localization for the page and of course, since this is a web page, inherits from `System.Web.UI.Page`.

The first procedure that is run in the page is the `Page_Init` method. Most of the action required to generate our request resides in this section. The first few lines of the method call the `InitializeComponent` method, which is a default web-form designer procedure, the `InializePage`, which generates the information to fill the meta-tags, and the `ManageRequest`, which collects the affiliate information and updates the site log.

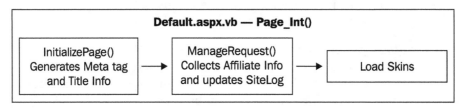

Default.aspx.vb — Page_Int()

| InitializePage()
Generates Meta tag
and Title Info | → | ManageRequest()
Collects Affiliate Info
and updates SiteLog | → | Load Skins |

If you look at a couple of pieces of code in, we can see some of the files we looked at earlier in use. In the `InitializePage` method, we make use of both the `PortalSettings` class and the `Current` property of the `HTTPContext` object to retrieve the `TabName`:

```
objTab = objTabs.GetTabByName(Request.QueryString("TabName"), _
CType(HttpContext.Current.Items("PortalSettings"), _
PortalSettings).PortalId)
```

The `ManageRequest` method on the other hand makes use of the `Globals` class to find the `SiteLogStorate` setting:

```
If Convert.ToString(Common.Globals.HostSettings("SiteLogStorage")) _
    <> "" Then
```

```
    strSiteLogStorage = _
      Convert.ToString(Common.Globals.HostSettings("SiteLogStorage"))
  End If
```

When these two methods complete, the process of loading the skin begins. The process starts by creating a user control to hold the skin and a `SkinControler` that will do the work of loading the skin.

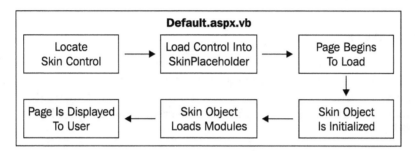

After determining whether the request is a skin preview, the code moves on to load the skin. There are three possible outcomes when loading the skin: it is for an admin page, it is for a regular page, or there was an error and it loads the default skin. Regardless of which section is invoked, the skin is loaded using the `LoadSkin` method.

```
ctlSkin = LoadSkin(PortalSettings.ActiveTab.SkinSrc)
```

This method reads the physical path of the skin control and loads it into our `ctlSkin` variable. And finally, after calls to `ManageStyleSheets` and `ManageFavicon`, the control is added to the page by using the `SkinPlaceholder` that we looked at earlier in the HTML page:

```
' add skin to page
SkinPlaceHolder.Controls.Add(ctlSkin)
```

At this point, you may be thinking to yourself, "I understand how the skin is dynamically added to the page for a user's request, but how are the modules dynamically added?" Well, to get the answer to that question, we will need to look at the skin control itself. You can find the skin control (`skin.vb`) in the `admin\Skins` folder. We will not look at this entire class, but if you look closely at the `Page_Init` method, which is called when the control is instantiated, you will see how the modules are created. The method first determines the number of panes available on the skin and then dynamically populates the modules assigned to each pane. It will check for the authorization of the user as it goes and then finally inject the module into the skin (found in `Skin.vb`).

```
' inject the module into the skin
InjectModule(parent, objModule, PortalSettings)
```

This procedure will be repeated for all of the modules associated with that page, and the request is finally completed and presented to the user. We did not, of course, cover every piece of code that is called in the process, but hopefully have given you a path to follow to continue researching the core architecture on your own.

Summary

In this chapter we have taken a look at how the core of DotNetNuke works. We looked at a general overview, examined important pieces of the framework, and finally followed a request through its paces. We will be expanding on this knowledge as we venture into the world of custom-module creation in Chapter 7.

Custom Module Development

7

In this chapter, we will be creating a custom module for the Coffee Connections portal. A custom module can consist of one or more custom web controls. The areas that will be covered are:

- Setting up the development environment
- Creating a "Hello World!" View Control
- Creating a "Hello Edit" Edit control

Setting up the Development Environment

To develop modules for DotNetNuke you must first have a DotNetNuke installation running on the computer on which you intend to develop them.

DotNetNuke comes in two versions, a *source* version, and an *install* version. The *install* version is also packaged as the *DotNetNuke Starter Kit*. They are functionally the same. Surprisingly, it is recommended that you use the *install* version to develop modules. The reason for this is that the *source* version should only be used if you intend to change the DotNetNuke core code. This is not recommended as it may not allow you to upgrade your installation in the future.

In this chapter, **Visual Web Developer Express 2005** will be used (hereafter referred to as Visual Studio); however, the instructions are the same for all versions of Visual Studio 2005.

Download and install the **DotNetNuke Starter Kit**. Then open Visual Studio and from the **File** menu select **New Web Site**.

Select the **DotNetNuke Web Application Framework** template that was installed by the **DotNetNuke Starter Kit**. Ensure that the **Location** is set to **File System**.

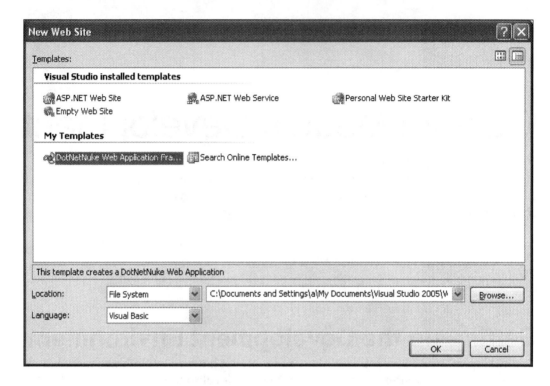

Follow the directions on the page that will appear after installation to complete any configuration and launch your DotNetNuke website.

> DotNetNuke is constantly changing as it evolves and the best way to get up-to-date help and information is to use the DotNetNuke message board at DotNetNuke.com. There are installation documents available at DotNetNuke.com that you can download that will assist you.

The Coffee Shop Listing Module

In this chapter, we will go through the process of creating a DotNetNuke module from top to bottom. Although we will go through quite a bit of code in this chapter, we do not cover every single line. To help you as you work through the chapter, the complete source code is available for download from the publisher's site (http://www.PacktPub.com/support).

One of the main attractions for the Coffee Shop Listing module is that users will be able to search, by zip code, for coffee shops in their area. After searching, the users will be presented with the shops in their area. This will be accomplished using the View control.

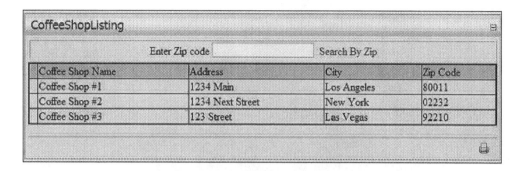

In addition, the module will be configurable to allow certain users to add coffee shops using the Edit control.

CoffeeShop Edit	
ShopName	Coffee Shop #1
Address1	1234 Main
Address2	
City	Los Angeles
State	CA
zip	80011
WiFi Yes or No	⊙ Yes ○ No
Extra Details	This place is great
	Update Cancel Delete

The administrator of the site will be able to configure which users are allowed to add coffee shops using the Settings control.

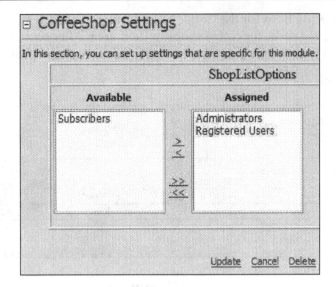

To allow the focus of this chapter to be on module development, we will not spend time on validation of the various controls, instead we will focus only on what is necessary to create the module.

Creating the View Control

Our first example will be the traditional *Hello World!* example. Later, we will alter this control to complete the Coffee Shop Listing module.

1. Open Visual Studio and select **File** from the toolbar, then click **Open Web Site**.

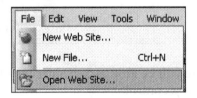

2. Next, select the root directory of the DotNetNuke website and click the **Open** button.

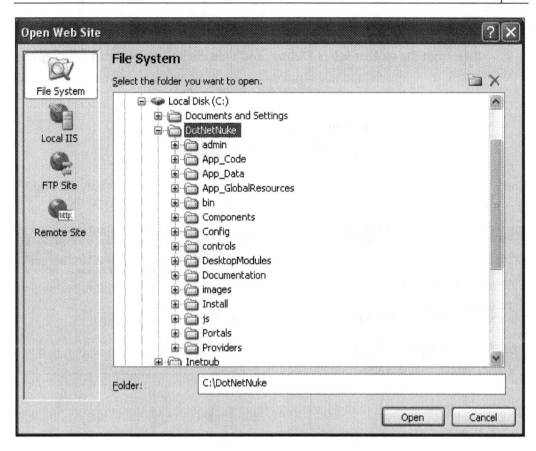

The website will open and display in the **Solution Explorer** window.

3. To ensure that your development environment is configured properly, from the toolbar select **View**, then click **Output** to display the output window, then from the toolbar select **Debug**, and then click **Start Without Debugging**.

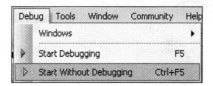

You might have a long wait while Visual Studio builds the website. When the build is complete the output windows should show no errors (**failed** should be 0).

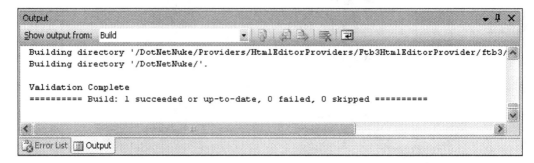

When the build is complete the website will automatically launch.

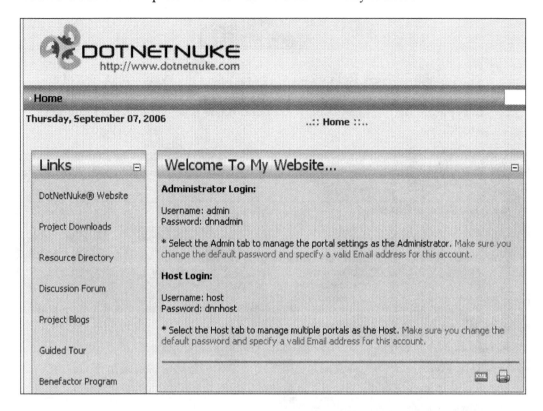

4. Now close your web browser and return to Visual Studio. In the **Solution Explorer**, right-click on the **DesktopModules** folder and select **New Folder**.

5. Name the folder **CoffeeShopListing**

6. Next, right-click on the **CoffeeShopListing** folder and select **Add New Item**.

7. When the **Add New Item** menu appears, select the **Web User Control** and enter ShopList.ascx in the **Name** box and check the box next to **Place code in separate file**. Also, ensure that **Visual Basic** is selected in the **Language** dropdown.

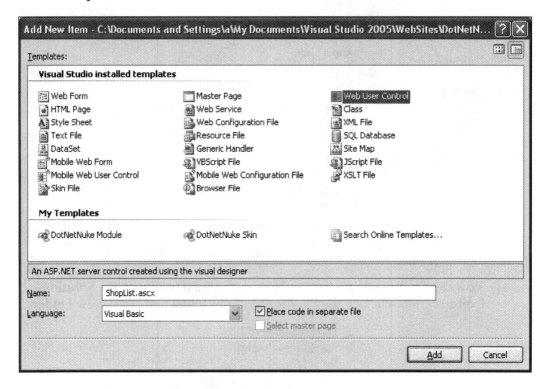

The ShopList.ascx file will now appear under the **CoffeeShopListing** folder.

The source for the ShopList.ascx will also appear in the main window. If it is in the design view, click the **Source** button in the lower left-hand corner of the window to switch to the **Source** view.

8. Replace all the code with this code:

```
<%@ Control language="vb" AutoEventWireup="false"
          Inherits="EganEnterprises.CoffeeShopListing.ShopList"
          CodeFile="ShopList.ascx.vb"%>
<asp:Label ID="Label1" runat="server" Text="Label"></asp:Label>
```

 You will see wavy blue lines that indicate errors. These errors will be cleared up when we replace the code in the code-behind file.

9. Now, right-click on the ShopList.ascx file and select **View Code**.

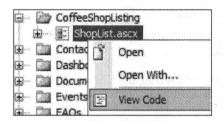

10. Replace all the code with the following code:

```
Imports DotNetNuke
Imports DotNetNuke.Security.Roles
Imports System.Collections.Generic

Namespace EganEnterprises.CoffeeShopListing
    Partial Class ShopList
        Inherits Entities.Modules.PortalModuleBase
        Protected Sub Page_Load(ByVal sender As System.Object, _
        ByVal e As System.EventArgs) Handles MyBase.Load
            Try
                Label1.Text = "Hello World!"
            Catch exc As Exception
                Exceptions.ProcessModuleLoadException(Me, exc)
            End Try
        End Sub
    End Class
End Namespace
```

11. Select **File** then **Save All** to save the changes. Now, from the toolbar select **Build,** then click on **Build Page**.

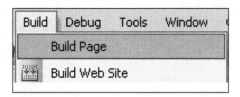

If you have build errors it is best to download the code using the link noted at the beginning of the chapter and compare it to your own.

Displaying the Module

We will now walk through the steps needed to configure the module and view it in your DotNetNuke website.

1. In Visual Studio, select **Debug** then **Start Without Debugging**. When the site comes up click the **Login** link.

2. Log in as the *host* user.

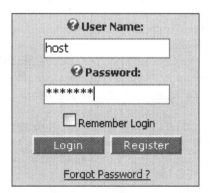

The password for the host account is usually *dnnhost*. However, refer to the first page of your DotNetNuke website as this may change.

3. Click on the **Host** menu and select **Module Definitions**.

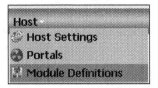

4. From the **Module Definitions** menu (click on the small black down-pointing arrow in the upper left-hand corner) select **Add New Module Definition**.

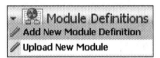

5. When the Module Definition screen comes up:
    ° Enter **CoffeeShopListing** for **Module Name**.
    ° Enter **CoffeeShopListing** for **Folder Name**.
    ° Enter **CoffeeShopListing** for **Friendly Name**.
    ° Enter **CoffeeShopListing** for **Description**.
    ° Enter **01.00.00** for **Version**.
    ° Click the **Update** button.

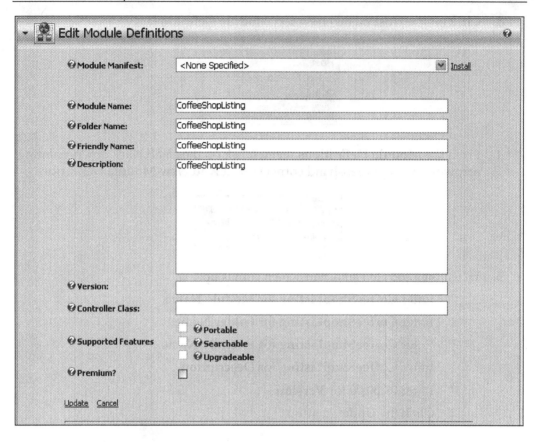

6. Near the bottom of the **Edit Module Definitions** form, enter
   CoffeeShopListing in the **New Definition** box and click the **Add
   Definition link**.

7. Click the **Add Control** link.

8. When the **Edit Module Control** form appears:

   ° Enter **CoffeeShopListing** for **Title**.

   ° Use the dropdown to select **DesktopModules/
     CoffeeShopListing/ShopList.ascx** for **Source**.

- ° Use the dropdown to select **View** for **Type**.
- ° Click the **Update** button.

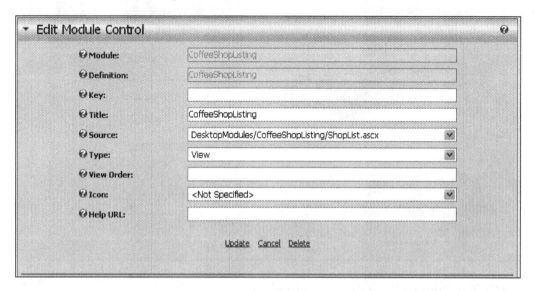

9. On the **Admin** menu select **Pages**.

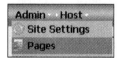

10. On the Pages form click **Add New Page**.

11. On the **Edit Page** form:
    - ° Enter **Coffee Shop Listing** for **Page Name**.
    - ° Enter **Coffee Shop Listing** for **Page Title**.
    - ° Enter **Coffee Shop Listing** for **Description**.
    - ° Check the box for **All Users** under **View Page**.
    - ° Then click the **Update** button.

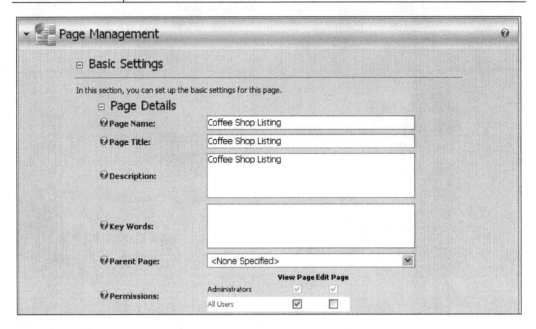

The **Coffee Shop Listing** tab will now appear on the toolbar.

12. Click on it to navigate to that page.
13. From the administration bar at the top of the site, select **CoffeeShopListing** from the **Module** dropdown and click **Add**.

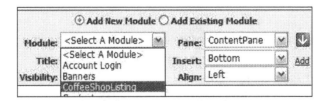

The module will now appear.

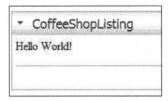

Next, we will intentionally generate an error to explore the functionality of the **Log Viewer**. Leave the website open and return to Visual Studio. In Visual Studio, add the following, highlighted line into your code as shown:

```
Label1.Text = "Hello World!"
Throw New Exception("Something didn't work right.")
Catch exc As Exception
    Exceptions.ProcessModuleLoadException(Me, exc)
End Try
```

Save the page and return to the site in the web browser and click on the **Coffee Shop Listing** tab to refresh the page. The page will now show an error message.

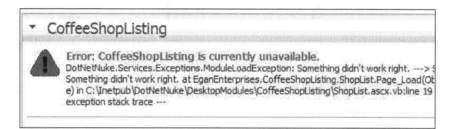

Select **Log Viewer** from the **Admin** menu. Locate the most recent entry for **Module Load Exception** and click on it to expand it. We can see it indicates that the error is in the ShopList.ascx.vb file and indicates the line number.

```
 7/20/2006 6:47:57 PM          Module Load Exception          host
ModuleId: 369
ModuleDefId: 127
FriendlyName: CoffeeShopListing
ModuleControlSource: DesktopModules/CoffeeShopListing/ShopList.ascx
AssemblyVersion: 04.03.02
Method: EganEnterprises.CoffeeShopListing.ShopList.Page_Load
FileName: C:\Inetpub\DotNetNuke\DesktopModules\CoffeeShopListing\ShopList.ascx.vb
FileLineNumber: 19
FileColumnNumber: 17
PortalID: 0
PortalName: My Website
UserID: 1
UserName: host
ActiveTabID: 53
ActiveTabName: Coffee Shop Listing
AbsoluteURL: /DNN4/Default.aspx
```

You may see multiple General Exceptions errors for
System.IO.Path.NormalizePathFast. To prevent this,
develop DotNetNuke in a much shorter physical path
folder to reduce the total number of characters that
compose the path and filename (for instance
`C:\DotNetNuke`).

Return to Visual Studio and remove the **Throw New Exception("Something didn't
work right.")** line. Save the page and return to the site in the web browser and click
on the **Coffee Shop Listing** tab to refresh the page.

What we have Accomplished

We have just explored a few core concepts of DotNetNuke module development:

- The DotNetNuke module folder structure
- Inheriting from PortalModuleBase
- Module configuration
- Diagnosing errors using the Log Viewer

The Module Folder Structure

A DotNetNuke module is made up of User Controls and their associated code-behind
files that reside in folders in the `DesktopModules` directory. Optionally, other code files
for the module that are not associated with a User Control (for example, Data Access
Layer and Business Logic Layer code) reside in the `App_Code` directory. In later steps
we will create code that will reside in the `App_Code` directory.

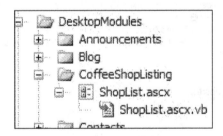

Inheriting from PortalModuleBase

The most important item for making your User Control integrate well with the
DotNetNuke framework is this:

```
Inherits Entities.Modules.PortalModuleBase
```

Inheriting from `PortalModuleBase` is essential because it is the base class for all User Controls in DotNetNuke. Using the base class is what gives our control consistency in its appearance with the portal it resides in, and provides functionality such as the menu and portal access security.

This class also gives us access to useful items such as the current user and the current **ModuleId**. In later steps you will see how these items allow the User Control to interact with the DotNetNuke framework to provide most of the functionality you would desire.

Module Configuration

Adding module definitions makes the module appear in the control panel module dropdown when you are signed on as host or admin. It connects your controls to the portal framework. In the walk-through we configured the module to have one User Control. In later steps, we will create and configure two additional User Controls.

Diagnosing Errors using the Log Viewer

The **ProcessModuleLoadException** method of the **DotNetNuke.Services.Exceptions** class offers a simple way to send errors to the Log Viewer.

```
Catch exc As Exception
    Exceptions.ProcessModuleLoadException(Me, exc)
```

This is useful during module development as well as to assist an administrator in diagnosing problems when the module is deployed to production.

Navigation and Localization

At this stage you can see that creating a module from a User Control is relatively straightforward. Programming multiple User Controls to interact with each other is not as straightforward. The next walk-through will be devoted to this subject as well as demonstrating *Localization*, which allows your module to display its text in multiple languages.

We will create an Edit User Control. For now it will just say *Hello Edit!* Later we will alter it to complete the Coffee Shop Listing module.

Create EditShopList.ascx

1. In Visual Studio, right-click on the **CoffeeShopListing** folder and select **Add New Item**.

2. When the **Add New Item** menu comes up, select **Web User Control** and enter EditShopList.ascx in the **Name** box. Ensure that the **Place code in separate file** box is checked and click the **Add** button.

3. When the page comes up in source view, replace all the code with the following code:

```
<%@ Control language="vb" AutoEventWireup="false"
Inherits="EganEnterprises.CoffeeShopListing.EditShopList"
CodeFile="EditShopList.ascx.vb"%>
<asp:Label ID="Label1" runat="server" Text="Label"></asp:Label>
<br />
<br />
<asp:LinkButton id="cmdReturn" runat="server" Text="Return"
BorderStyle="none" CssClass="CommandButton"
CausesValidation="False"></asp:LinkButton>
```

4. Right-click on EditShopList.ascx in the Solution Explorer and select **View Code**. When the source code is displayed, replace all the code with the following code:

```
Imports DotNetNuke
Namespace EganEnterprises.CoffeeShopListing
    Partial Class EditShopList
        Inherits Entities.Modules.PortalModuleBase
        Protected Sub Page_Load(ByVal sender As System.Object, _
        ByVal e As System.EventArgs) Handles MyBase.Load
            Label1.Text = "Hello Edit!"
        End Sub
        Protected Sub cmdDelete_Click( _
            ByVal sender As System.Object, _
            ByVal e As System.EventArgs) Handles cmdReturn.Click
            ' Redirect back to the portal
            Response.Redirect(NavigateURL())
        End Sub
    End Class
End Namespace
```

5. Save and build the page.

Navigation

The `EditShopList.ascx` page doesn't do much at this point. For now, it is being used to demonstrate how to navigate between User Controls (or pages) of your module. Now we will place a link and a menu item on the ShopList page that will navigate to the EditShopList page.

1. Right-click on `ShopList.ascx` and select **View Code**.

2. When the source code is displayed, add the highlighted line as shown:

    ```
    Inherits Entities.Modules.PortalModuleBase
    Implements Entities.Modules.IActionable
    ```

3. Next, insert the following code above the line: `End Class`.

    ```
    #Region "Optional Interfaces"
      Public ReadOnly Property ModuleActions() As _
      DotNetNuke.Entities.Modules.Actions.ModuleActionCollection _
         Implements DotNetNuke.Entities.Modules.IActionable.
            ModuleActions
      Get
        Dim Actions As New _
        Entities.Modules.Actions.ModuleActionCollection
        Actions.Add(GetNextActionID, Localization.
        GetString(Entities.Modules.Actions.ModuleActionType.
        AddContent, LocalResourceFile), Entities.Modules.Actions.
        ModuleActionType.AddContent, "", "", EditUrl(), False,
        Security.SecurityAccessLevel.Edit, True, False)
                Return Actions
            End Get
         End Property

    #End Region
    ```

4. Save and build the page.

Localization

In the final step for this section we will create a resource file that can be used to replace the text of one of the links (for example to change the language). For now the link will be in English and we will only localize one link. Normally you would localize all the text elements of your module so that it can be used in any language.

1. Right-click on the CoffeeShopListing folder and select **Add ASP.NET Folder** and then **App_LocalResources**.

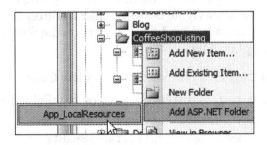

2. When the **App_LocalResources** folder appears, select **Add New Item**.

3. When the **Add New Item** box comes up, select **Resource File** as the template, enter ShopList.ascx.resx in the **Name** box, and click the **Add** button.

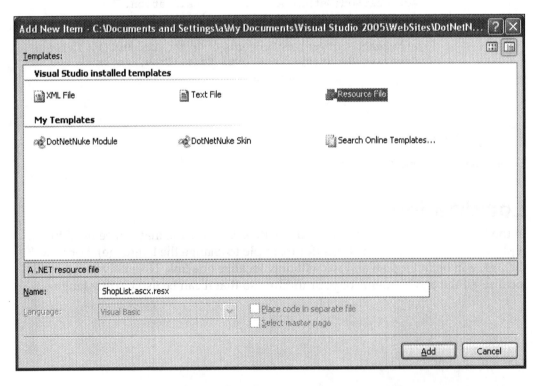

4. When the resource editor window appears, enter **AddContent.Action** in the **Name** column and **Add Coffee Shop** in the **Value** column.

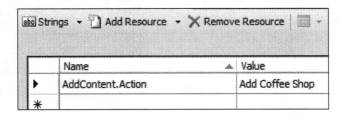

5. Save the file and close it.

Update the Configuration

In Visual Studio, press *Ctrl+F5* to start the DotNetNuke site.

1. Log in as host.
2. From the **Host** menu select **Module Definitions**.
3. From the **Module Definitions** click the edit symbol next to the **CoffeeShopListing** module to select it.
4. Click the **Add Control** link toward the bottom of the **CoffeeShopListing** module definition.
5. When the control configuration screen appears, configure it with the following settings:
    ° Enter **Edit** for **Key**.
    ° Enter **Edit Shoplist** for **Title**.
    ° Use the dropdown to select **DesktopModules/ CoffeeShopListing/EditShopList.ascx** for **Source**.
    ° Use the dropdown to select **Edit** for **Type**.
    ° Click the **Update** button.

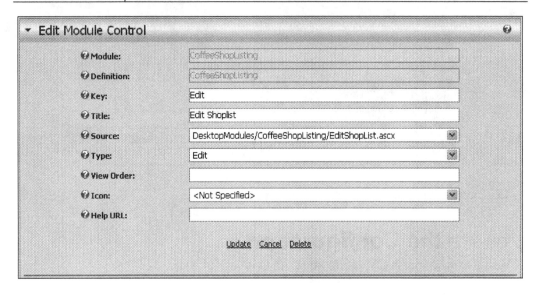

Navigate from ShopList to EditShopList

Next, click the **Coffee Shop Listing** link on the menu bar in the DotNetNuke site. On the **CoffeeShopListing** module, you will see that there is now a link to **Add Coffee Shop.**

Click on the link and you will navigate to the Edit page.

Click the **Return** button and you will navigate back to the ShopList page. Click the menu icon in the corner of the **Coffee Shop Listing** module and notice that there is also an **Add Coffee Shop** link there.

What we have Accomplished

We have explored a few additional concepts of DotNetNuke module development:

- IActionable
- NavigateURL
- Localization

IActionable

We only implemented the `IActionable` interface in one place in the code yet the **Add Coffee Shop** link shows up in two places on the module. It shows up on the ShopList page and on the modules menu. This demonstrates the benefit of the DotNetNuke API. The link and the menu item not only show up in standardized places, but they also show up based on the security roles that you indicate. For example, currently the **Add Coffee Shop** link will only show up if you are logged in as the host or administrator account.

To add an action menu item to the module actions menu, we create an instance of a `ModuleActionCollection`. This is done in the `ModuleActions` property declaration.

```
Public ReadOnly Property ModuleActions() As _
DotNetNuke.Entities.Modules.Actions.ModuleActionCollection _
Implements DotNetNuke.Entities.Modules.IActionable.ModuleActions
    Get
        Dim Actions As New _
        Entities.Modules.Actions.ModuleActionCollection
```

We then use the `Add` method of this object to add an item to the menu.

```
Actions.Add(GetNextActionID, _
Localization.GetString( _
Entities.Modules.Actions.ModuleActionType.AddContent, _
LocalResourceFile), _
```

```
      Entities.Modules.Actions.ModuleActionType.AddContent, _
      "", _
      "", _
      EditUrl(), _
      False, _
      Security.SecurityAccessLevel.Edit, _
      True, _
      False)
      Return Actions
   End Get
   End Property
```

The parameters of the `Actions.Add` method are:

Parameter	Type	Description
ID	Integer	The `GetNextActionID` function (found in the `ActionsBase.vb` file) will retrieve the next available ID for your `ModuleActionCollection`. This works like an auto-increment field, adding one to the previous action ID.
Title	String	The title is what is displayed in the context menu form your module.
CmdName	String	If you want your menu item to call client-side code (JavaScript), then this is where you will place the name of the command. This is used for the delete action on the context menu. When the delete item is selected, a message asks you to confirm your choice before executing the command. For the menu items we are adding we will leave this blank.
CmdArg	String	This allows you to add additional arguments for the command.
Icon	String	This allows you to set a custom icon to appear next to your menu option.
URL	String	This is where the browser will be redirected to when your menu item is clicked. You can use a standard URL or use the `EditURL` function to direct it to another module. The `EditURL` function finds the module associated with your view module by looking at the key passed in. These keys are entered in the Module Definition.
ClientScript	String	As the name implies, this is where you would add the client-side script to be run when this item is selected. This is paired with the `CmdName` attribute above. We are leaving this blank for your actions.

Parameter	Type	Description
UseActionEvent	Boolean	This determines if the user will receive notification when a script is being executed.
Secure	SecurityAccessLevel	This is an Enum that determines the access level for this menu item.
Visible	Boolean	Determines whether this item will be visible.
New Window	Boolean	Determines whether information will be presented in a new window.

NavigateUrl

If you want to create a link that you do not want to appear as a menu item, you can simply use code such as `Response.Redirect(NavigateURL())`.

The `NavigateURL` function works in conjunction with DotNetNuke URL rewriting. URL rewriting is a function DotNetNuke performs to create URL's that are more easily indexed by search engines.

If we run the code in Debug mode we can see that `NavigateURL()` resolves to `http://localhost:1545/DotNetNuke/CoffeeShopListing/tabid/53/Default.aspx`. Your instance will certainly have a different URL, but the result will be the same that directs the user back to the default page of your module, which in this case is the ShopList User Control.

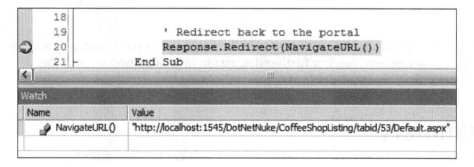

We can see in the Visual Studio object browser that the `NavigateURL()` method has multiple overloads.

```
⊞ { } DotNetNuke                          ⋯♦ ManageUploadDirectory(String, String) As String
⊟ { } DotNetNuke.Common                    ⋯♦ NavigateURL() As String
  ⊞ ·⚙ FileItem                            ⋯♦ NavigateURL(Integer) As String
  ·♣ Globals                               ⋯♦ NavigateURL(Integer, Boolean) As String
  ·⚙ Globals.PerformanceSettings           ⋯♦ NavigateURL(Integer, Boolean, DotNetNuke.Entities.Portals.PortalSettings, String, ParamArray String()) As String
  ·⚙ Globals.PortalRegistrationType        ⋯♦ NavigateURL(Integer, DotNetNuke.Entities.Portals.PortalSettings, String, ParamArray String()) As String
  ·⚙ Globals.UpgradeStatus                 ⋯♦ NavigateURL(Integer, String) As String
  ⊞ ·⚙ XmlValidatorBase                    ⋯♦ NavigateURL(Integer, String, ParamArray String()) As String
⊞ { } DotNetNuke.Common.Controls           ⋯♦ NavigateURL(String) As String
```

Adding Localization

You will notice that the second parameter of the `Add()` method in the `IActionable` interface asks for a title. This is the text that will be displayed. In our code you will notice that instead of using a string, we use the `Localization.GetString()` method to get the text from the local resource file.

```
Actions.Add(GetNextActionID, _
    Localization.GetString( _
    Entities.Modules.Actions.ModuleActionType.AddContent, _
    LocalResourceFile), _
    Entities.Modules.Actions.ModuleActionType.AddContent, _
    "", _
    "", _
    EditUrl(), _
    False, _
    Security.SecurityAccessLevel.Edit, _
    True, _
    False)
```

This allows the portal administrator to set the language of their choice by simply replacing the resource file. For further discussion of localization refer to the localization document available at `DotNetNuke.com`.

Summary

The module is not complete, however, we have covered many important concepts that you will most likely use in every module you create. Essentially a DotNetNuke module is made up of web controls that inherit from *Entities.Modules. PortalModuleBase*. Navigation and localization were covered because their proper use will allow you to create modules that integrate well into your portal. In addition, we also covered exception handling that will aid you in your module development.

In the next chapter we will cover connecting to the database. We will also cover optional interfaces that will allow you to import and export module data and to integrate the module into the DotnetNuke portal search.

8
Connecting to the Database

In this chapter, we are going to complete the custom module for the Coffee Connections portal. In the previous chapter, we set up our development environment, and created custom web controls. In this chapter, we will cover the methods used to connect to the database. The areas that will be covered are:

- Using the **DAL+** — a simplified data access method that still allows your module to support multiple data sources.

- Using the **DAL** — a more robust data access method that allows your modules to have 100% *portability*.

- Implementing optional interfaces
    - `ISearchable`
    - `IPortable`

- Packaging and uploading the module

DotNetNuke Data Access Layer (DAL)

We are now ready to create code that will communicate with the database. To do this we will create a Settings page for the module that will use the DotNetNuke **Data Access Layer** (DAL).

The DAL's purpose is to allow DotNetNuke (and its modules) to communicate with any data source. It consists of an Abstract Data Provider and a Concrete Provider.

For the Settings page we will use the DAL+. The DAL+ is an alternative method of communicating with the database. With the DAL+ you will not need to write code for an Abstract Data Provider or a Concrete Provider. Instead, you use a subset of methods that are a part of the DAL. These methods will still allow you to create modules that can communicate with an alternative database. However, unlike the traditional DAL the DAL+ is not 100% portable to other data sources.

The reason it is not 100% portable is that a situation can exist where one stored procedure or SQL statement is needed to perform an action using one data source (for example Microsoft SQL Server), but more than one is needed for another data source (for example, MySQL). In cases such as this, the DAL+ will not work. The traditional DAL will work in all situations with all data sources.

The DAL+ is best used for modules that will not need to run on a database other than the database you develop the module on.

The traditional DAL will be covered later in this chapter.

Create the Database Elements

First, we will execute a SQL script that will create all the tables and stored procedures needed for the module. Only some of the database elements will be used in the Settings page. The remaining database elements will be used by the module code that will be covered later in this chapter.

Execute the SQL Script

1. Log in as host.
2. From the **Host** menu select **SQL**.
3. Check the **Run As Script** box.
4. Enter the following code sections in the main window (only enter the code, not the narration that explains each section) and click the Execute link (remember you can obtain this script and all the code from http://www.packtpub.com/support):

First we create the two tables that the module will use. One table will be used to hold the listings of coffee shops and the other will be used to hold the information on the security roles that will be allowed to add coffee shops.

```
CREATE TABLE {databaseOwner}{objectQualifier}
                              [EganEnterprises_CoffeeShopInfo] (
   [coffeeShopID] [int] IDENTITY (1, 1) NOT NULL ,
   [moduleID] [int] NOT NULL ,
   [coffeeShopName] [varchar] (100) NOT NULL ,
   [coffeeShopAddress1] [varchar] (150) NULL ,
   [coffeeShopAddress2] [varchar] (150) NULL ,
   [coffeeShopCity] [varchar] (50) NULL ,
   [coffeeShopState] [char] (2) NULL ,
   [coffeeShopZip] [char] (11) NULL ,
   [coffeeShopWiFi] [smallint] NOT NULL ,
```

```
    [coffeeShopDetails] [varchar] (250) NULL
) ON [PRIMARY]
GO
CREATE TABLE {databaseOwner}{objectQualifier}
                             [EganEnterprises_CoffeeShopModuleOptions] (
    [ModuleID] [int] NOT NULL ,
    [AuthorizedRoles] [varchar] (200) NULL
) ON [PRIMARY]
GO
```

Next, we will create the stored procedures.

```
CREATE procedure {databaseOwner}{objectQualifier}EganEnterprises_
AddCoffeeShopInfo
@moduleID    int,
@coffeeShopName          varchar(100)    ,
@coffeeShopAddress1      varchar(150),
@coffeeShopAddress2      varchar(150),
@coffeeShopCity          varchar(50)   ,
@coffeeShopState           char(2),
@coffeeShopZip           char(11),
@coffeeShopWiFi          bit,
@coffeeShopDetails       varchar(250)

AS
insert into EganEnterprises_CoffeeShopInfo (
    moduleID,
    coffeeShopName,
    coffeeShopAddress1,
    coffeeShopAddress2,
    coffeeShopCity,
    coffeeShopState,
    coffeeShopZip,
    coffeeShopWiFi,
    coffeeShopDetails
)
values (
    @moduleID,
    @coffeeShopName,
    @coffeeShopAddress1,
    @coffeeShopAddress2,
    @coffeeShopCity,
    @coffeeShopState,
    @coffeeShopZip,
    @coffeeShopWiFi,
```

```
    @coffeeShopDetails
)

select SCOPE_IDENTITY()
GO
CREATE procedure {databaseOwner}{objectQualifier}
                        EganEnterprises_AddCoffeeShopModuleOptions
@moduleID         int,
@authorizedRoles varchar(250)

AS
    INSERT INTO
      EganEnterprises_CoffeeShopModuleOptions
      (moduleId, AuthorizedRoles)
    VALUES
      (@moduleID, @authorizedRoles)
GO
create procedure {databaseOwner}{objectQualifier}
                            EganEnterprises_DeleteCoffeeShop
@coffeeShopID   int
AS
delete
from    EganEnterprises_CoffeeShopInfo
where   coffeeShopID = @coffeeShopID
GO
CREATE procedure {databaseOwner}{objectQualifier}
                        EganEnterprises_GetCoffeeShopModuleOptions
@moduleId int
AS
select  *
from    EganEnterprises_CoffeeShopModuleOptions
where
     moduleID = @moduleID
GO
CREATE procedure {databaseOwner}{objectQualifier}
                                EganEnterprises_GetCoffeeShops
@moduleId int
AS
select coffeeShopID,
     coffeeShopName,
     coffeeShopAddress1,
     coffeeShopAddress2,
     coffeeShopCity,
     coffeeShopState,
     coffeeShopZip,
```

```
        coffeeShopWiFi,
        coffeeShopDetails
from    EganEnterprises_CoffeeShopInfo
where
        moduleID = @moduleID
GO
CREATE procedure {databaseOwner}{objectQualifier}
                                EganEnterprises_GetCoffeeShopsByID
@coffeeShopID int
AS
select coffeeShopID,
        coffeeShopName,
        coffeeShopAddress1,
        coffeeShopAddress2,
        coffeeShopCity,
        coffeeShopState,
        coffeeShopZip,
        coffeeShopWiFi,
        coffeeShopDetails
from    EganEnterprises_CoffeeShopInfo
where
        coffeeShopID = @coffeeShopID
GO
CREATE procedure {databaseOwner}{objectQualifier}
                                EganEnterprises_GetCoffeeShopsByZip
@moduleID int,
@coffeeShopZip      char(11)

AS
select coffeeShopID,
        coffeeShopName,
        coffeeShopAddress1,
        coffeeShopAddress2,
        coffeeShopCity,
        coffeeShopState,
        coffeeShopZip,
        coffeeShopWiFi,
        coffeeShopDetails
from    EganEnterprises_CoffeeShopInfo
where
        coffeeShopZip = @coffeeShopZip AND moduleID = @moduleID
GO
CREATE procedure {databaseOwner}{objectQualifier}
                                EganEnterprises_UpdateCoffeeShopInfo
```

```
@coffeeShopID          int,
@coffeeShopName        varchar(100),
@coffeeShopAddress1     varchar(150),
@coffeeShopAddress2     varchar(150),
@coffeeShopCity        varchar(50),
@coffeeShopState        char(2),
@coffeeShopZip         char(11),

@coffeeShopWiFi        int ,
@coffeeShopDetails      varchar(250)

AS
update EganEnterprises_CoffeeShopInfo
set  coffeeShopName = isnull(@coffeeShopName,coffeeShopName),
     coffeeShopAddress1 =
                    isnull(@coffeeShopAddress1,coffeeShopAddress1),
     coffeeShopAddress2 =
                    isnull(@coffeeShopAddress2,coffeeShopAddress2),
     coffeeShopCity = isnull(@coffeeShopCity,coffeeShopCity),
     coffeeShopState = isnull(@coffeeShopState,coffeeShopState),
     coffeeShopZip = isnull(@coffeeShopZip,coffeeShopZip),
     coffeeShopWiFi = isnull(@coffeeShopWiFi,coffeeShopWiFi),
     coffeeShopDetails = isnull(@coffeeShopDetails,coffeeShopDetails)
where  coffeeShopID = @coffeeShopID
GO


CREATE procedure {databaseOwner}{objectQualifier}EganEnterprises_
UpdateCoffeeShopModuleOptions
@moduleID        int,
@authorizedRoles varchar(250)

AS
    UPDATE
      EganEnterprises_CoffeeShopModuleOptions
    SET   AuthorizedRoles = @AuthorizedRoles

    WHERE  moduleID = @moduleID
GO
```

Create the Class Files

Now, we will create the module Settings page. This page will allow you to indicate the user roles that will be able to add Coffee Shops.

First, we will create two class files. We will create methods that the Settings page will use to connect to the database. These two classes will be placed in the **App_Code** folder because they are classes that are not code behind for User Controls.

1. In the **Solution Explorer** in Visual Studio, **right-click** on the **App_Code** folder and create a new folder called **CoffeeShopListing**.

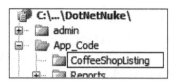

2. Now, right-click on the **CoffeeShopListing** folder and select **Add New Item**.

3. When the **Add New Item** menu appears, select the **Class** template and enter **CoffeeShopListingOptionsInfo.vb** in the **Name** box. Also, ensure that **Visual Basic** is selected in the **Language** drop-down and click the **Add** button.

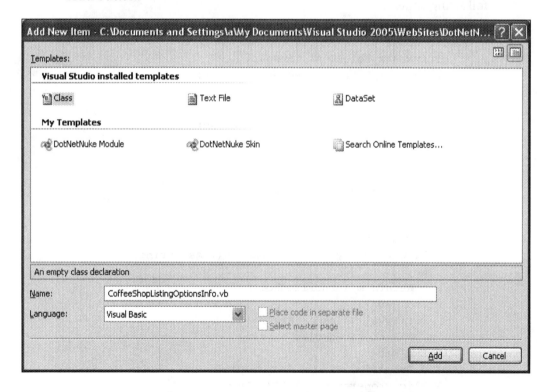

4. Repeat the same process to create a **CoffeeShopListingOptionsController. vb** file.

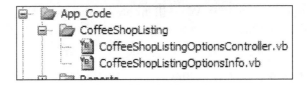

Insert the DAL+ Code

We will now insert the code for the two class files. The
`CoffeeShopListingOptionsInfo` class is a simple class that exposes
fields that will be used to pass data between the Setting page and the
CoffeeShopListingOptionsController. It will use the DAL+ methods to
communicate with the database.

1. In Visual Studio, in the **Solution Explorer**, right-click on the
    `CoffeeShopListingOptionsInfo.vb` file and select **Open**.

2. When the source code is displayed, replace all the code with the
    following code:

```vb
Namespace EganEnterprises.CoffeeShopListing
Public Class CoffeeShopListingOptionsInfo
    Private m_RoleID As Integer
    Private m_AuthorizedRoles As String
    Private m_moduleID As Integer

    Public Property RoleID() As Integer
      Get
        Return m_RoleID
      End Get
      Set(ByVal Value As Integer)
        m_RoleID = Value
      End Set
    End Property
    Public Property AuthorizedRoles() As String
      Get
        Return m_AuthorizedRoles
      End Get
      Set(ByVal Value As String)
        m_AuthorizedRoles = Value
      End Set
    End Property
    Public Property moduleID() As Integer
      Get
        Return m_moduleID
```

```
        End Get
        Set(ByVal Value As Integer)
          m_moduleID = Value
        End Set
      End Property
    End Class
End Namespace
```

3. Save the file.

4. Right-click on the `CoffeeShopListingOptionsController.vb` file and select **Open**.

5. When the source code is displayed, replace all the code with the following code:

```
Imports System
Imports System.Data
Imports System.Collections.Generic


Namespace EganEnterprises.CoffeeShopListing
  Public Class CoffeeShopListingOptionsController
    Public Function EganEnterprises_GetCoffeeShopModuleOptions( _
        ByVal ModuleId As Integer) _
        As List(Of CoffeeShopListingOptionsInfo)
        Return CBO.FillCollection( _
                       Of CoffeeShopListingOptionsInfo)(CType( _
        DotNetNuke.Data.DataProvider.Instance(). _
        ExecuteReader( _
        "EganEnterprises_GetCoffeeShopModuleOptions", ModuleId), _
          IDataReader))
    End Function
    Public Function _
              EganEnterprises_UpdateCoffeeShopModuleOptions( _
        ByVal objShopListOptions As EganEnterprises. _
        CoffeeShopListing.CoffeeShopListingOptionsInfo) _
        As Integer
        Return CType(DotNetNuke.Data.DataProvider.Instance(). _
        ExecuteScalar( _
             "EganEnterprises_UpdateCoffeeShopModuleOptions", _
        objShopListOptions.moduleID, _
          objShopListOptions.AuthorizedRoles), _
          Integer)
    End Function
    Public Function EganEnterprises_AddCoffeeShopModuleOptions( _
        ByVal objShopListOptions As EganEnterprises. _
        CoffeeShopListing.CoffeeShopListingOptionsInfo) _
```

```
        As Integer
        Return CType(DotNetNuke.Data.DataProvider.Instance(). _
        ExecuteScalar(
                "EganEnterprises_AddCoffeeShopModuleOptions", _
        objShopListOptions.moduleID, _
        objShopListOptions.AuthorizedRoles), Integer)
    End Function
  End Class
End Namespace
```

6. Save the page.

Create the Settings Page

We will now create the Settings page. Unlike the `ShopList.ascx` and `EditShopList.ascx` pages, this will be the final code that will be used in the final Coffee Shop Listing module (we will update and complete the `ShopList.ascx` and `EditShopList.ascx` pages later in this chapter).

1. In Visual Studio, right-click on the **CoffeeShopListing** folder and select **Add New Item**.

2. When the **Add New Item** menu comes up, select **Web User Control** and enter `Settings.ascx` in the **Name** box. Ensure that the **Place code in a separate file** box is checked and click the **Add** button.

3. When the page comes up in source view, replace all the code with the following code:

```
<%@ Control language="vb" AutoEventWireup="false"
Inherits="EganEnterprises.CoffeeShopListing.Settings"
CodeFile="Settings.ascx.vb"%>
<%@ Register TagPrefix="Portal" TagName="DualList"
Src="~/controls/DualListControl.ascx" %>
<TABLE id="Table1" cellSpacing="1" cellPadding="1"
                                        width="100%" border="1">
  <TR>
    <TD>
      <P align="center">ShopListOptions</P>
    </TD>
  </TR>
  <TR>
    <td><portal:duallist id="ctlAuthRoles" runat="server"
    ListBoxWidth="130"
                    ListBoxHeight="130" DataValueField="Value"
        DataTextField="Text" /></td>
```

```
    </TR>
  </TABLE>
```

4. Right-click on the **Settings.ascx** file and select **View Code**. When the source code is displayed, replace all the code with the following code:

```
Imports System.Web
Imports DotNetNuke.Security.Roles
Imports System.Collections.Generic
Imports System.Web.UI.WebControls

Namespace EganEnterprises.CoffeeShopListing
  Partial Class Settings
    Inherits DotNetNuke.Entities.Modules.ModuleSettingsBase
#Region "Base Method Implementations"
    Public Overrides Sub LoadSettings()
      Try
        ' declare roles
        Dim arrAvailableAuthRoles As New ArrayList
        Dim arrAssignedAuthRoles As New ArrayList
        ' Get list of possible roles
        Dim objRoles As New RoleController
        Dim objRole As RoleInfo
        Dim arrRoles As ArrayList = _
        objRoles.GetPortalRoles(PortalId)

        'String of roles for shoplist
Dim objShopRoles As New CoffeeShopListingOptionsController
        Dim objShopRole As CoffeeShopListingOptionsInfo
Dim arrShopRoles As List(Of CoffeeShopListingOptionsInfo) =
objShopRoles.EganEnterprises_GetCoffeeShopModuleOptions _
        (ModuleId)
        'Put roles into a string
        Dim shopRoles As String = ""

        For Each objShopRole In arrShopRoles
          'If it makes it here then we will be updating
          shopRoles = objShopRole.AuthorizedRoles.ToString
        Next

        'Now loop through all available roles in portal
        For Each objRole In arrRoles
          Dim objListItem As New ListItem
          objListItem.Value = objRole.RoleID.ToString()
          objListItem.Text = objRole.RoleName.ToString()
```

```
                          'If it matches a role in the ShopRoles string put
                          'it in the assigned box
                          If shopRoles.IndexOf(objRole.RoleID & ";") _
                          <> -1 Or objRole.RoleID = _
                          PortalSettings.AdministratorRoleId Then
                            arrAssignedAuthRoles.Add(objListItem)
                          Else ' put it inthe avalible box
                            arrAvailableAuthRoles.Add(objListItem)
                          End If
                      Next
                      ' assign to duallist controls
                      ctlAuthRoles.Available = arrAvailableAuthRoles
                      ctlAuthRoles.Assigned = arrAssignedAuthRoles
                  Catch exc As Exception  'Module failed to load
                      ProcessModuleLoadException(Me, exc)
                  End Try
              End Sub


          Public Overrides Sub UpdateSettings()
              Try
      Dim objShopRoles As New CoffeeShopListingOptionsController
                  Dim objShopRole As New CoffeeShopListingOptionsInfo
                  Dim item As ListItem
                  Dim strAuthorizedRoles As String = ""
                  For Each item In ctlAuthRoles.Assigned
                    strAuthorizedRoles += item.Value & ";"
                  Next item
                  objShopRole.AuthorizedRoles = strAuthorizedRoles
                  objShopRole.moduleID = ModuleId
                  Dim intExists As Integer
                  intExists = objShopRoles. _
                  EganEnterprises_UpdateCoffeeShopModuleOptions(
                                                        objShopRole)
                  If intExists = 0 Then 'New record
                    objShopRoles.
                            EganEnterprises_AddCoffeeShopModuleOptions _
                    (objShopRole)
                  End If
              Catch exc As Exception  'Module failed to load
                  ProcessModuleLoadException(Me, exc)
              End Try
          End Sub


      #End Region
```

```
End Class
End Namespace
```

13. Save the page.

Update the Configuration

In Visual Studio, press *Ctrl+F5* to build the code and start the DotNetNuke site.

1. Log in as host.
2. From the **Host** menu select **Module Definitions**.
3. From the **Module Definitions** click the edit symbol next to the **CoffeeShopListing** module to select it.
4. Click the **Add Control** link toward the bottom of the **CoffeeShopListing** module definition.
5. When the control configuration screen appears, configure it with the following settings:
   - Enter **Settings** for **Key**.
   - Enter **CoffeeShop Settings** for **Title**.
   - Use the dropdown to select **DesktopModules/ CoffeeShopListing/Settings.ascx** for **Source**.
   - Use the dropdown to select **View** for **Type**.
   - Click the **Update** button.

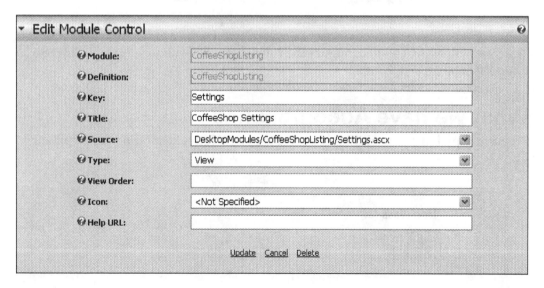

View the Settings Page

Click the **Coffee Shop Listing** link on the menu bar in the DotNetNuke site to display the Coffee Shop Listings module, then click on the Coffee Shop Listing module's menu and select **Settings**.

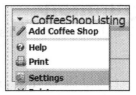

Now expand the **CoffeeShop Settings** section.

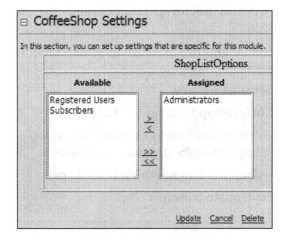

The form will allow you to configure the roles that will be allowed to add **Coffee Shop listings**.

What we have Accomplished

We have explored a few additional concepts of DotNetNuke module development:

- SQL scripts
- DAL+
  - ° Info class
  - ° CBO
  - ° Controller class

- Module Settings page
    - ° Inheriting from `ModuleSettingsBase`
    - ° Overriding `LoadSettings` and `UpdateSettings`
    - ° Built-in DotNetNuke User Controls

SQL Scripts

We ran an SQL script that created the tables and the stored procedures. You will notice that the script is written in this syntax:

```
CREATE TABLE {databaseOwner}{objectQualifier}[EganEnterprises_
CoffeeShopInfo]
```

Rather than the normal SQL syntax such as:

```
CREATE TABLE [dbo][EganEnterprises_CoffeeShopInfo]
```

The script tokens `{databaseOwner}` and `{objectQualifier}` indicate that they are to be replaced by configuration settings in the `web.config` file. Normally `{databaseOwner}` is set to `.dbo` and `{objectQualifier}` is set to nothing (it would not have a setting). However, if alternative settings were indicated in the `web. config` file, those settings would be inserted into the script.

You must have the **Run as Script** box checked for this replacement to happen.

The DAL+

The purpose of the DAL+ is to simplify module development by a reduction in code and complexity. The DAL+ allows you to make calls to the database directly from the controller class. This means that you do not have to code a separate data provider, yet you will still be able to support different data sources in most situations.

The DAL+ achieves this by providing the following generic methods:

- **ExecuteNonQuery** — Used to execute a stored procedure that will not return a value.
- **ExecuteReader** — Used to execute a stored procedure that will return multiple records.
- **ExecuteScalar** — Used to execute a stored procedure that will return a single value.
- **ExecuteSQL** — Used to execute an SQL statement.

The explanation of the format used to implement the DAL+ is given below. The `ExecuteReader` method is used in the example to call a stored procedure named `EganEnterprises_GetCoffeeShopModuleOptions`:

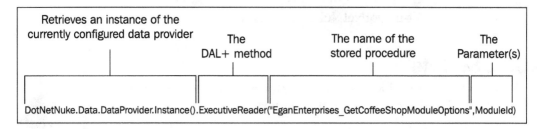

The Business Logic Layer (BLL)

The DAL+ code resides in the Business Logic Layer (BLL). The BLL is code that sits between the DAL+ (or the DAL that will be presented later) and the presentation layer. The BLL has three main components:

- Info Class (`CoffeeShopListingOptionsInfo`)
- Custom Business Objects (`DotNetNuke.Common.Utilities.CBO`)
- Controller Class (`CoffeeShopListingOptionsController`)

The CoffeeShopListingOptionsInfo class

The `CoffeeShopListingOptionsInfo` class is a very simple class that holds the information used to pass information to the database layer. It is used to pass a hydrated (populated with data) object instead of individual parameters.

Custom Business Objects (CBO)

To help minimize the task of populating custom business objects from the data layer, the DotNetNuke core API offers a generic utility class to help hydrate your business objects, the `CBO` class found in the `DotNetNuke.Common.Utilities` namespace.

This class primarily performs two functions; hydrating a single object instance (`FillObject`) and hydrating a collection of objects (`FillCollection`). As you can see, the `CBO` class contains a number of overloaded methods for `FillCollection` and `FillObject`.

```
CloneObject(Object) As Object
FillCollection(Of T)(System.Data.IDataReader) As System.Collections.Generic.List(Of T)
FillCollection(Of T)(System.Data.IDataReader, ByRef System.Collections.Generic.IList(Of T)) As System.Collections
FillCollection(System.Data.IDataReader, System.Type) As System.Collections.ArrayList
FillCollection(System.Data.IDataReader, System.Type, ByRef System.Collections.IList) As System.Collections.IList
FillObject(Of T)(System.Data.IDataReader) As T
FillObject(Of T)(System.Data.IDataReader, Boolean) As T
FillObject(System.Data.IDataReader, System.Type) As Object
FillObject(System.Data.IDataReader, System.Type, Boolean) As Object
GetPropertyInfo(System.Type) As System.Collections.ArrayList
InitializeObject(Object, System.Type) As Object
New()
Serialize(Object) As System.Xml.XmlDocument
```

```
Public Class CBO
    Inherits System.Object
    Member of: DotNetNuke.Common.Utilities
```

The `FillCollection` method is used in the
`CoffeeShopListingOptionsController` class to hydrate the
`CoffeeShopListingOptionsInfo` class.

```
Return CBO.FillCollection(
                    Of CoffeeShopListingOptionsInfo)(CType( _
        DotNetNuke.Data.DataProvider.Instance(). _
        ExecuteReader("EganEnterprises_
    GetCoffeeShopModuleOptions", ModuleId), _
            IDataReader))
```

Using these methods allows you to write less code to hydrate your custom business
objects (info classes) than you would have to without them.

> For more information on custom business objects refer to
> DotNetNuke Data Access.doc available for download at
> DotNetNuke.com.

The CoffeeShopListingOptionsController Class

The `CoffeeShopListingOptionsController` class provides methods for the
Settings page (the Settings page is in the presentation layer) that allow it to connect
to the database.

```
EganEnterprises_GetCoffeeShopModuleOptions( _
        ByVal ModuleId As Integer) _
        As List(Of CoffeeShopListingOptionsInfo)
EganEnterprises_UpdateCoffeeShopModuleOptions( _
        ByVal objShopListOptions As EganEnterprises. _
        CoffeeShopListing.CoffeeShopListingOptionsInfo) _
```

```
        As Integer
EganEnterprises_AddCoffeeShopModuleOptions( _
        ByVal objShopListOptions As EganEnterprises. _
        CoffeeShopListing.CoffeeShopListingOptionsInfo) _
        As Integer
```

As you can see, other than the tables and stored procedures that also make up the Data Access layer, the DAL+ is comprised of very minimal code.

The Settings Page

The Settings page is in the presentation layer. The code covered in the walk-through covers these concepts and controls:

- Inheriting from `ModuleSettingsBase`
- Overriding `LoadSettings` and `UpdateSettings`
- Built-in DotNetNuke User Controls

Inheriting from ModuleSettingsBase

Unlike the other User Controls, the Settings page inherits from `ModuleSettingsBase`. `ModuleSettingsBase` inherits from `PortalModuleBase` and contains all of its useful properties such as `ModuleId` but it also has two abstract methods that we implement: `LoadSettings` and `UpdateSettings`.

Overriding LoadSettings and UpdateSettings

`LoadSettings` is called when the module settings page is accessed, and `UpdateSettings` is called when the update button is clicked on the module settings page. In the `LoadSettings` method in the `Settings.ascx.vb` page, we load all the user roles and bind them to a Dual List Control. In the `UpdateSettings` method we save any changes.

Built-in DotNetNuke User Controls

In our implementation we use the Dual List Control to move the roles between the lists to give or remove the ability to add coffee shops. The Dual List Control is one of many built-in DotNetNuke User Controls that are available in the `/controls` directory. Using the object browser we can browse the definitions of the various controls in the `DotNetNuke.UI.UserControls` namespace.

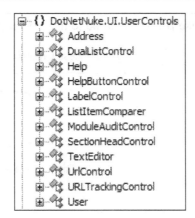

In addition, there are useful Web Controls such as `DNNLabelEdit` and `DNNTextSuggest` that are available in the `DotNetNuke.WebControls` assembly.

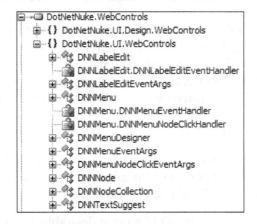

Using these controls saves a lot of code and provides a consistent look that better integrates your module into the DotNetNuke framework.

Comparing the DAL to the DAL+

We will now cover the traditional DotNetNuke DAL. This is the coding pattern that the core DotNetNuke code uses. First, let us compare the DAL+ we have just covered to the DAL.

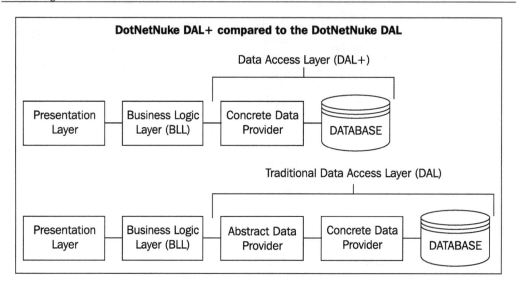

As you can see in the graphic above, the difference is the inclusion of an Abstract Data Provider in the DAL. However, an additional difference is that the Concrete Data Provider of the DAL+ is created by the database provider that the DotNetNuke installation is running on, and not the module developer. For example, a MySQL Concrete Data Provider that allowed you to run DotNetNuke on the MySQL server would implement the four methods of the DAL+. The module developer would only have to write the code for the BLL.

With the DAL, both the Abstract Data Provider and the Concrete Data Provider are written by the module developer. For example, for MySQL you would have to write all the code that connected to the database yourself.

While this would seem to make the DAL+ more desirable, it actually highlights its weakness. The Concrete Data Provider of the DAL+ only exposes four methods. For most cases this is enough, however, in those situations where it is not (for example when running a module on a different database than the one it was developed on) the DAL provides the only solution that will work 100% of the time.

The DAL allows your module to run on different data sources by simply replacing the Concrete Data Provider. This is how the DotNetNuke core code is written. Developers have created providers to allow DotNetNuke to run on Oracle, Firebird, and MySQL by simply creating a Concrete Data Provider for those data sources. In some cases a method that only needs a single stored procedure in Microsoft SQL Server needs two stored procedures in Firebird. This is not a problem with the DAL because the Concrete Data Provider for Firebird simply specifies two calls to the database to support the method in the BLL. This would not be possible with the DAL+.

A Close-up Look at the DAL

The following diagram shows how the pages that we will alter and create will fit in the DAL structure. The Settings page and its supporting classes will remain as they are in the DAL+ format so that you will have a module that has both coding examples for reference.

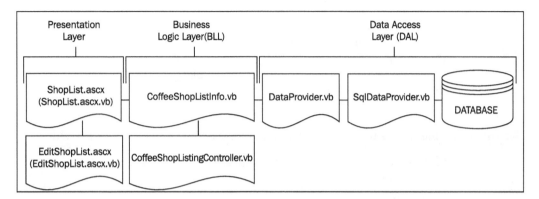

Create the DataProvider.vb

We will now insert the code for the `DataProvider.vb` class. This abstract class will be used as the base class for our provider, so we will declare this class as `MustInherit`. This means we will not be able to instantiate this class; it can only be used as the base class for our provider.

1. In Visual Studio, in the **Solution Explorer**, right-click on the **CoffeeShopListing** folder that is under the **App_Code** directory and select **Add New Item**.

2. When the **Add New Item** menu **appears**, select the **Class** template and enter **DataProvider.vb** in the **Name** box. Also, ensure that **Visual Basic** is selected in the **Language** drop-down and click the **Add** button.

3. When the source code is displayed, replace all the code with the following code (only enter the code, not the narration that explains each section):

```
Imports System
Imports DotNetNuke

Namespace EganEnterprises.CoffeeShopListing
   Public MustInherit Class DataProvider
#Region "Shared/Static Methods"
      ' singleton reference to the instantiated object
      Private Shared objProvider As DataProvider = Nothing
```

```
' constructor
Shared Sub New()
  CreateProvider()
End Sub
```

The `CreateProvider` method uses reflection to create an instance of the data provider being created. We pass it the provider type, the namespace, and the assembly name.

```
Private Shared Sub CreateProvider()
  objProvider = _
  CType(Framework.Reflection.CreateObject _
  ("data", "EganEnterprises.CoffeeShopListing", ""), DataProvider)
End Sub
```

The `Instance` method is used to actually create the instance of our data provider.

```
Public Shared Shadows Function Instance() As DataProvider
  Return objProvider
End Function


#End Region
```

The following methods are created as `MustOverride` because we will need to implement them in our provider object.

Since any data source may be used, the implementation of these methods will reside in the provider created in the next step. Here we will only create the signature of the methods. The parameter names match those in our stored procedures (minus the @).

```
#Region "Abstract methods"
    Public MustOverride Function EganEnterprises_GetCoffeeShops( _
        ByVal ModuleId As Integer) _
        As IDataReader
    Public MustOverride Function
                            EganEnterprises_GetCoffeeShopsByZip( _
        ByVal ModuleId As Integer, _
        ByVal coffeeShopZip As String) _
        As IDataReader
    Public MustOverride Function EganEnterprises_GetCoffeeShopsByID( _
        ByVal coffeeShopID As Integer) _
        As IDataReader
    Public MustOverride Function EganEnterprises_AddCoffeeShopInfo( _
        ByVal ModuleId As Integer, _
        ByVal coffeeShopName As String, _
        ByVal coffeeShopAddress1 As String, _
```

```
            ByVal coffeeShopAddress2 As String, _
            ByVal coffeeShopCity As String, _
            ByVal coffeeShopState As String, _
            ByVal coffeeShopZip As String, _
            ByVal coffeeShopWiFi As System.Int16, _
            ByVal coffeeShopDetails As String) _
            As Integer
        Public MustOverride Sub EganEnterprises_UpdateCoffeeShopInfo( _
            ByVal coffeeShopID As Integer, _
            ByVal coffeeShopName As String, _
            ByVal coffeeShopAddress1 As String, _
            ByVal coffeeShopAddress2 As String, _
            ByVal coffeeShopCity As String, _
            ByVal coffeeShopState As String, _
            ByVal coffeeShopZip As String, _
            ByVal coffeeShopWiFi As System.Int16, _
            ByVal coffeeShopDetails As String)
        Public MustOverride Sub EganEnterprises_DeleteCoffeeShop( _
            ByVal coffeeShopID As Integer)
    #End Region
        End Class
    End Namespace
```

Create the SqlDataProvider.vb

We will now insert the code for the `SqlDataProvider.vb` class. This class will serve as our Concrete Data Provider and override the methods in the `DataProvider.vb` file we have just created. This is the class that is specific to our data source.

Most of the Imports statements in this class should be familiar, but one that stands out is `Microsoft.ApplicationBlocks.Data`. This is an assembly created by Microsoft to help with the connections and commands needed to work with SQL Server. It is used to facilitate calls to the database without having to create all of the ADO.NET code manually.

1. In Visual Studio, in the **Solution Explorer**, right-click on the **CoffeeShopListing** folder that is under the **App_Code** directory and select **Add New Item**.

2. When the **Add New Item** menu appears, select the **Class** template and enter **SqlDataProvider.vb** in the **Name** box. Also, ensure that **Visual Basic** is selected in the **Language** dropdown and click the **Add** button.

3. When the source code is displayed, replace all the code with the following code sections from `Imports System` to `End Namespace` (only enter the code, not the narration that explains each section) :

```
Imports System
Imports System.Data
Imports System.Data.SqlClient
Imports Microsoft.ApplicationBlocks.Data
Imports DotNetNuke
Imports DotNetNuke.Common.Utilities
Imports DotNetNuke.Framework.Providers

Namespace EganEnterprises.CoffeeShopListing
  Public Class SqlDataProvider
```

As you can see, we will inherit from the `DataProvider` base class created earlier:

```
Inherits EganEnterprises.CoffeeShopListing.DataProvider
#Region "Private Members"
```

We also need to declare a constant variable that will hold the type of the provider. There are many different providers used in DotNetNuke so we need to specify the type. This is done by assigning it the simple lowercase string data.

```
Private Const ProviderType As String = "data"
```

We then use this type to instantiate a data provider configuration:

```
Private _providerConfiguration As _
ProviderConfiguration = _
ProviderConfiguration.GetProviderConfiguration _
(ProviderType)
```

Next, we declare variables that will hold the information necessary for us to connect to the database:

```
Private _connectionString As String
Private _providerPath As String
Private _objectQualifier As String
Private _databaseOwner As String
#End Region
#Region "Constructors"
```

In the constructor for the class we read the attributes that we set in the `web.config` file to gather the database-specific information like connection string and database owner.

```
Public Sub New()
' Read the configuration specific information for this provider
  Dim objProvider As Provider = _
  CType(_providerConfiguration.Providers _
```

```vbnet
            (_providerConfiguration.DefaultProvider), _
              Provider)
        ' Read the attributes for this provider
        If objProvider.Attributes("connectionStringName") <> "" _
        AndAlso _
          System.Configuration.ConfigurationManager.AppSettings _
          (objProvider.Attributes("connectionStringName")) <> "" _
          Then
          _connectionString = _
          System.Configuration.ConfigurationManager.AppSettings _
          (objProvider.Attributes("connectionStringName"))
        Else
          _connectionString = _
          objProvider.Attributes("connectionString")
        End If
        _providerPath = objProvider.Attributes("providerPath")
        _objectQualifier = _
        objProvider.Attributes("objectQualifier")
      If _objectQualifier <> "" And _objectQualifier.EndsWith("_") _
      = False Then
          _objectQualifier += "_"
        End If
        _databaseOwner = objProvider.Attributes("databaseOwner")
        If _databaseOwner <> "" And _databaseOwner.EndsWith(".") _
        = False Then
          _databaseOwner += "."
        End If
    End Sub
#End Region
#Region "Properties"


    Public ReadOnly Property ConnectionString() As String
      Get
        Return _connectionString
      End Get
    End Property

    Public ReadOnly Property ProviderPath() As String
      Get
        Return _providerPath
      End Get
    End Property
```

```
Public ReadOnly Property ObjectQualifier() As String
  Get
    Return _objectQualifier
  End Get
End Property

Public ReadOnly Property DatabaseOwner() As String
  Get
    Return _databaseOwner
  End Get
End Property

#End Region
```

As you recall, in the base provider class we declared our methods as MustOverride. In this section, we are doing just that. We override the methods from the base class and use the Microsoft.ApplicationBlocks.Data class to make the calls to the database.

The GetNull function is used to convert an application-encoded null value to a database null value that is defined for the datatype expected. We will be utilizing this throughout the rest of this section.

```
' general
Private Function GetNull(ByVal Field As Object) As Object
  Return Null.GetNull(Field, DBNull.Value)
End Function
Public Overrides Function EganEnterprises_GetCoffeeShops( _
   ByVal ModuleId As Integer) _
   As IDataReader
   Return CType(SqlHelper.ExecuteReader(ConnectionString, _
      DatabaseOwner & _
      ObjectQualifier & _
      "EganEnterprises_GetCoffeeShops", _
      ModuleId), _
      IDataReader)
End Function
Public Overrides Function EganEnterprises_GetCoffeeShopsByZip( _
   ByVal ModuleId As Integer, _
   ByVal coffeeShopZip As String) _
   As IDataReader
   Return CType(SqlHelper.ExecuteReader(ConnectionString, _
      DatabaseOwner & _
      ObjectQualifier & _
      "EganEnterprises_GetCoffeeShopsByZip", _
```

```
            ModuleId, _
            coffeeShopZip), _
            IDataReader)
     End Function
     Public Overrides Function EganEnterprises_GetCoffeeShopsByID( _
        ByVal coffeeShopID As Integer) _
        As IDataReader
        Return CType(SqlHelper.ExecuteReader(ConnectionString, _
            DatabaseOwner & _
            ObjectQualifier & _
            "EganEnterprises_GetCoffeeShopsByID", _
            coffeeShopID), _
            IDataReader)
     End Function
     Public Overrides Function EganEnterprises_AddCoffeeShopInfo( _
        ByVal ModuleId As Integer, _
        ByVal coffeeShopName As String, _
        ByVal coffeeShopAddress1 As String, _
        ByVal coffeeShopAddress2 As String, _
        ByVal coffeeShopCity As String, _
        ByVal coffeeShopState As String, _
        ByVal coffeeShopZip As String, _
        ByVal coffeeShopWiFi As System.Int16, _
        ByVal coffeeShopDetails As String) _
        As Integer
        Return CType(SqlHelper.ExecuteScalar(ConnectionString, _
            DatabaseOwner & _
            ObjectQualifier & _
            "EganEnterprises_AddCoffeeShopInfo", _
            ModuleId, _
            coffeeShopName, _
            GetNull(coffeeShopAddress1), _
            GetNull(coffeeShopAddress2), _
            coffeeShopCity, _
            coffeeShopState, _
            coffeeShopZip, _
            coffeeShopWiFi, _
            coffeeShopDetails), _
            Integer)
     End Function
     Public Overrides Sub EganEnterprises_UpdateCoffeeShopInfo( _
        ByVal coffeeShopID As Integer, _
        ByVal coffeeShopName As String, _
        ByVal coffeeShopAddress1 As String, _
```

```
              ByVal coffeeShopAddress2 As String, _
              ByVal coffeeShopCity As String, _
              ByVal coffeeShopState As String, _
              ByVal coffeeShopZip As String, _
              ByVal coffeeShopWiFi As System.Int16, _
              ByVal coffeeShopDetails As String)
           SqlHelper.ExecuteNonQuery(ConnectionString, _
              DatabaseOwner & _
              ObjectQualifier & _
              "EganEnterprises_UpdateCoffeeShopInfo", _
              coffeeShopID, _
              coffeeShopName, _
              GetNull(coffeeShopAddress1), _
              GetNull(coffeeShopAddress2), _
              coffeeShopCity, _
              coffeeShopState, _
              coffeeShopZip, _
              coffeeShopWiFi, _
              coffeeShopDetails)
        End Sub
        Public Overrides Sub EganEnterprises_DeleteCoffeeShop( _
           ByVal coffeeShopID As Integer)
           SqlHelper.ExecuteNonQuery(ConnectionString, _
              DatabaseOwner & _
              ObjectQualifier & _
              "EganEnterprises_DeleteCoffeeShop", _
              coffeeShopID)
        End Sub
     End Class
  End Namespace
```

Create the BLL Layer

We will now insert the code for the two class files of the BLL layer. The
`CoffeeShopListingInfo` class is a simple class that exposes fields that will
be used to pass data between the Shoplist and EditShopList pages and the
CoffeeShopListingController. The CoffeeShopListingController will connect
to the `dataprovider` class, which contains methods that are overridden by the
`SqlDataProvider` class, which then connects to the database.

1. Right-click on the **CoffeeShopListing** folder that is under the **App_Code**
    directory and select **Add New Item**.

2. When the **Add New Item** menu appears, select the **Class** template and enter **CoffeeShopListingInfo.vb** in the **Name** box. Also, ensure that **Visual Basic** is selected in the **Language** dropdown and click the **Add** button.

3. When the source code is displayed, replace all the code with the following code:

```
Imports System
Imports System.Configuration
Imports System.Data
Namespace EganEnterprises.CoffeeShopListing


  Public Class CoffeeShopListingInfo
#Region "Private Members"

    Private m_moduleID As Integer
    Private m_coffeeShopID As Integer
    Private m_coffeeShopName As String
    Private m_coffeeShopAddress1 As String
    Private m_coffeeShopAddress2 As String
    Private m_coffeeShopCity As String
    Private m_coffeeShopState As String
    Private m_coffeeShopZip As String
    Private m_coffeeShopWiFi As System.Int16
    Private m_coffeeShopDetails As String

#End Region
#Region "Constructors"
    Public Sub New()
    End Sub

#End Region
#Region "Properties"
    Public Property moduleID() As Integer
      Get
        Return m_moduleID
      End Get
      Set(ByVal Value As Integer)
        m_moduleID = Value
      End Set
    End Property
    Public Property coffeeShopID() As Integer
      Get
        Return m_coffeeShopID
```

```
         End Get
         Set(ByVal Value As Integer)
            m_coffeeShopID = Value
         End Set
     End Property
     Public Property coffeeShopName() As String
        Get
            Return m_coffeeShopName
        End Get
        Set(ByVal Value As String)
            m_coffeeShopName = Value
        End Set
     End Property
     Public Property coffeeShopAddress1() As String
        Get
            Return m_coffeeShopAddress1
        End Get
        Set(ByVal Value As String)
            m_coffeeShopAddress1 = Value
        End Set
     End Property
     Public Property coffeeShopAddress2() As String
        Get
            Return m_coffeeShopAddress2
        End Get
        Set(ByVal Value As String)
            m_coffeeShopAddress2 = Value
        End Set
     End Property
     Public Property coffeeShopCity() As String
        Get
            Return m_coffeeShopCity
        End Get
        Set(ByVal Value As String)
            m_coffeeShopCity = Value
        End Set
     End Property
     Public Property coffeeShopState() As String
        Get
            Return m_coffeeShopState
        End Get
        Set(ByVal Value As String)
            m_coffeeShopState = Value
        End Set
```

```
      End Property
      Public Property coffeeShopZip() As String
        Get
          Return m_coffeeShopZip
        End Get
        Set(ByVal Value As String)
          m_coffeeShopZip = Value
        End Set
      End Property
      Public Property coffeeShopWiFi() As System.Int16
        Get
          Return m_coffeeShopWiFi
        End Get
        Set(ByVal Value As System.Int16)
          m_coffeeShopWiFi = Value
        End Set
      End Property
      Public Property coffeeShopDetails() As String
        Get
          Return m_coffeeShopDetails
        End Get
        Set(ByVal Value As String)
          m_coffeeShopDetails = Value
        End Set
      End Property
  #End Region
    End Class
End Namespace
```

4. Next, right-click on the **CoffeeShopListing** folder that is under the **App_ Code** directory and select **Add New Item**.

5. When the **Add New Item** menu appears, select the **Class** template and enter **CoffeeShopListingController.vb** in the **Name** box. Also, ensure that **Visual Basic** is selected in the **Language** dropdown and click the **Add** button.

6. When the source code is displayed, replace all the code with the following code:

```
Imports DotNetNuke.Services.Search
Imports DotNetNuke.Common.Utilities.XmlUtils
Imports System.Collections.Generic
Imports System
Imports System.Configuration
Imports System.Data
Imports System.XML
```

```
Namespace EganEnterprises.CoffeeShopListing

Public Class CoffeeShopListingController
#Region "Public Methods"
    Public Function EganEnterprises_GetCoffeeShops( _
      ByVal ModuleId As Integer)
                                As List(Of CoffeeShopListingInfo)
      Return CBO.FillCollection( _
                                Of CoffeeShopListingInfo)(CType( _
        DataProvider.Instance(). _
        EganEnterprises_GetCoffeeShops _
        (ModuleId), IDataReader))
    End Function
    Public Function EganEnterprises_GetCoffeeShopsByZip( _
    ByVal ModuleId As Integer, _
    ByVal coffeeShopZip As String) _
    As List(Of CoffeeShopListingInfo)
    Return CBO.FillCollection(Of CoffeeShopListingInfo)(CType( _
        DataProvider.Instance(). _
        EganEnterprises_GetCoffeeShopsByZip _
        (ModuleId, coffeeShopZip), _
        IDataReader))
    End Function
    Public Function EganEnterprises_GetCoffeeShopsByID( _
    ByVal coffeeShopID As Integer) As CoffeeShopListingInfo
      Return CType(CBO.FillObject _
      (EganEnterprises.CoffeeShopListing. _
      DataProvider.Instance(). _
      EganEnterprises_GetCoffeeShopsByID( _
      coffeeShopID), GetType(CoffeeShopListingInfo)), _
      CoffeeShopListingInfo)
    End Function
    Public Function EganEnterprises_AddCoffeeShopInfo( _
    ByVal objShopList As _
    EganEnterprises.CoffeeShopListing.CoffeeShopListingInfo) _
    As Integer
      Return CType(EganEnterprises.CoffeeShopListing. _
      DataProvider.Instance(). _
      EganEnterprises_AddCoffeeShopInfo( _
      objShopList.moduleID, _
      objShopList.coffeeShopName, _
      objShopList.coffeeShopAddress1, _
      objShopList.coffeeShopAddress2, _
      objShopList.coffeeShopCity, _
```

```
                objShopList.coffeeShopState, _
                objShopList.coffeeShopZip, _
                objShopList.coffeeShopWiFi, _
                objShopList.coffeeShopDetails), Integer)
        End Function
        Public Sub EganEnterprises_UpdateCoffeeShopInfo( _
        ByVal objShopList As _
        EganEnterprises.CoffeeShopListing.CoffeeShopListingInfo)
            EganEnterprises.CoffeeShopListing. _
            DataProvider.Instance(). _
            EganEnterprises_UpdateCoffeeShopInfo( _
            objShopList.coffeeShopID, _
            objShopList.coffeeShopName, _
            objShopList.coffeeShopAddress1, _
            objShopList.coffeeShopAddress2, _
            objShopList.coffeeShopCity, _
            objShopList.coffeeShopState, _
            objShopList.coffeeShopZip, _
            objShopList.coffeeShopWiFi, _
            objShopList.coffeeShopDetails)
        End Sub
        Public Sub EganEnterprises_DeleteCoffeeShop( _
        ByVal coffeeShopID As Integer)
            EganEnterprises.CoffeeShopListing. _
            DataProvider.Instance(). _
            EganEnterprises_DeleteCoffeeShop(coffeeShopID)
        End Sub
    #End Region
      End Class
    End Namespace
```

DAL Summary

The CoffeeShopListingController makes calls to the data source much like the CoffeeShopOptionsController made with the exception that it does not invoke a DAL+ method. Instead it simply calls a method in the `DataProvider`.

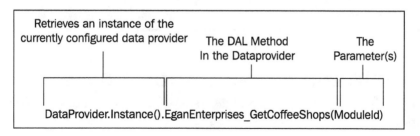

The purpose of the DAL is to allow a module to run on an alternative data source by only replacing the Concrete Data provider. The `DataProvider` is an abstract class that defines a contract that the Concrete Data provider fulfils by overriding the methods that it defines.

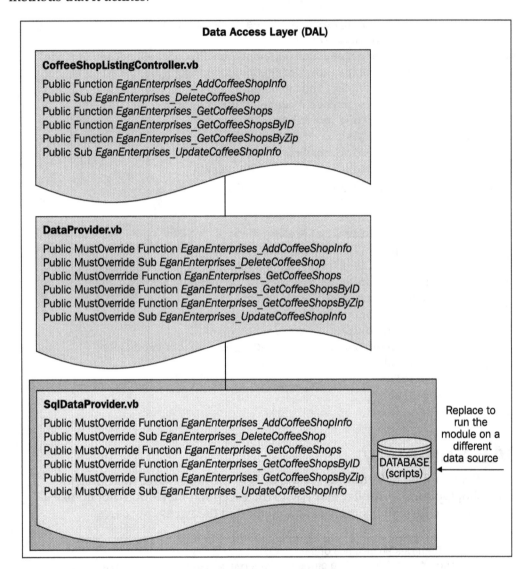

Complete the Presentation Layer

We will now alter `ShopList.ascx` and `EditShopList.ascx` (and their code-behind files `ShopList.ascx.vb` and `EditShopList.ascx.vb`) with their final code.

Alter and Complete ShopList

1. In Visual Studio, right-click on ShopList.ascx in the **Solution Explorer** and select **Open**. When the page is displayed in the editing window, ensure that you are in source mode and replace all the code with the following code:

```
<%@ Control language="vb" AutoEventWireup="false"
Inherits="EganEnterprises.CoffeeShopListing.ShopList"
CodeFile="ShopList.ascx.vb"%>
<asp:Panel id="pnlGrid" runat="server">
  <TABLE id="Table1" cellSpacing="1"
                       cellPadding="1" width="100%" border="1">
    <TR>
      <TD>
        <P align="center">Enter Zip code
          <asp:TextBox id="txtZipSearch"
                              runat="server"></asp:TextBox> 
          <asp:LinkButton id="lbSearch"
                runat="server">Search By Zip</asp:LinkButton></P>
      </TD>
    </TR>
    <TR>
      <TD>
        <P align="center">
          <asp:linkbutton id="lbAddNewShop"
                runat="server">Add New Shop</asp:linkbutton></P>
      </TD>
    </TR>
  </TABLE>
  <asp:datagrid id="dgShopLists" runat="server"
                AutoGenerateColumns="False"
                BorderColor="Blue" BorderWidth="2px"
    Width="100%">
    <AlternatingItemStyle BackColor="Lavender"></
                                      AlternatingItemStyle>
    <HeaderStyle BackColor="Silver"></HeaderStyle>
    <Columns>
      <asp:TemplateColumn>
        <ItemTemplate>
          <asp:HyperLink id=hlcoffeeShopID
              runat="server" Visible="<%# IsEditable %>"
              NavigateUrl='<%# EditURL("coffeeShopID",
              DataBinder.Eval(Container.DataItem,
              "coffeeShopID")) %>' ImageUrl="~/images/edit.gif">
          </asp:HyperLink>
        </ItemTemplate>
```

```
        </asp:TemplateColumn>
        <asp:BoundColumn DataField="coffeeShopName"
              ReadOnly="True" HeaderText="Coffee Shop Name"></
                 asp:BoundColumn>
        <asp:BoundColumn DataField="coffeeShopAddress1"
              ReadOnly="True" HeaderText="Address"></
                 asp:BoundColumn>
        <asp:BoundColumn DataField="coffeeShopCity"
              ReadOnly="True" HeaderText="City"></asp:BoundColumn>
        <asp:BoundColumn DataField="coffeeShopZip" ReadOnly="True"
              HeaderText="Zip Code"></asp:BoundColumn>
    </Columns>
</asp:datagrid></asp:Panel>
                              <asp:Panel id="pnlAdd" runat="server">
<TABLE id="Table2" cellSpacing="1"
                       cellPadding="1" width="100%" border="1">
  <TR>
    <TD align="center" bgColor="lavender" colSpan="2"><STRONG>
            <FONT color="#000000">Enter A New
            Coffee Shop</FONT></STRONG></TD>
  </TR>
  <TR>
    <TD>
      <P align="center">ShopName</P>
    </TD>
    <TD>
      <asp:textbox id="txtcoffeeShopName"
                            runat="server"></asp:textbox></TD>
  </TR>
  <TR>
    <TD>
      <P align="center">Address1</P>
    </TD>
    <TD>
      <asp:textbox id="txtCoffeeShopAddress1"
                            runat="server"></asp:textbox></TD>
  </TR>
  <TR>
    <TD>
      <P align="center">Address2</P>
    </TD>
    <TD>
      <asp:textbox id="txtCoffeeShopAddress2"
                            runat="server"></asp:textbox></TD>
  </TR>
```

```
<TR>
  <TD>
    <P align="center">City</P>
  </TD>
  <TD>
    <asp:textbox id="txtcoffeeShopCity" runat="server"></
                                  asp:textbox></TD>
</TR>
<TR>
  <TD>
    <P align="center">State</P>
  </TD>
  <TD>
    <asp:textbox id="txtcoffeeShopState" runat="server"></
                                  asp:textbox></TD>
</TR>
<TR>
  <TD>
    <P align="center">zip</P>
  </TD>
  <TD>
    <asp:textbox id="txtcoffeeShopZip" runat="server"></
                                  asp:textbox></TD>
</TR>
<TR>
  <TD height="31">
    <P align="center">WiFi Yes or No</P>
  </TD>
  <TD height="31">
    <asp:RadioButtonList id="rblWiFi" runat="server"
                            RepeatDirection="Horizontal">
      <asp:ListItem Value="1">Yes</asp:ListItem>
      <asp:ListItem Value="0">No</asp:ListItem>
    </asp:RadioButtonList></TD>
</TR>
<TR>
  <TD>
    <P align="center">Extra Details</P>
  </TD>
  <TD>
    <asp:TextBox id="txtcoffeeShopDetails" runat="server"></
                                  asp:TextBox></TD>
</TR>
<TR>
  <TD>
```

```
          <P align="center"> </P>
      </TD>
      <TD>
        <P>
          <asp:LinkButton id="cmdAdd" runat="server"
                Text="Update" BorderStyle="none"
                CssClass="CommandButton">Add</
                asp:LinkButton> 
          <asp:LinkButton id="cmdCancel" runat="server"
                Text="Cancel" BorderStyle="none"
                CssClass="CommandButton"
                CausesValidation="False"></asp:LinkButton> 
        </P>
      </TD>
    </TR>
  </TABLE>
</asp:Panel>
```

2. Next, right-click on **ShopList.ascx.vb** and select **View Code**. When the
    source code is displayed, replace all the code with the following code:

```
Imports DotNetNuke
Imports DotNetNuke.Security.Roles
Imports System.Collections.Generic

Namespace EganEnterprises.CoffeeShopListing
  Partial Class ShopList
    Inherits Entities.Modules.PortalModuleBase
    Implements Entities.Modules.IActionable
    Dim coffeeShopID As Integer = -1
    Protected Sub Page_Load(ByVal sender As System.Object, _
    ByVal e As System.EventArgs) Handles MyBase.Load
      'If we are not adding show the grid
      If (Request.Params("Add") Is Nothing) Then
        'Grid panel is visible
        pnlAdd.Visible = False
        pnlGrid.Visible = True

        'Then fill the grid
        If Not Page.IsPostBack Then
      Dim objCoffeeShops As New CoffeeShopListingController
      Dim myList As List(Of CoffeeShopListingInfo)
      myList = objCoffeeShops.EganEnterprises_GetCoffeeShops _
          (ModuleId)
          Me.dgShopLists.DataSource = myList
          Me.dgShopLists.DataBind()
```

```
                  End If
'Check roles to see if the user can add items to the listing
'String of roles for shoplist
Dim objShopRoles As New CoffeeShopListingOptionsController
Dim objShopRole As CoffeeShopListingOptionsInfo
Dim arrShopRoles As List(Of CoffeeShopListingOptionsInfo) =
   objShopRoles.EganEnterprises_GetCoffeeShopModuleOptions _
   (ModuleId)
      'Put roles into a string
      Dim shopRoles As String = ""
      For Each objShopRole In arrShopRoles
        shopRoles += objShopRole.AuthorizedRoles.ToString
      Next


      '
      Dim bAuth = False
      If UserInfo.UserID <> -1 Then
        If UserInfo.IsSuperUser = True Then
          bAuth = True
        Else
         Dim objRoles As New RoleController
         Dim Roles As String() = objRoles.GetRolesByUser _
           (UserInfo.UserID, PortalSettings.PortalId)
           Dim maxRows As Integer = UBound(Roles)
           Dim i As Integer
           For i = 0 To maxRows
             Dim objRoleInfo As RoleInfo
  objRoleInfo = objRoles.GetRoleByName(PortalId, Roles(i))
  If shopRoles.IndexOf(objRoleInfo.RoleID & ";") <> -1 Then
             bAuth = True
             Exit For
           End If
         Next
       End If
     End If
     If bAuth Then
       lbAddNewShop.Visible = True
     Else
       lbAddNewShop.Visible = False
     End If
   Else ' If we are adding...
     'Add panel is visible
     pnlAdd.Visible = True
     pnlGrid.Visible = False
```

```
            End If
      End Sub
      Protected Sub lbAddNewShop_Click( _
         ByVal sender As System.Object, _
         ByVal e As System.EventArgs) Handles lbAddNewShop.Click
         Response.Redirect(NavigateURL(TabId, "", _
                                          "Add=YES"), True)
      End Sub
      Protected Sub cmdAdd_Click( _
         ByVal sender As System.Object, _
         ByVal e As System.EventArgs) Handles cmdAdd.Click
         Dim objShopList As New CoffeeShopListingInfo
         With objShopList
           .moduleID = ModuleId
           .coffeeShopID = coffeeShopID
           .coffeeShopName = txtcoffeeShopName.Text
           .coffeeShopAddress1 = txtCoffeeShopAddress1.Text
           .coffeeShopAddress2 = txtCoffeeShopAddress2.Text
           .coffeeShopCity = txtcoffeeShopCity.Text
           .coffeeShopState = txtcoffeeShopState.Text
           .coffeeShopZip = txtcoffeeShopZip.Text
           .coffeeShopDetails = txtcoffeeShopDetails.Text
           .coffeeShopWiFi = rblWiFi.SelectedValue
         End With

         Dim objShopLists As New CoffeeShopListingController

         coffeeShopID = _
         objShopLists.EganEnterprises_AddCoffeeShopInfo(objShopList)
         ' Redirect back to the portal
         Response.Redirect(NavigateURL())
      End Sub

      Protected Sub cmdCancel_Click( _
         ByVal sender As System.Object, _
         ByVal e As System.EventArgs) Handles cmdCancel.Click
         ' Redirect back to the portal
         Response.Redirect(NavigateURL())
      End Sub

      Protected Sub lbSearch_Click( _
         ByVal sender As System.Object, _
         ByVal e As System.EventArgs) Handles lbSearch.Click
         Dim objCoffeeShops As New CoffeeShopListingController
```

```
        Dim myList As List(Of CoffeeShopListingInfo)
        myList = _
        objCoffeeShops.EganEnterprises_GetCoffeeShopsByZip _
        (ModuleId, txtZipSearch.Text)
        Me.dgShopLists.DataSource = myList
        Me.dgShopLists.DataBind()
    End Sub


#Region "Optional Interfaces"
    Public ReadOnly Property ModuleActions() As _
    DotNetNuke.Entities.Modules.Actions.ModuleActionCollection _
    Implements DotNetNuke.Entities.Modules.
                                    IActionable.ModuleActions
      Get
        Dim Actions As New _
        Entities.Modules.Actions.ModuleActionCollection
        Actions.Add(GetNextActionID,
        Localization.GetString(Entities.Modules.Actions.
        ModuleActionType.AddContent, LocalResourceFile),
        Entities.Modules.Actions.ModuleActionType.AddContent,
        "", "", EditUrl(), False, Security.SecurityAccessLevel.
        Edit, True, False)
        Return Actions
      End Get
    End Property
#End Region
  End Class
End Namespace
```

Alter and Complete EditShopList

1. Right-click on `EditShopList.ascx` and select **Open**. When the page is displayed in the editing window, ensure that you are in source mode and replace all the code with the following code:

```
<%@ Control language="vb" AutoEventWireup="false"
Inherits="EganEnterprises.CoffeeShopListing.EditShopList"
CodeFile="EditShopList.ascx.vb"%>
<TABLE id="Table1" cellSpacing="1"
cellPadding="1" width="100%" border="1">
  <TR>
    <TD>
      <P align="center">ShopName</P>
    </TD>
    <TD><asp:textbox id="txtcoffeeShopName" runat="server">
```

```
        </asp:textbox></TD>
  </TR>
  <TR>
    <TD>
      <P align="center">Address1</P>
    </TD>
    <TD><asp:textbox id="txtCoffeeShopAddress1" runat="server">
    </asp:textbox></TD>
  </TR>
  <TR>
    <TD>
      <P align="center">Address2</P>
    </TD>
    <TD><asp:textbox id="txtCoffeeShopAddress2" runat="server">
    </asp:textbox></TD>
  </TR>
  <TR>
    <TD>
      <P align="center">City</P>
    </TD>
    <TD><asp:textbox id="txtcoffeeShopCity" runat="server">
    </asp:textbox></TD>
  </TR>
  <TR>
    <TD>
      <P align="center">State</P>
    </TD>
    <TD><asp:textbox id="txtcoffeeShopState" runat="server">
    </asp:textbox></TD>
  </TR>
  <TR>
    <TD>
      <P align="center">zip</P>
    </TD>
    <TD><asp:textbox id="txtcoffeeShopZip" runat="server">
    </asp:textbox></TD>
  </TR>
  <TR>
    <TD height="31">
      <P align="center">WiFi Yes or No</P>
    </TD>
    <TD height="31">
      <asp:RadioButtonList id="rblWiFi" runat="server"
      RepeatDirection="Horizontal">
```

```
        <asp:ListItem Value="1">Yes</asp:ListItem>
        <asp:ListItem Value="0">No</asp:ListItem>
      </asp:RadioButtonList></TD>
  </TR>
  <TR>
    <TD>
      <P align="center">Extra Details</P>
    </TD>
    <TD>
      <asp:TextBox id="txtcoffeeShopDetails" runat="server">
      </asp:TextBox></TD>
  </TR>
  <TR>
    <TD>
      <P align="center"> </P>
    </TD>
    <TD>
      <P>
        <asp:LinkButton id="cmdUpdate" runat="server"
        Text="Update" BorderStyle="none"
        CssClass="CommandButton"></asp:LinkButton> 
        <asp:LinkButton id="cmdCancel" runat="server"
        Text="Cancel" BorderStyle="none"
        CssClass="CommandButton"
          CausesValidation="False"></asp:LinkButton> 
        <asp:LinkButton id="cmdDelete" runat="server"
        Text="Delete" BorderStyle="none" CssClass="CommandButton"
          CausesValidation="False"></asp:LinkButton></P>
        </TD>
      </TR>
</TABLE>
```

2. Next, right-click on `EditShopList.ascx.vb` and select **View Code**. When the source code is displayed, replace all the code with the following code:

```
Imports DotNetNuke
Namespace EganEnterprises.CoffeeShopListing
  Partial Class EditShopList
    Inherits Entities.Modules.PortalModuleBase
    Dim coffeeShopID As Integer = -1
    Protected Sub Page_Load(ByVal sender As System.Object, _
    ByVal e As System.EventArgs) Handles MyBase.Load
      ' get parameter
      If Not (Request.Params("coffeeShopID") Is Nothing) Then
        coffeeShopID = _
        Integer.Parse(Request.Params("coffeeShopID"))
```

```
            Else
              coffeeShopID = Null.NullInteger
            End If
            If Page.IsPostBack = False Then
              cmdDelete.Attributes.Add("onClick", _
              "javascript:return confirm('Are You Sure You Wish To
                Delete This Item ?');")
If Not DotNetNuke.Common.Utilities.Null.IsNull(coffeeShopID) Then
Dim objCoffeeShops As New CoffeeShopListingController
Dim objCoffeeShop As CoffeeShopListingInfo = _
        objCoffeeShops.EganEnterprises_GetCoffeeShopsByID( _
                                        coffeeShopID)
If Not objCoffeeShop Is Nothing Then
txtcoffeeShopName.Text = objCoffeeShop.coffeeShopName
txtCoffeeShopAddress1.Text = objCoffeeShop.coffeeShopAddress1
txtCoffeeShopAddress2.Text = objCoffeeShop.coffeeShopAddress2
txtcoffeeShopCity.Text = objCoffeeShop.coffeeShopCity
txtcoffeeShopState.Text = objCoffeeShop.coffeeShopState
txtcoffeeShopZip.Text = objCoffeeShop.coffeeShopZip
If objCoffeeShop.coffeeShopWiFi Then
    rblWiFi.Items(0).Selected = True
Else
    rblWiFi.Items(1).Selected = True
End If
txtcoffeeShopDetails.Text = objCoffeeShop.coffeeShopDetails

Else
' security violation attempt to access item not related to this
' Module
            Response.Redirect(NavigateURL())
          End If
        Else
          ' This is new item
          cmdDelete.Visible = False

      End If
    End If
  End Sub
  Private Sub cmdCancel_Click( _
    ByVal sender As System.Object, _
    ByVal e As System.EventArgs) Handles cmdCancel.Click
    ' Redirect back to the portal
    Response.Redirect(NavigateURL())
  End Sub
```

```
Protected Sub cmdUpdate_Click( _
  ByVal sender As System.Object, _
  ByVal e As System.EventArgs) Handles cmdUpdate.Click
Try
  Dim objShopList As New CoffeeShopListingInfo
  objShopList.moduleID = ModuleId
  objShopList.coffeeShopID = coffeeShopID
  objShopList.coffeeShopName = txtcoffeeShopName.Text
  objShopList.coffeeShopAddress1 = txtCoffeeShopAddress1.
  TextobjShopList.coffeeShopAddress2 =
  txtCoffeeShopAddress2.Text
  objShopList.coffeeShopCity = txtcoffeeShopCity.Text
  objShopList.coffeeShopState = txtcoffeeShopState.Text
  objShopList.coffeeShopZip = txtcoffeeShopZip.Text
  objShopList.coffeeShopDetails = txtcoffeeShopDetails.Text
  objShopList.coffeeShopWiFi = rblWiFi.SelectedValue
  Dim objShopLists As New CoffeeShopListingController
  If Null.IsNull(coffeeShopID) Then
    coffeeShopID = _ objShopLists.
          EganEnterprises_AddCoffeeShopInfo(objShopList)
  Else
    objShopLists.EganEnterprises_UpdateCoffeeShopInfo( _
                                    objShopList)
  End If


  ' Redirect back to the portal
  Response.Redirect(NavigateURL())
Catch ex As Exception
  ProcessModuleLoadException(Me, ex)
End Try
End Sub
Protected Sub cmdDelete_Click( _
  ByVal sender As System.Object, _
  ByVal e As System.EventArgs) Handles cmdDelete.Click
If Not Null.IsNull(coffeeShopID) Then
  Dim objShopLists As New CoffeeShopListingController
  objShopLists.EganEnterprises_DeleteCoffeeShop( _
                                    coffeeShopID)
End If
' Redirect back to the portal
Response.Redirect(NavigateURL())
End Sub

End Class
End Namespace
```

Build and View the Module

In Visual Studio, press *Ctrl+F5* to start the DotNetNuke site. When it starts, log in as host. Next, click the **Coffee Shop Listing** link on the menu bar in the DotNetNuke site to navigate to the module.

You will now be able to explore the functionality of the working module.

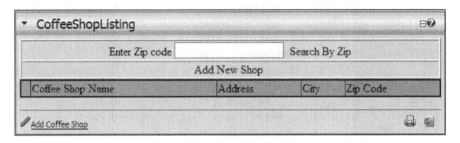

 Leaving fields blank when submitting data using the forms in the module could cause various run-time errors; in a real-world application it would be necessary to add validation to all user input. You could use ASP.NET validation controls to accomplish this task.

Implementing Optional Interfaces

In the final step we will complete the **Coffee Shop Listing** module by implementing two optional interfaces, IPortable and ISearchable.

Implementing IPortable

The IPortable interface can be implemented to allow a user to transfer data from one module instance to another. This is accessed on the context menu of the module.

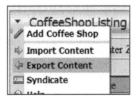

To use this interface, you will need to implement two different methods, `ExportModule` and `ImportModule`. The implementation of these methods will be slightly different depending on the data that is stored in the module. Since we will be holding information about certain coffee shops in our module this is the information we need to import and export. This is accomplished using the .NET `System.XML` namespace.

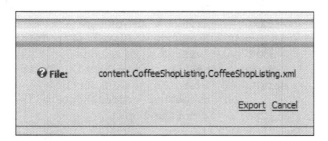

The `ExportModule` method uses our `EganEnterprises_GetCoffeeShops` stored procedure to build a collection of `CoffeeShopListingInfo` objects. The objects are then converted to XML nodes and returned to the caller. We don't need to call the `ExportModule` function ourselves; the DotNetNuke framework adds the Import and Export options to the module's context menu and performs this function when the **Export** link is clicked, and the data is exported to a physical file.

1. Add the following line of code to the `CoffeeShopListingController` class under the line `Public Class CoffeeShopListingController`.

    ```
    Implements Entities.Modules.IPortable
    ```

    Visual Studio will create "stubs" for the `ExportModule` and `ImportModule` methods when the "Implements" line is added.

2. Update the module code so that the code appears as below:

    ```
    Public Function ExportModule(ByVal ModuleID As Integer) _
        As String Implements _
        DotNetNuke.Entities.Modules.IPortable.ExportModule
        Dim strXML As String = ""
        Dim arrCoffeeShops As List(Of CoffeeShopListingInfo) = _
        EganEnterprises_GetCoffeeShops(ModuleID)
        If arrCoffeeShops.Count <> 0 Then
          strXML += "<coffeeshops>"
          Dim objCoffeeShop As CoffeeShopListingInfo
          For Each objCoffeeShop In arrCoffeeShops
            strXML += "<coffeeshop>"
            strXML += "<name>" & XMLEncode( _
                      objCoffeeShop.coffeeShopName) & "</name>"
    ```

```
        strXML += "<address1>" & XMLEncode( _
              objCoffeeShop.coffeeShopAddress1) & "</address1>"
        strXML += "<address2>" & XMLEncode(_
              objCoffeeShop.coffeeShopAddress2) & "</address2>"
        strXML += "<city>" & XMLEncode(_
                    objCoffeeShop.coffeeShopCity) & "</city>"
        strXML += "<state>" & XMLEncode(_
                    objCoffeeShop.coffeeShopState) & "</state>"
        strXML += "<zip>" & XMLEncode(_
              objCoffeeShop.coffeeShopZip.ToString) & "</zip>"
        strXML += "<wifi>" & XMLEncode(_
            objCoffeeShop.coffeeShopWiFi.ToString) & "</wifi>"
        strXML += "<details>" & XMLEncode(_
              objCoffeeShop.coffeeShopDetails) & "</details>"
        strXML += "</coffeeshop>"
    Next
    strXML += "</coffeeshops>"
  End If
  Return strXML
End Function
```

The `ImportModule` method does just the opposite; it takes the XML file created by the `ExportModule` method and creates `CoffeeShopListingInfo` items. Then it uses the `EganEnterprises_AddCoffeeShopInfo` method to add them to the database, thus filling the module with transferred data.

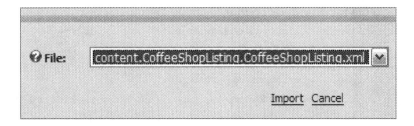

3. Update the module code so that the code appears as below:

```
Public Sub ImportModule(ByVal ModuleID As Integer, _
    ByVal Content As String, ByVal Version As String, _
    ByVal UserID As Integer) _
    Implements DotNetNuke.Entities.Modules.IPortable.ImportModule
    Dim xmlCoffeeShop As XmlNode
```

```
        Dim xmlCoffeeShops As XmlNode = _
        GetContent(Content, "coffeeshops")

        For Each xmlCoffeeShop In xmlCoffeeShops
            Dim objCoffeeShop As New CoffeeShopListingInfo
            objCoffeeShop.moduleID = ModuleID
            objCoffeeShop.coffeeShopName = _
                          xmlCoffeeShop.Item("name").InnerText
            objCoffeeShop.coffeeShopAddress1 = _
                          xmlCoffeeShop.Item("address1").InnerText
            objCoffeeShop.coffeeShopAddress2 = _
                          xmlCoffeeShop.Item("address2").InnerText
            objCoffeeShop.coffeeShopCity = _
                          xmlCoffeeShop.Item("city").InnerText
            objCoffeeShop.coffeeShopState = _
                          xmlCoffeeShop.Item("state").InnerText
            objCoffeeShop.coffeeShopZip = _
                          xmlCoffeeShop.Item("zip").InnerText
            objCoffeeShop.coffeeShopWiFi = _
                          xmlCoffeeShop.Item("wifi").InnerText
            objCoffeeShop.coffeeShopDetails = _
                          xmlCoffeeShop.Item("details").InnerText
            EganEnterprises_AddCoffeeShopInfo(objCoffeeShop)
        Next
    End Sub
```

4. Save the page.

Implementing ISearchable

To allow your modules to be searched, you need to implement the `ISearchable` interface. This interface has only one method you need to implement: `GetSearchItems`.

This method uses a `SearchItemCollection`, which can be found in the `DotNetNuke.Services.Search` namespace, to hold a list of the items available in the search. In our implementation, we use the `EganEnterprises_GetCoffeeShops` method to fill a `collection` with the coffee shops in our database. We then use the objects returned to the `collection` to add to a `SearchItemInfo` object. The constructor for this object is overloaded and it holds items such as `Title`, `Description`, `Author`, and `SearchKey`. What you place in these properties depends on your data. For our coffee shop items we will be using `coffeeShopName`, `coffeeShopID`, and `coffeeShopCity` to fill the object.

Each time it loops through the collection it will add a search item to the `SearchItemCollection`. The core framework takes care of all the other things needed to implement this on your portal.

1. Add the following line of code to the CoffeeShopListingController class under the line `Implements Entities.Modules.IPortable`.

   ```
   Implements Entities.Modules.ISearchable
   ```

   Visual Studio will create a "stub" for the `GetSearchItems` method when the "Implements" line is added.

2. Update the module code so that the code appears as below:

   ```
   Public Function GetSearchItems _
       (ByVal ModInfo As DotNetNuke.Entities.Modules.ModuleInfo) _
       As DotNetNuke.Services.Search.SearchItemInfoCollection _
     Implements _
     DotNetNuke.Entities.Modules.ISearchable.GetSearchItems
         Dim SearchItemCollection As New SearchItemInfoCollection
         Dim CoffeeShops As List(Of CoffeeShopListingInfo) = _
         EganEnterprises_GetCoffeeShops(ModInfo.ModuleID)
         Dim objCoffeeShop As Object
         For Each objCoffeeShop In CoffeeShops
           Dim SearchItem As SearchItemInfo
           With CType(objCoffeeShop, CoffeeShopListingInfo)
             SearchItem = New SearchItemInfo _
             (ModInfo.ModuleTitle & " - " & .coffeeShopName, _
             .coffeeShopName, _
             Convert.ToInt32(10), _
             DateTime.Now, ModInfo.ModuleID, _
             .coffeeShopID.ToString, _
             .coffeeShopName & " - " & .coffeeShopCity)
             SearchItemCollection.Add(SearchItem)
           End With
         Next
         Return SearchItemCollection
     End Function
   ```

3. Save the page.

Making IPortable and ISearchable Work

In Visual Studio, press *Ctrl+F5* to start the DotNetNuke site. When it starts, log in as host. Next, click the **Coffee Shop Listing** link on the menu bar in the DotNetNuke site to navigate to the module.

Click on the menu link for the module and you will not see the **Import Content** and **Export Content** options.

Navigate to the configuration settings for the **Coffee Shop Listing** module (**Host | Module Definitions | CoffeeShopListing**) and you will see the reason. **Portable** and **Searchable** are not indicated in our module configuration.

 Upgradeable is also an optional interface called IUpgradable, but its use is beyond the scope of this discussion.

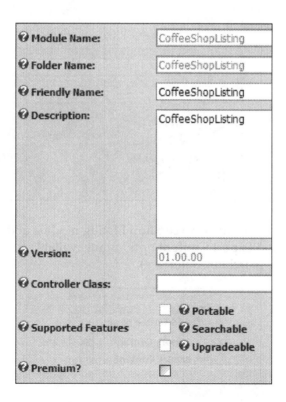

Normally, we would indicate these settings in the module definition when we initially create it. However, there are instances, such as now, where we decide to implement the optional interfaces after we have created the module definition and begun development.

In the module definition, enter **EganEnterprises.CoffeeShopListing. CoffeeShopListingController** in the **Controller Class** box and click the **Update** link. The module defintion will be updated and **Portable** and **Searchable** will be checked.

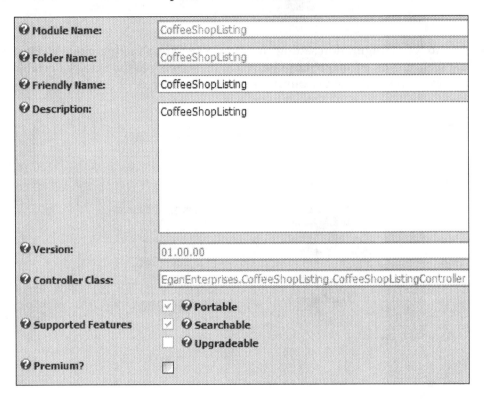

Now return to the menu for the **Coffee Shop Listing** module and you will see that the **Import Content** and **Export Content** options are available (the module is now also implementing the searchable interface).

Testing Your Module

Throughout the development process you should use all of Visual Studio's debugging capabilities to make sure that your code is working correctly.

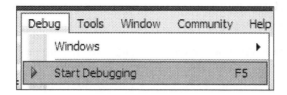

You will be able to set breakpoints and view your code in the various watch windows. When you have finished debugging your module, you are ready to package it and get it ready for distribution.

Packaging Your Module for Distribution

You now have a finished module. It is advisable to develop your module on a separate development machine then deploy it to production using a Private Assembly package (called a PA).

This PA package is a `.zip` file that contains all the elements needed to install the module on a DotNetNuke installation. These elements include the code and the installation scripts.

Installation Scripts

The first step in preparing your module for distribution is to create the installation scripts needed to create the tables and stored procedures required by your module. There should be at least two files: an installation script and an uninstallation script. You should name your scripts in the following manner.

Type of Script	Description	Example
Installation Script	Concatenate the version number of your module with the type of provider the script represents eg. Sql.	`01.00.00.SqlDataProvider`
Uninstallation Script	Concatenate the word `Uninstall` with the type of provider the script represents.	`Uninstall.SqlDataProvider`

These scripts are similar to the code run for creating your tables at the beginning of this chapter. The scripts for your PA installation should use the `databaseOwner` and `objectQualifier` variables as well as including code to check if the database objects you are creating already exist in the database. This will help to ensure that uploading your module will not overwrite previous data. The full scripts can be found in the code download for this chapter.

The version number for your scripts is very important. If a version of the module is already installed on your portal, the framework checks the version number on the script file to determine whether to run the script. If the number on the file matches the number in the database then the script will not be run. In this way, you can have one package work as an installation and upgrade package.

Create the Installation Scripts

The first step of creating the installation scripts will be to create the folder that will contain them. We will place them in the **CoffeeShopListing folder that is under the** DesktopModules **folder.**

1. In Visual Studio, in the **Solution Explorer**, right-click on the **CoffeeShopListing** folder that is under the **DesktopModules** folder and select **New Folder**.

2. Name the folder **Providers**.

3. Now, right-click on the **Providers** folder that you have just created and select **New Folder**.

4. Name the folder **DataProviders**.

5. Next, right-click on the **DataProviders** folder that you have just created and select **New Folder**.

6. Name the folder **SqlDataProvider**.

The reason we have created the multiple folders is because you may want to create additional data providers for your module. This is the recommended way of organizing them.

Now we will create the installation scripts. We will create an install script (`01.01.00.SqlDataProvider`) and an uninstall script (`uninstall.SqlDataProvider`). The install script will be processed by the DotNetNuke installation when the module is installed, and the uninstall script will be processed by the DotNetNuke installation when the module is uninstalled.

The complete scripts can be found in the code download for this chapter.

1. Right-click on the **SqlDataProvider** folder and select **Add New Item**.

2. Select **Text File** as the template and enter `01.01.00.SqlDataProvider` in the **Name** field.

3. Right-click on the `01.01.00.SqlDataProvider` and select Open.

4. When the file opens in the editor window, place the contents of the script file (that can be found in the code download for this chapter) and save the file.

5. Right-click on the **SqlDataProvider** folder and select **Add New Item**.

6. Select **Text File** as the template and enter **uninstall.SqlDataProvider** in the **Name** field.

7. Right-click on the **uninstall.SqlDataProvider** and select Open.

8. When the file opens in the editor window, place the contents of the script file (that can be found in the code download for this chapter) and save the file.

The Install ZIP File

Now it is time to package all of the files into a PA `.zip` file to enable them to be uploaded and installed on another DotNetNuke installation.

1. In Visual Studio, press *Ctrl+F5* to start the DotNetNuke site. When it starts, log in as host.

2. Navigate to the configuration settings for the **Coffee Shop Listing** module (**Host | Module Definitions | CoffeeShopListing**) and select **Package Module** from the module configuration menu:

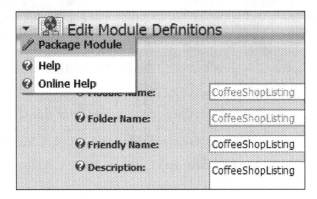

3. Name the package `CoffeeShopListing_PA.zip` and click the **Create** link.

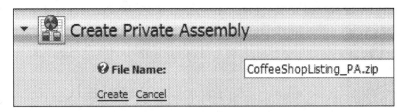

A screen will appear indicating that the module elements have been successfully placed in the `.zip` file.

```
Successfully created the Private Assembly:

StartJob  Create manifest file. CoffeeShopListing
EndJob    Create manifest file. CoffeeShopListing


StartJob  Creating Private Assembly: CoffeeShopListing
Info      Adding files to the Private Assembly: CoffeeShopListing
Info      File ShopList.ascx.resx saved to Private Assembly.
Info      File 01.01.00.SqlDataProvider saved to Private Assembly.
Info      File uninstall.SqlDataProvider saved to Private Assembly.
Info      File EditShopList.ascx saved to Private Assembly.
Info      File EditShopList.ascx.vb saved to Private Assembly.
Info      File Settings.ascx saved to Private Assembly.
Info      File Settings.ascx.vb saved to Private Assembly.
Info      File ShopList.ascx saved to Private Assembly.
Info      File ShopList.ascx.vb saved to Private Assembly.
Info      File CoffeeShopListingController.vb saved to Private Assembly.
Info      File CoffeeShopListingInfo.vb saved to Private Assembly.
Info      File CoffeeShopListingOptionsController.vb saved to Private Assembly.
Info      File CoffeeShopListingOptionsInfo.vb saved to Private Assembly.
Info      File DataProvider.vb saved to Private Assembly.
Info      File SqlDataProvider.vb saved to Private Assembly.
Info      File CoffeeShopListing.dnn saved to Private Assembly.
EndJob    Creating Private Assembly: CoffeeShopListing
```

You can retrieve the .zip file by navigating to the root of the portal (usually at
\Portals_default) using the Windows File Manager.

Testing Your Installation

This is the final step. At this stage, all of your coding should work fine because you
have tested it in your Visual Studio .NET environment. Now you need to test if
uploading your module will work for you. You have a couple of options. Since you
have already set up this module manually in your Visual Studio environment you
would have to remove the module code and delete the tables in your database to fully
test whether your PA package works. However, it is recommended that you set up a
separate instance of DotNetNuke that is only used for testing uploads of modules.

Uploading the module is simple. Sign in as host and select Module Definitions on the
host menu. Hover the cursor over the context menu and select **Upload New Module**.

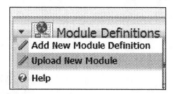

Click the **Browse** button to browse to your .zip file and add it to the file
download box by clicking the **Add** link. Next, click on **Upload New File** link to
load your module.

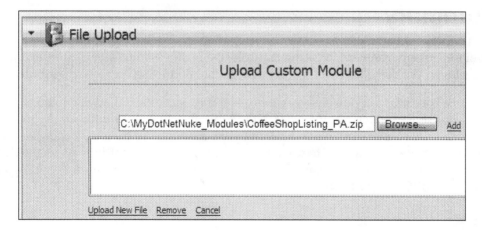

This will create a file-upload log, which will then be displayed. Search the log for any errors that may have occurred and fix the errors.

```
Info       Created C:\Inetpub\DotNetNuke\DesktopModules\CoffeeShopListing\
Info       Created C:\Inetpub\DotNetNuke\App_Code\CoffeeShopListing\Coffee
Info       Created C:\Inetpub\DotNetNuke\App_Code\CoffeeShopListing\Coffee
Info       Created C:\Inetpub\DotNetNuke\App_Code\CoffeeShopListing\Coffee
Info       Created C:\Inetpub\DotNetNuke\App_Code\CoffeeShopListing\Coffee
Info       Created C:\Inetpub\DotNetNuke\App_Code\CoffeeShopListing\DataP
Info       Created C:\Inetpub\DotNetNuke\App_Code\CoffeeShopListing\SqlDat
Info       Created C:\Inetpub\DotNetNuke\DesktopModules\CoffeeShopListing\
EndJob     Files created


StartJob   Registering DesktopModule
Info       Registering Definitions
Info       Registering Controls
EndJob     Registering finished


EndJob     Installation successful.
```

Add your module to a tab and put it through its paces. Make sure to try out all the features. It is advisable to have others test it. You will be surprised at the things that users will do with your module. When all features have been tested, you are ready to distribute it to the DotNetNuke world.

Summary

We have covered a lot of code in the last two chapters, including setting up our development environment, creating controls, the business logic layer, and the data access layer. We then showed how to package the module so it can be distributed.

Since this code was very extensive, we broke it into sections and advised you to build your project at regular intervals. Doing this should give you the ability to solve any issues you come across while building your module. We then took things a bit further and showed you how to use a few extra items like the settings page, the dual-list box, and the optional interfaces. This should give you a sound understanding of how all the different parts work together.

9
Skinning Your Site

Skinning your site can be one of the most rewarding aspects of your portal administration process. It is your chance to be visually creative and personalize your DotNetNuke installation. Literally speaking, a skin is a collection of physical files that, together, form a skin package. This package contains all of the files and information needed to completely describe the look and feel of your site. When this complete package is uploaded into the portal framework, it is put through a parsing process that places the skin, as well as any containers, into the list of available display choices for your site. At the heart of the upload process is the DotNetNuke 4.0 skinning engine, which maintains the same level of separation between the presentation layer and application layer of your site as the previous version while exposing additional enhancements that leverage the flexibility of the DotNetNuke Provider Model.

Whether you are a user who has downloaded a third-party skin package or a developer looking to develop your own skin, this abstraction of the presentation layer from the logic layer provides a great deal of freedom. In the case of a third-party skin package, it provides you with the freedom to upload and apply a skin package that changes the look and feel of your site without worrying about breaking any existing modules. Similarly, when developing a custom skin from scratch, this abstraction provides you with the freedom to use an editor of your choice while you to focus on the design of your site. In this chapter, we will cover:

- An overview of Skin Packages
- How to upload a Skin Package
- How to apply your Skin
- An overview of the concepts involved in Custom Skinning
- How to create your Custom Skin using HTML, Tokens, and XML
- How to create your Custom Skin using ASP.NET User Controls

- How to create the Cascading Style Sheets to support your Skin
- How to create your Skin Package

What Are Skin Packages?

Let us begin with the basic concept of what a skin package is and how it works. A skin package contains a collection of many different files. These include HTML layout files, Cascading Style Sheets, Images, .NET User Controls and XML layout files. These all work together to form the foundation of the skin, which can be further divided into two basic components, skins, and containers. The role the skin plays in the package is directly related to the general structure of your site. Think of it in terms of an outer layer for your pages that provides information about how each page will look while not affecting the way the page functions. In order to illustrate this concept, let us take a look at an example. This first example is a screenshot of a page with the default DotNetNuke installation skin applied.

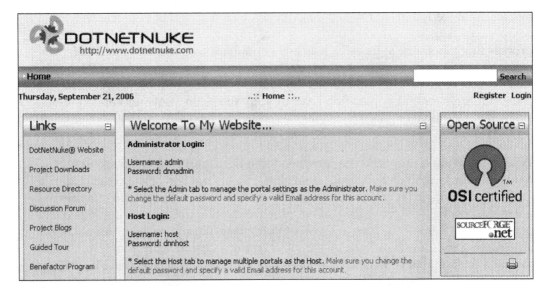

Notice the layout of the page has the main menu aligned along the left edge of the page with what should be a familiar banner right above it. There is a single **Links** module placed on the left side of the page with a **Content** area to the right. The next screenshot shows how the very same page would look with a custom skin applied. Pay particular attention to the placement and alignment of the main menu as well as the look of the **Links** module in the left content pane.

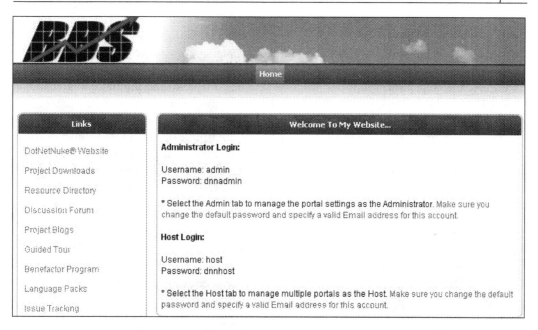

With this package applied, the main menu is now centered on the page and there is a different banner image across the top. In this example, the banner images and main menu are elements of the skin. The rounded borders around the **Links** module and **Content** area are the containers. Notice that while the look of the page has changed a great deal, the function of the page remains identical. The **Links** module still resides on the left-hand side of the page with the content area to the right. All we have done is change the structure of the page, the skin, and the borders around the modules, the containers. Now let us take a look specifically at how the **Links** module is displayed in both examples.

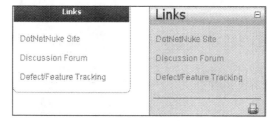

Notice how only the border is changing while the data, the list of site links in this case, does not change. The example on the left is meant to fit within a very different skin theme than the one on the right. For this reason, containers are frequently packaged along with skins so that the containers support the overall look and feel of the skin within which they are meant to fit.

Uploading a Skin Package

Now that we understand the contents of a skin package and how they are meant to work, we can now discuss the specifics of how we use the package. Before we can apply the skin package to our site, we must first upload the package into the DotNetNuke framework. The upload can be performed either using Administrator or Host-level access. Uploading the package using Administrator access would restrict us to using the skin on a single portal while uploading as Host would grant us a greater degree of flexibility since we would be able to apply the skin to any parent or child portal we later create. For this reason, we will be using Host-level permission and we start by logging into our DotNetNuke installation with this higher level of access.

Now that we are logged in with Host access, we have two options that allow us to upload our skin. The first involves hovering over the **Host** menu and clicking on **Host Settings** in the dropdown. By default, this will be the first menu selection under the **Host** sub-menu. Under the **Appearance** section of our **Host Settings** page, we find the following:

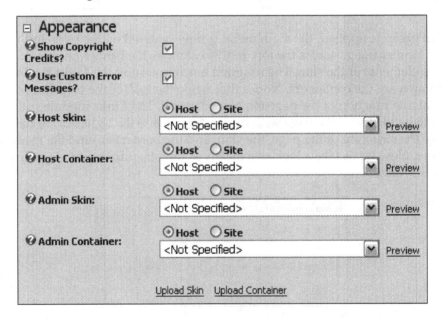

This is the section of the Settings page that deals with the look and feel of our site. We then click on the **Upload Skin** link, which will take us to the following file upload interface.

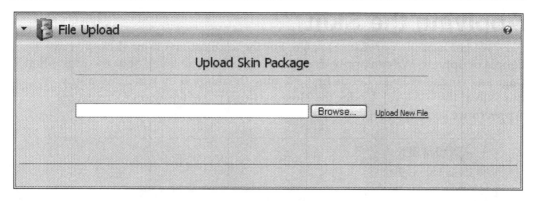

We first click on the **Browse** button to bring up a file dialog box that allows us to navigate to our skin project root directory. We then select our skin package ZIP file and click the **Add** link. At this point, the name of our skin package ZIP file will be displayed in the textbox above. At this point, we are ready to upload the new skin. We now click on the **Upload New File** link at the bottom of the **Upload Skin Package** page and let the DotNetNuke skinning engine do its work. At the end of the file upload process, we will be presented with a log of the actions that the engine performed in parsing and creating the skin objects similar to the following image. We will also see any errors that may have occurred.

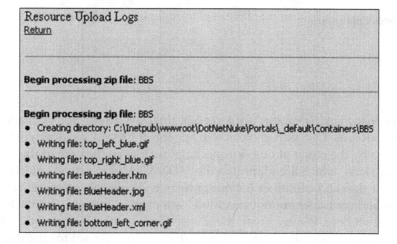

Applying the Skin

Now we get to apply our skin package. For the application of our skin, we have a couple of options. We can apply the skin at either the site level, or at the individual page and container level. Let us first examine the method by which we apply our skin at the site level. Under the **Host Settings** page, we again focus on the **Appearance** section.

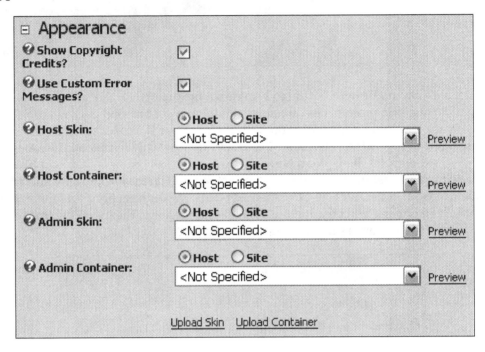

Now, rather than clicking on the **Upload Skin** link, we choose our skin and container with the dropdowns. Our skin choices will appear in these drop-down lists as items prefixed by the name of our skin package such as in the case of the default DotNetNuke skins, which are all prefixed by "DNN". Making these selections will set the default skin and container for our entire site. What this means is whenever a specific skin and container are not specified for a page in our site, they will default to the values we set here. We are given the ability to set a default skin and container for the public section of our site that is different than the one we set for the display of the administrative elements.

The second way we could apply our skin at the site level is via the **Skins** page accessible from the **Host** main menu dropdown.

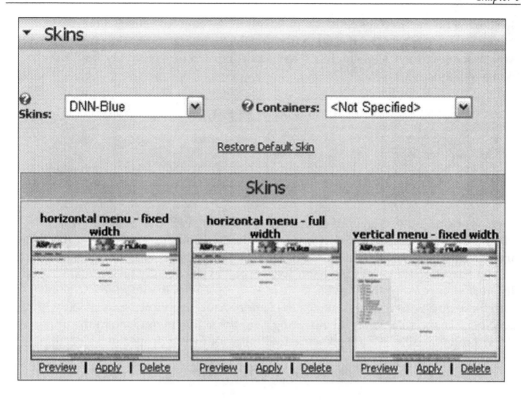

From this interface, we first scroll to the bottom and make sure the appropriate checkboxes are checked, which correspond to where we would like to apply the skin. The choices are **Host** and **Admin** and they function the same way as the set of four dropdowns in our previous example, which allow us to define a default skin for the user areas of our site that is different than the default skin for the administrative areas. Once we have decided on where we want to apply our skin, we then simply click the **Apply** link below the thumbnail preview image.

To apply the skin at a page and container level, we first make sure that we are logged in with administrator or host-level access then navigate to the page we wish to work with. We access the page settings from the icon bar on the left side of the administration panel at the top of the page.

By clicking on the **Settings** link, we are taken to the page administration page. By expanding the **Advanced** section, we are able to interact with the page **Appearance** settings. Here again we have a dropdown for specifying both the Skin and Container.

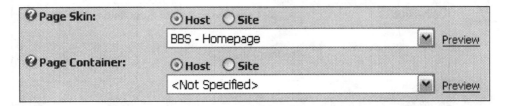

There is one additional layer of customization that is available to us for our site. Obviously there must be a way to specify individual container skins since the above dropdown will set the default container for the whole page. What if our skin calls for three different containers? Or what if we wanted to use a really nice container from a different skin package that has been previously uploaded to our site? The answer to both these questions is accessible via the action menu dropdown associated with the DotNetNuke module object. By hovering over the action menu icon in the upper left of our **Links** module, we are presented with the following drop-down selection.

From this list, we select the **Settings** option, which takes us to the settings page for our Links module. We then expand the "Page Settings" section and look for the following section.

From this dropdown list, we can choose the container to display around our **Links** module.

Creating a Custom Skin

At this point, you should be able to take any skin package, upload it, and apply it to your site. But what would you do if you wanted to create your own skin package from scratch? The act of creating a custom skin package is referred to as **skinning**. We begin our custom skinning process by first taking a step backward and re-examining the question of what a skin is; but this time let us answer the question from more of a conceptual point of view.

Imagine that a close friend is in dire need of a creative individual to help build a new home. Since you are a close friend and have the utmost faith in your creative ability, you approach your friend and agree to lend a hand. Imagine that you are then presented with a floor plan that describes in painstaking detail not only where all the rooms will be placed, but also how all of the furniture will be arranged. You might be tempted to make the assumption that your friend left no room for creativity. That is, of course, until you realize that the floor plan contains no detail describing how the exterior will look. You are free to be as creative as you like with the exterior of the new home provided you can cover all the rooms in the floor plan.

Buoyed by your renewed enthusiasm, you then set out to design the exterior of the new home with your floor plan in hand. You obviously have to design the placement of doors in the exterior because your friend would have to enter and exit somehow. You also have to decide where to place windows on the exterior to allow people to see from the outside in as well as vice-versa. Having become comfortable with where the doors and windows are placed, you then decide on the colors for the walls and the trim. Maybe you add decorations above the front door or design ornate trimmings around the roof. All these choices have no bearing on the rooms and the furniture that will ultimately reside within the new home, but they each make a big difference to the individual walking by on the street. You choose obnoxious colors and place no windows around the first floor and chances are your friend will grow old and lonely and never get any visitors.

The choices you make in terms of the use of colors and the placement of such things as the doors and windows are all examples of what DotNetNuke skinning really means. You are given a very detailed floor plan that covers all of the inner-workings of the architecture itself as well as the placement of the objects within and then you are left with an enormous amount of flexibility in terms of how you can make the walls look. You can choose where to place doors and windows and how to decorate the outside so that it is as appealing as possible to people walking by on the street provided that you include three required elements. You need a door that the owner will use to enter, at least one window for the display of content, and a directory, consisting of a menu, that describes how to get from room to room while inside.

What Tools can we Use?

Now that the basics are out of the way, let us dig a little deeper and start to understand the materials we are provided to build our exterior. Let us start with the building blocks we use to develop the skin structure. Depending on our choice of method, our structure will either take shape within HTML files or .NET .ASCX User Controls. In either case, within this structure, we will insert directions that will be used by the DotNetNuke 4.0 skinning engine to create and format the skin objects that will be presented visually to the user. Skin objects, as we will see illustrated later, consist of big things such as our main menu and content panes, as well as little things like the frame or border around our various modules. These building blocks form the foundation of a skin package and work together to control the visual presentation of your site. All we need to do now is decide on a way that we will create the structure and insert the skin object information. This leads us to the first really important question we have to ask ourselves; what editor will we use?

Making our decision easy are two very significant qualities of the DotNetNuke skinning engine. The first significant quality revolves around the ability to use HTML to create the skin structure. Suddenly this opens up a world of possibilities for us. Anything that can create HTML formatting can be used to create the structure of the skin, but what about the formatting directions for the skin objects? The answer to that question leads us to the next significant quality of the skinning engine.

The skin objects we will use are implemented as Web User Controls within the DotNetNuke architecture. In the HTML designer method of creating the skin, this quality may not seem that important, but to those with a programming background, the Web User Control implementation means we have the option of creating our skin in an editor such as Visual Web Developer Express, which will allow us to simply drag the chosen skin objects onto our skin structure.

Together, we will go through both methods of skin creation. In the end, the skins that emerge will be identical. The choice of what method will work for you depends largely on the background you bring with you to the project. If you come from a web designer background, the example using Macromedia's Dreamweaver will seem very comfortable to you. If you come from a programming background and are comfortable with working with web user controls, then you will probably prefer the example using Visual Web Developer Express.

Creating a Skin Using HTML

We begin the HTML method by creating a new site in Macromedia's Dreamweaver. The first elements we create are folders that will contain the resource elements of our skin project. To simplify the process of creating more skins, we start with a Skin Packages site to which we add a folder named BBS that will contain our first skin. Within this BBS folder, we create a folder named Containers and another named Skins. The following figure illustrates how our project looks at this point.

We start with the Skins folder and begin by adding the required file resources for our project. It is a good idea to begin with a page that has the highest degree of flexibility. All DotNetNuke portals have distinct user pages and Admin/Host pages. We will want a generic page with a single content pane to apply to the Admin/Host pages of our site. With this in mind, we well start with the files for an Admin skin page. These include an Admin.htm file that will contain the HTML structure of our skin page, an Admin.xml file that will be used by the DotNetNuke skinning engine to format the skin objects we use, and a Skin.css file that will be responsible for the style formatting on our page. By naming the .css file in this way, the styles in the stylesheet will be used on all of the pages we later create in our package. Alternatively, we could have named this file Admin.css. This results in a .css file that is specific to a skin page, Admin.htm in our current example. We will dig deeper into the .css inclusion chain later in the chapter; for now, let us continue setting up our skin folder. We then add, to this folder, any additional image files that we will use in our skin.

Within the `Containers` folder we add similar file resources. These include a `BlueHeader.htm` file that will hold the HTML structure of our container, a file to be used to format the skin objects called `BlueHeader.xml`, and a stylesheet for our container called `Container.css`. Just as in our skin folder, we could have named our container stylesheet `BlueHeader.css` so that it would be applied specifically to our container. We will, however, start with a generic `.css` file that will be applied to all of our containers. Now we add any additional image files that we will need for the display of our container.

The following figure illustrates how our project will look with the `Skins` folder expanded. Notice the inclusion of an `Admin.jpg` file in the directory. This file will be used by the skinning engine as a thumbnail preview of our page. We will discuss this file in greater detail when we are ready to create our deployment package.

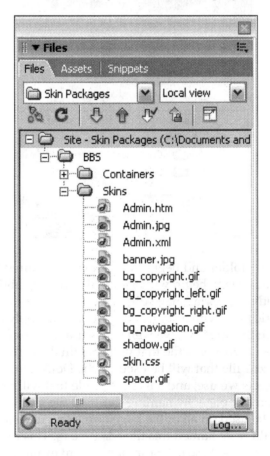

Creating the HTML Files

For the first page of our skin project, we have a specific goal in mind. We want our skin package to be applied to the entire site, including the administrative pages. In order to allow the DotNetNuke portal the greatest flexibility in rendering the administrative modules without breaking our skin, we will use a simple page layout consisting of a banner at the top with a single content area beneath.

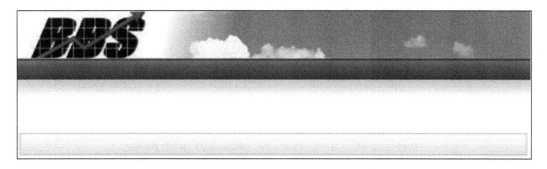

The following is the complete source code for the Admin.htm file that renders the page above:

```
<table cellpadding="0" cellspacing="0" border="0" width="100%">
  <tr>
    <td>
      <table cellpadding="0" cellspacing="0" border="0" width="100%">
        <tr>
          <td width="50%" bgcolor="#FFFFFF"> </td>
          <td width="760" height="70">
            <img src="banner.jpg" width="760" height="70">
          </td>
          <td width="50%" bgcolor="#73ABE4"> </td>
        </tr>
      </table>
    </td>
  </tr>
  <tr>
    <td background="bg_navigation.gif" height="30">
      <table cellpadding="0" cellspacing="0" border="0"
             align="center">
        <tr><td>[SOLPARTMENU]</td></tr>
      </table>
    </td>
  </tr>
  <tr>
```

```
          <td background="shadow.gif" height="30">
            <img src="spacer.gif" width="5" height="30" />
          </td>
        </tr>
        <tr>
          <td>
            <table cellpadding="0" cellspacing="0" border="0" width="760">
              <tr>
                <td width="5"><img src="spacer.gif"
                                        width="5" height="5" /></td>
                <td colspan="2">[CONTENTPANE:1]</td>
                <td width="5"><img src="spacer.gif"
                                        width="5" height="5" /></td>
              </tr>
              <tr>
                <td height="10" colspan="4">
                  <img src="spacer.gif" height="10" width="5" />
                </td>
              </tr>
              <tr>
                <td width="5" height="32"
                              background="bg_copyright.gif" align="left">
                  <img src="bg_copyright_left.gif" width="5" height="32" />
                </td>
                <td width="375" height="32" background="bg_copyright.gif">
                  [COPYRIGHT]
                </td>
                <td width="375" height="32"
                              background="bg_copyright.gif" align="right">
                  [LOGIN]
                </td>
                <td width="5" height="32"
                              background="bg_copyright.gif" align="right">
                  <img src="bg_copyright_right.gif" width="5" height="32" />
                </td>
              </tr>
            </table>
          </td>
        </tr>
        <tr>
          <td height="10"><img src="spacer.gif" height="10" width="5" /></td>
        </tr>
      </table>
```

The bulk of the file, as you can see, is simply HTML used to layout the structure of our page. Notice how images are referenced via a relative path indicating that they are found in the same directory as the HTML file. Going back to the home exterior analogy, think of the HTML contained above as the frame over which we are placing our nice wall. Of significance to our framing structure above, is the use of an image file called `spacer.gif`. This is a single transparent pixel image used to simply space out table cells and ensure that when the page is rendered by a web browser, it retains a rigid structure that preserves our desired look and feel. Within the structure, we then place our three required elements needed to make our skin work; the door, the window, and the directory.

```
<td width="375" height="32" background="bg_copyright.gif"
    align="right">
  [LOGIN]
</td>
```

The code segment above illustrates how skin objects are placed using our HTML designer approach. [LOGIN] is called a token and is used during the package deployment process to tell the skinning engine to inject a login Web User Control into our page. The formatting of the controls is accomplished via our associated XML file that we will discuss later. Without the login user control on the skin, you will nearly lock everyone out of the DotNetNuke back-end interface, including yourself. If this ever happens to you, simply add `"default.aspx?ctl=login"` at the end of your base URL. For example, if you are running your DotNetNuke portal from your local web server, your direct URL to the login control would be `http://localhost/website/default.aspx?ctl=login`.

```
<tr>
  <td width="5"><img src="spacer.gif"
                                   width="5" height="5" /></td>
  <td colspan="2">[CONTENTPANE:1]</td>
  <td width="5"><img src="spacer.gif"
                                   width="5" height="5" /></td>
</tr>
```

The next required element is a window. In the above code segment, notice how we use a similarly formatted token to indicate a content pane. The content pane is where modules will be rendered allowing users to see and interact with the data within the site. In this example, [CONTENTPANE:1] illustrates how we can designate more than one content pane within a page. Creating additional pages with more than one content area would be accomplished by adding tokens such as [CONTENTPANE:2] and [CONTENTPANE:3].

```
<table cellpadding="0" cellspacing="0"
                                   border="0" align="center">
  <tr><td>[SOLPARTMENU]</td></tr>
</table>
```

The last required element for our skin is a directory. In the code segment above, we indicate where we want the skinning engine to inject the main menu by using the [SOLPARTMENU] token. This is not only how users will navigate within the site, but also how site administrators will get to the control panels. The following illustrates how our skin file looks with the tokens in place.

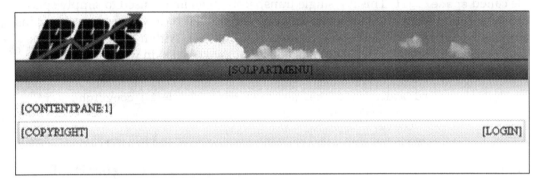

Creating the Container

Now we turn our attention to the creation of the BlueHeader.htm container file. Just as we did in the previous file, we begin by deciding on a look for our container that will fit within the overall look and feel of our skin. The following illustrates the container we will create:

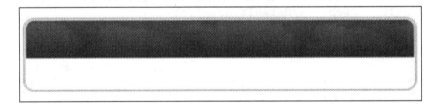

Remember that we are dealing only with the frame that will be displayed around the modules in our site. In this case, we are decorating our frame with a colored background behind the area where we will render our module title, and surrounding it with a square border with rounded edges. The following is the source for our BlueHeader.htm file.

```
<table cellpadding="0" cellspacing="0" width="100%" border="0">
  <tr>
    <td valign="top" colspan="5"><img src="spacer.gif"
                                      height="10" width="5"></td>
  </tr>
  <tr>
    <td width="12" height="30" align="left">
```

```
      <img src="top_left_blue.gif" width="12" height="30">
    </td>
    <td height="20" valign="middle"
                              background="top_blue_bg.gif" nowrap>
[SOLPARTACTIONS]
    </td>
    <td height="20" valign="middle" background="top_blue_bg.gif"
                  width="100%" align="center" nowrap>[TITLE]</td>
    <td width="12" height="30" align="right">
      <img src="top_right_blue.gif" width="12" height="30">
    </td>
  </tr>
  <tr>
    <td width="12" background="left_tile.gif">
      <img src="spacer.gif" width="12" height="5" border="0">
    </td>
    <td colspan="2" bgcolor="#FFFFFF">
      <img src="spacer.gif" height="10" width="5" border="0">
    </td>
    <td width="12" background="right_tile.gif">
      <img src="spacer.gif" width="12" height="5" border="0">
    </td>
  </tr>
  <tr>
    <td width="12" background="left_tile.gif">
      <img src="spacer.gif" width="12" height="5" border="0"></td>
    <td colspan="2" bgcolor="#FFFFFF">[CONTENTPANE]</td>
    <td width="12" background="right_tile.gif">
      <img src="spacer.gif" width="12" height="5" border="0">
    </td>
  </tr>
  <tr>
    <td width="12" height="10">
      <img src="bottom_left_corner.gif" width="12" height="10">
    </td>
    <td colspan="2" background="bottom_tile.gif">
      <img src="spacer.gif" height="10" width="5">
    </td>
    <td width="12" height="10">
      <img src="bottom_right_corner.gif" width="12" height="10">
    </td>
  </tr>
  <tr>
    <td valign="top" colspan="5"><img src="spacer.gif"
                                  height="5" width="5"></td>
  </tr>
</table>
```

Again, the majority of the content of this file is HTML mark-up. The elements that are significant to the DotNetNuke skinning structure are the tokens we use. There are skin object elements that are required for a container to function, just as in our skin; however, unlike in our skin, there are only two. Viewing the container as a window frame, we need to include a latch with which we can open the window if we ever need to change something on the inside. The following code segment provides the latch.

```
<td height="20" valign="middle"
                                 background="top_blue_bg.gif" nowrap>
[SOLPARTACTIONS]
  </td>
```

The [SOLPARTACTIONS] token refers to the icon element that will generate the administrator drop-down menu allowing us to change the settings of the modules contained within. Without including this token, the container would restrict access to module customization features. Needless to say, this would result in a very inflexible module. The second thing we need is a region where the module contents will be rendered. We accomplish this with the following segment.

```
<td colspan="2" bgcolor="#FFFFFF">[CONTENTPANE]</td>
```

With the action menu in place and the content area defined, our container is now ready to provide the required functionality. There are a number of optional token elements that we could choose to include in our container. For our example, let us assume we would like to display the title of the module that will be rendered within our container in the blue region at the top. We accomplish this with the following code segment.

```
<td height="20" valign="middle" background="top_blue_bg.gif"
width="100%" align="center" nowrap>[TITLE]</td>
```

The following table lists the tokens that are provided for defining skin objects in our containers.

Token	Description
[SOLPARTACTIONS]	Popup module actions menu (formerly [ACTIONS])
[DROPDOWNACTIONS]	Simple drop-down combo box for module actions
[LINKACTIONS]	Links list of module actions
[ICON]	Displays the icon related to the module
[TITLE]	Displays the title of the module
[VISIBILITY]	Displays an icon representing the minimized or maximized state of a module
[PRINTMODULE]	Displays a new window with only the module content displayed

Chapter 9

Creating the XML Support Files

Now that we have our HTML file created with our required tokens in place, we turn our attention toward creating the XML support file that will tell the skinning engine how to format our skin objects. The following is the source for the Admin.xml file that formats the skin elements of our Admin.htm page.

```
<Objects>
  <Object>
    <Token>[SOLPARTMENU]</Token>
    <Settings>
      <Setting>
        <Name>separatecss</Name>
        <Value>true</Value>
      </Setting>
      <Setting>
        <Name>display</Name>
        <Value>horizontal</Value>
      </Setting>
        <Setting>
        <Name>menucontainercssclass</Name>
        <Value>MainMenu_MenuContainer</Value>
      </Setting>
      <Setting>
        <Name>menubarcssclass</Name>
        <Value>MainMenu_MenuBar</Value>
      </Setting>
      <Setting>
        <Name>menuitemcssclass</Name>
        <Value>MainMenu_MenuItem</Value>
      </Setting>
      <Setting>
        <Name>menuiconcssclass</Name>
        <Value>MainMenu_MenuIcon</Value>
      </Setting>
      <Setting>
        <Name>menuitemselcssclass</Name>
        <Value>MainMenu_MenuItemSel</Value>
      </Setting>
      <Setting>
        <Name>submenucssclass</Name>
        <Value>MainMenu_SubMenu</Value>
      </Setting>
      <Setting>
        <Name>rootmenuitemactivecssclass</Name>
```

[285]

```
                <Value>MainMenu_ItemActive</Value>
              </Setting>
              <Setting>
                <Name>usearrows</Name>
                <Value>false</Value>
              </Setting>
            </Settings>
        </Object>
        <Object>
          <Token>[LOGIN]</Token>
          <Settings>
            <Setting>
              <Name>Text</Name>
              <Value>Login</Value>
            </Setting>
          <Setting>
              <Name>CssClass</Name>
              <Value>FooterText</Value>
          </Setting>
              <Setting>
                <Name>LogoffText</Name>
                <Value>Logoff</Value>
              </Setting>
            </Settings>
        </Object>
        <Object>
          <Token>[COPYRIGHT]</Token>
          <Settings>
            <Setting>
              <Name>CssClass</Name>
              <Value>FooterText</Value>
            </Setting>
          </Settings>
        </Object>
        <Object>
          <Token>[CONTENTPANE:1]</Token>
          <Settings>
            <Setting>
              <Name>ID</Name>
              <Value>ContentPane</Value>
            </Setting>
          </Settings>
        </Object>
      </Objects>
```

As you can see from the source, the format of the XML file consists of a single collection of items surrounded by the `<Objects></Objects>` tags. The format of each of the individual object elements is illustrated in the following example focussing on the object associated with our content pane.

```
<Object>
  <Token>[CONTENTPANE:1]</Token>
  <Settings>
    <Setting>
      <Name>ID</Name>
      <Value>ContentPane</Value>
    </Setting>
  </Settings>
</Object>
```

Each object has a `<Token>` node that corresponds to the token we placed in our HTML file. In this case, our object corresponds to the `[CONTENTPANE:1]` token. In addition to the token node, we have another collection of items designated by the `<Settings></Settings>` tags. Each setting consists of a name and value pair corresponding to an attribute of the skin object. These attributes are pre-defined by the available editable attributes of the user controls that will render our skin object on the page. In our example above, we have a single setting for our pane which indicates that an attribute called `ID` will be set equal to `ContentPane` as a result of the skinning engine parsing the XML file and injecting the user control. Similarly, the `[LOGIN]` token has three attributes corresponding to the text that a user will see displayed both before and after they log in as well as the CSS style that will be used to format the text.

For a list of available tokens that can be used in the creation of your supporting XML files as well as the editable attributes associated with them, refer to the *DotNetNuke Skinning Guide* by Shaun Walker available at `http://www.dotnetnuke.com`.

The creation of the `BlueHeader.xml` support file for our container follows a similar design pattern with fewer elements. The following is the source code for our `BlueHeader.xml` file.

```
<Objects>
  <Object>
    <Token>[TITLE]</Token>
    <Settings>
      <Setting>
        <Name>CssClass</Name>
        <Value>BBSHead</Value>
      </Setting>
    </Settings>
```

```
    </Object>
    <Object>
      <Token>[CONTENTPANE]</Token>
      <Settings>
        <Setting>
          <Name>ID</Name>
          <Value>ContentPane</Value>
        </Setting>
      </Settings>
    </Object>
  </Objects>
```

Again, we define the content pane that will be used to render modules within our container, with an identical structure as before. It contains a single ID attribute to which we set the value ContentPane. Notice that we omit an object node corresponding to our [SOLPARTACTIONS] token. There are no editable attributes of the [SOLPARTACTIONS] skin object and, as a result, we can omit any supporting XML attribute definitions. The skinning engine will recognize our token and inject the appropriate icon that will generate the module actions drop-down menu when a user hovers over it. Our [TITLE] token contains a settings node named CssClass. This attribute of the user control allows us to set the name of the CSS style that will be used to format the display of our module title text. In our container project, we set it to BBSHead rather than the default value, Head. The reason we do this, is so that we can define a custom style solely for the purpose of formatting the display of a module title within our container.

This leads to the next step in our skin creation process, which deals with the Skin. css and Container.css files that will format our skin elements. The creation of these CSS files is identical for both the HTML and web user control methods of skin development and, as a result, will be treated seperately following the Visual Web Developer example.

Creating a Skin Using Visual Web Developer

To create our skin project using Microsoft's Visual Web Developer Express, we start by opening our DotNetNuke 4.0 local web project. With the project open, we then right-click on the root of our web project and select **New Folder** as illustrated in the following image.

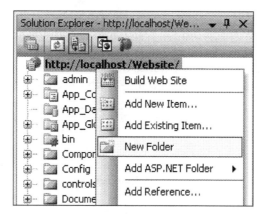

At this point, you will be creating a place for not only this project, but also for all future skin projects, so you will want to give a generic name to this first folder. For example, this folder is named **SkinProjects** and it will be placed at the root directory level of our local web project. Within this folder, we will create another folder that will contain the actual skin project and, to keep our example consistent with the previous method, we will again name the folder **BBS**. Next, we create the standard folders named **Skins**, into which we will place the files and supporting images that manage the look and feel of our pages, and **Containers**, which will hold the files and supporting images that will control the look and feel of the borders around our modules. The following image illustrates how our project will look in Visual Web Developer at this point.

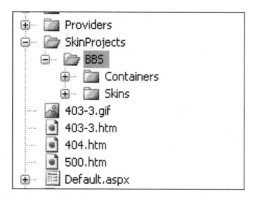

Just as we did in the HTML example, we now fill the **Skins** folder with all the required elements that we will need and then perform the same process for our **Containers** folder. We include all the images that we need as well as our two CSS files named Skin.css and Container.css, which we place into the **Skins** and **Containers** folders respectively.

Unlike in our previous HTML example where we dealt with HTML files, with XML formatting, we will be creating our skin structure within the context of a web user control named `Admin.ascx`. For our Container, we create another web user control named `BlueHeader.ascx` and place it into our **Containers** folder. The following image illustrates how our project would look with the **Skins** folder expanded.

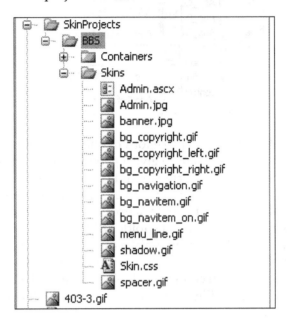

At this point, we are ready to begin working with our web user controls to create our skin structure. We will first walk through the steps of creating the `Admin.ascx` control and then we will turn our attention to the creation of the container web user control, `BlueHeader.ascx`.

Creating the Web User Controls

We will begin process of creating our structure by focussing on a layout that includes a banner at the top with a single content area beneath, just as we did in the example in which we created our skin in an HTML file.

With our target skin in mind, we start by expanding the **HTML** section of our toolbox on the left side of our interface and select the **Table** tool as illustrated in the following image.

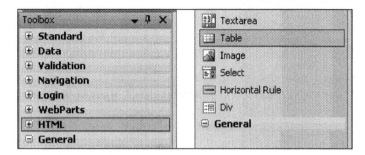

We then drag the **Table** tool onto our page and lay out the cells that will hold our skin objects. Think of this in terms of the home exterior analogy since all we are doing at this point is framing the areas where our skin objects will be placed. Since we are going for a simple layout with a banner across the top, the first part of our layout will handle the placement of the banner image. Immediately following the banner placement, we will create a cell where we will place the menu. Finally, we will create a cell that will serve as the content pane.

The following is the complete source of our `Admin.ascx` file once we have completed the HTML layout and the placement of our skin images.

```
<%@ Control language="vb" CodeBehind="~/admin/Skins/skin.vb"
AutoEventWireup="false" Explicit="True" Inherits="DotNetNuke.UI.Skins.
Skin" %>
<table cellpadding="0" cellspacing="0" border="0" width="100%">
  <tr>
    <td>
      <table cellpadding="0" cellspacing="0" border="0" width="100%">
        <tr>
          <td width="50%" bgcolor="#ffffff"> </td>
          <td width="760" height="70">
            <img src="<%= SkinPath %>banner.jpg"
                                          width="760" height="70">
          </td>
          <td width="50%" bgcolor="#73abe4"> </td>
        </tr>
      </table>
    </td>
  </tr>
  <tr>
```

```
<td background="<%= SkinPath %>bg_navigation.gif" height="30">
  <table cellpadding="0" cellspacing="0"
                                  border="0" align="center">
    <tr><td></td></tr>
  </table>
</td>
</tr>
<tr>
  <td background="<%= SkinPath %>shadow.gif" height="30">
    <img src="<%= SkinPath %>spacer.gif" width="5" height="30">
  </td>
</tr>
<tr>
  <td>
    <table cellpadding="0" cellspacing="0" border="0" width="760">
      <tr>
        <td width="5">
          <img src="<%= SkinPath %>spacer.gif" width="5" height="5">
        </td>
        <td colspan="2"></td>
        <td width="5"><img src="<%= SkinPath %>spacer.gif"
                                  width="5" height="5"></td>
      </tr>
      <tr>
        <td height="10" colspan="4">
          <img src="<%= SkinPath %>spacer.gif"
                                      height="10" width="5">
        </td>
      </tr>
      <tr>
        <td width="5" height="32" background="<%= SkinPath
                          %>bg_copyright.gif" align="left">
          <img src="<%= SkinPath %>bg_copyright_left.gif"
                                      width="5" height="32">
        </td>
        <td width="375" height="32"
                  background="<%= SkinPath %>bg_copyright.gif"></td>
        <td width="375" height="32"
                  background="<%= SkinPath %>bg_copyright.gif"></td>
        <td width="5" height="32" background="<%= SkinPath
                          %>bg_copyright.gif" align="right">
          <img src="<%= SkinPath %>bg_copyright_right.gif"
                                      width="5" height="32">
        </td>
      </tr>
    </table>
```

```
    </td>
  </tr>
  <tr>
    <td height="10"><img src="<%= SkinPath %>spacer.gif"
                                        height="10" width="5"></td>
  </tr>
</table>
```

While the format of our web user control is very similar to the HTML file that we created in our previous example, there are a couple of notable differences that should be mentioned. One occurs at the very first line of our Admin.ascx file.

```
<%@ Control language="vb" CodeBehind="~/admin/Skins/skin.vb"
AutoEventWireup="false" Explicit="True" Inherits="DotNetNuke.UI.Skins.
Skin" %>
```

In an ordinary web user control, this line would refer to the specific Visual Basic code-behind page associated with the control itself. In this case, it refers to a generic skin.vb class, which provides the glue between the portal architecture and our Admin.ascx web user control. This directive is required for our page to be able to interact with the DotNetNuke 4.0 portal framework.

Another difference is the inlusion of the <%= SkinPath %> server variable associated with every image in the file. This variable is evaluated as the path to the skin's directory and it allows us to use the relative image source path just like our previous HTML example.

Placing the Skin Objects

Once we are happy with the layout of our file and the placement of our images, we are ready to actually place the skin objects into the cells of our web user control. In our DotNetNuke web project, we expand the **~/admin/skins** folder as shown in the following illustration.

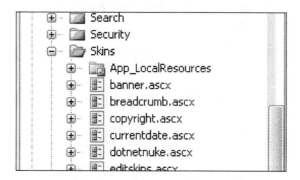

Within this folder, we find the physical web user controls that correspond to the skin objects we wish to use in our skin. Since we have created our `Admin.ascx` file within the DotNetNuke web project in Visual Web Developer, we are able to simply drag the chosen controls from the **Skins** folder into the desired cells in our layout.

Beginning with the `Admin.ascx` file, we start dragging our required elements onto our layout. We need the door that allows for access to the administrative interface of our site so we drag the `login.ascx` web user control onto our layout. We also need a directory that tells our visitors how to navigate within our site, so we drag the `solpartmenu.ascx` web user control from the `~/admin/skins` folder and place it into the desired cell on our layout. The following illustrates how our file looks at this point.

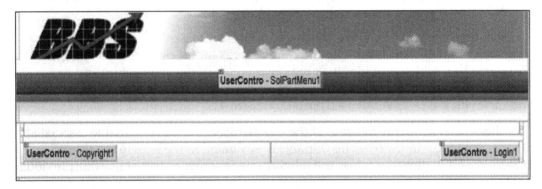

Also notice that we have placed an additional skin object on our page that corresponds to a copyright. This control will allow a site administrator to change the copyright display on the site via the back-end interface.

We still have one last required element to place within our file. We need a window in which to render content. Scanning the list of files in our `~/admin/skins` directory reveals that our content pane does not exist as a formal web user control. So how do we add it? The following code segment illustrates how we indicate the location of our content pane within our skin.

```
<table cellpadding="0" cellspacing="0" border="0" width="760">
  <tr>
    <td width="5">
      <img src="<%= SkinPath %>spacer.gif" width="5" height="5">
    </td>
    <td colspan="2" id="ContentPane" runat="Server"></td>
    <td width="5"><img src="<%= SkinPath %>spacer.gif"
                                   width="5" height="5"></td>
  </tr>
```

Once we have established where we would like the content to go, we add two attributes to the table cell. We add the `runat="Server"` attribute so that the server can inject content into the cell and we add the `id="ContentPane"` attribute so that our portal application has a way to reference our pane.

At this point, we have completed our `Admin.ascx` file and can now turn our attention to creating the container that will fit within the look and feel of our custom skin.

Placing the Container Objects

Again we start with a basic layout for our `BlueHeader.ascx` file that corresponds to the following image.

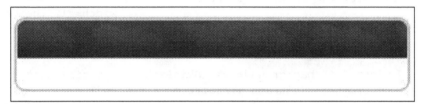

The web user controls corresponding to the skin objects that we can place in our container reside in the `~/admin/containers` folder. Using that same method we used for our skin elements, we drag our container user controls from the `~/admin/containers` folder and place them into the desired table cells in our `BlueHeader.ascx` file. This time, let us examine the contents of the `BlueHeader.ascx` file after our skin objects have been added to better understand what is going on behind the scenes when we drag and drop our skin object onto our web user control.

```
<!--<%@ Control language="vb"
              CodeBehind="~/admin/Containers/container.vb"
              AutoEventWireup="false" Explicit="True"
              Inherits="DotNetNuke.UI.Containers.Container" %>-->
                    <%@ Register TagPrefix="uc1" TagName="Title"
         Src="admin/Containers/Title.ascx" %>
            <%@ Register TagPrefix="uc1" TagName="SolPartActions"
         Src="admin/Containers/SolPartActions.ascx" %>
            <table style="BORDER-COLLAPSE: collapse" cellpadding="0"
      cellspacing="0" width="100%" border="0">
    <tr>
      <td valign="top" colspan="5"><img src="<%= SkinPath
                            %>spacer.gif" height="10" width="5"></td>
    </tr>
    <tr>
      <td width="12" height="30" align="left">
```

```
        <img src="<%= SkinPath %>top_left_blue.gif"
                                    width="12" height="30">
    </td>
    <td height="20" valign="middle" background="<%= SkinPath
                                %>top_blue_bg.gif" nowrap>
     <uc1:SolPartActions id="SolPartActions1"
                        runat="server"></uc1:SolPartActions>
    </td>
    <td height="20" valign="middle" background="<%= SkinPath
                %>top_blue_bg.gif" width="100%" align="center" nowrap>
     <uc1:Title id="Title1" runat="server"></uc1:Title>
    </td>
    <td width="12" height="30" align="right">
      <img src="<%= SkinPath %>top_right_blue.gif"
                                    width="12" height="30">
    </td>
  </tr>
  <tr>
    <td width="12" background="<%= SkinPath %>left_tile.gif">
      <img src="<%= SkinPath %>spacer.gif" width="12"
                                        height="5" border="0">
    </td>
    <td colspan="2" bgcolor="#ffffff">
      <img src="<%= SkinPath %>spacer.gif" height="10"
                                        width="5" border="0">
    </td>
    <td width="12" background="<%= SkinPath %>right_tile.gif">
      <img src="<%= SkinPath %>spacer.gif" width="12"
                                        height="5" border="0">
    </td>
  </tr>
  <tr>
    <td width="12" background="<%= SkinPath %>left_tile.gif">
      <img src="<%= SkinPath %>spacer.gif" width="12"
                                        height="5" border="0">
    </td>
    <td colspan="2" bgcolor="#ffffff" id="ContentPane"
                                        runat="server"></td>
    <td width="12" background="<%= SkinPath %>right_tile.gif">
      <img src="<%= SkinPath %>spacer.gif" width="12"
                                        height="5" border="0">
    </td>
  </tr>
  <tr>
    <td width="12" height="10">
      <img src="<%= SkinPath %>bottom_left_corner.gif"
                                        width="12" height="10">
```

```
      </td>
      <td colspan="2" background="<%= SkinPath %>bottom_tile.gif">
        <img src="<%= SkinPath %>spacer.gif" height="10" width="5">
      </td>
      <td width="12" height="10">
        <img src="<%= SkinPath %>bottom_right_corner.gif"
                                              width="12" height="10">
      </td>
    </tr>
    <tr>
      <td valign="top" colspan="5"><img src="<%= SkinPath
                        %>spacer.gif" height="5" width="5"></td>
    </tr>
  </table>
```

Recall that in our HTML example, we used a combination of HTML and XML to format the look of our skin objects. In our Visual Web Developer example, dragging the skin objects directly onto our container structure means we are able to interact directly with the attributes that contribute to the display of the skin objects without the need for a corresponding XML file. The following code segment illustrates how we can add a custom CSS style, named BBSHead just as in our HTML example, to our title control. The name and value pair that we used to create nodes in our XML file previously now becomes a more direct attribute name and value pair as seen below.

```
<td height="20" valign="middle" background="<%= SkinPath
            %>top_blue_bg.gif" width="100%" align="center" nowrap>
  <ucl:Title id="Title1" cssclass="BBSHead"
                                    runat="server"></ucl:Title>
</td>
```

In addition to the title control, we need to place the control that will allow us to interact with the administrative settings of any module rendered within our container. The following code segment illustrates how this is accomplished in our source.

```
<td height="20" valign="middle"
                  background="<%= SkinPath %>top_blue_bg.gif" nowrap>
  <ucl:SolPartActions id="SolPartActions1"
                              runat="server"></ucl:SolPartActions>
</td>
```

Now that we have a control placed that will render module titles and a way to access the module settings, we still need to designate a spot for the actual module contents. We accomplish this by editing the source of our BlueHeader.ascx file so that the code segment containing the table cell that will be our content pane looks like the following.

```
<td colspan="2" bgcolor="#ffffff"
                    id="ContentPane" runat="server"></td>
```

The following image illustrates how our `BlueHeader.ascx` web user control will look in design mode.

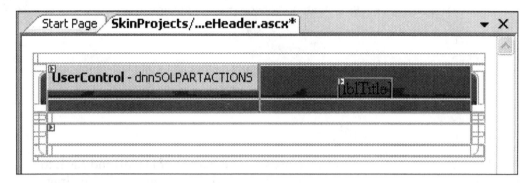

Our container now has all of the required elements in place. This leads us to the final step in the process before packaging and deployment. It is the step in which we fine-tune the visual presentation of our skin and add the last bit of customization.

Creating the Cascading Style Sheets

At this point, whether you have used the HTML method of creating your skin project in Dreamweaver, or you have used Visual Web Developer to interact with the skin objects directly, you now need to format the various text elements so that they look visually appealing and support the overall look and feel of your site. The best way that we can approach the daunting task of creating styles for all the various default administrator elements and content panes as well as our skin objects, is by agreeing on a common starting point upon which we can add our customizations. To that end, we copy the contents of the CSS file found within the `~/portals/_default/Skins/default.css` file into our own `Skin.css` file.

The `default.css` file contains all the necessary formatting for the DotNetNuke framework to display the administrative controls and default objects. This simplifies our development process a great deal by allowing us to focus only on the styles that concern our skin. In both our `Admin.htm` and `Admin.ascx` files, we included a login object, a main menu, and a single content pane. The following is a portion of the source code from our `Skin.css` file, which deals specifically with our skin objects.

```
.Normal {
  Font-weight: normal;
  Font-size: 12px;
  COLOR: #000000;
```

```
     Line-height: 16px;
     Font-style: normal;
     Font-family: Arial, Helvetica, sans-serif;
}
.MainMenu_MenuContainer {
   background-color: #4D75A3;
}
.MainMenu_MenuBar {
   cursor: pointer;
   cursor: hand;
   height:30;
   background-color: #4D75A3;
   background: url(bg_navigation.gif) repeat-x;
}
.MainMenu_MenuItem {
   cursor: pointer;
   cursor: hand;
   color: #FFFFFF;
   font-family: Tahoma, Arial, Helvetica, sans-serif;
   font-size: 11px;
   font-weight: bold;
   font-style: normal;
   background-color: #4D75A3;
}
.MainMenu_MenuIcon {
   cursor: pointer;
   cursor: hand;
   background-color: #4D75A3;
   border-left: #4D75A3 1px solid;
   border-bottom: #4D75A3 1px solid;
   border-top: #4D75A3 1px solid;
   text-align: center;
   width: 15;
   height: 30;
}
.MainMenu_SubMenu {
   z-index: 1000;
   cursor: pointer;
   cursor: hand;
   background-color: #4D75A3;
   filter:progid:DXImageTransform.Microsoft.Shadow(color='DimGray',
   Direction=135, Strength=3);
   border-bottom: #294363 1px solid;
   border-left: #294363 1px solid;
```

```
    border-top: #294363 1px solid;
    border-right: #294363 1px solid;
  }
.MainMenu_MenuItemSel {
  cursor: pointer;
  cursor: hand;
  color: #FFFFFF;
  height: 30;
  font-family: Tahoma, Arial, Helvetica, sans-serif;
  font-size: 11px;
  font-weight: bold;
  font-style: normal;
  background-color: #4D75A3;
  background: url(bg_navitem_on.gif) repeat-x;
  }
.MainMenu_ItemActive {
  cursor: pointer;
  cursor: hand;
  color: #FFFFFF;
  height: 30;
  font-family: Tahoma, Arial, Helvetica, sans-serif;
  font-size: 11px;
  font-weight: bold;
  font-style: normal;
  background-color: #4D75A3;
  background: url(bg_navitem_on.gif) repeat-x;
  }
.FooterText {
  height: 30px;
  padding-left: 10px;
  font-family: Tahoma, Arial, Helvetica, sans-serif;
  font-size: 10px;
  color: #454545;
  line-height: 28px;
  }
A.FooterText:link,  A.FooterText:visited,   A.FooterText:active   {
    text-decoration:    none;
    color:#454545;
  }
A.FooterText:hover     {
    text-decoration:    underline;
    color:#454545;
  }
```

The .normal CSS class is used to format all the default text in our site. Therefore, it is important that we define a text class that supports the overall look of our site. In our case, we define our default text to be preferrably Arial.

The next group of CSS classes deal with our main menu skin object. The real beauty of the main menu provided as a skin object in DotNetNuke lies in its enormous level of customizability. As can be seen in the CSS source file, we have the ability to control the display of the menu as a whole, via the .MainMenu_MenuContainer and .MainMenu_MenuBar classes, as well as the the sub-menu, via the .MainMenu_SubMenu class. In addition, classes like .MainMenu_MenuItem and .MainMenu_MenuItemSel give you the ability to customize the look of each individual menu element.

The last group of CSS styles deals with the display of our login skin object. In our example, we create a custom class called FooterText that is not included in the default CSS file. This gives us the freedom to alter the text style of our login control without worrying that we are inadvertantly changing other elements in our skin.

To really explore the power of CSS styles, we would have to spend a great deal of time discussing the nature of the connection between CSS and the way our pages are rendered. For our purposes, however, we will focus on the concepts that pertain to DotNetNuke's interaction with CSS and how this interaction is involved in our skinning project.

If you recall, in our Admin.xml file, we included setting nodes that associated the attributes of the SolPartMenu Web User Control with these CSS styles. By associating the attributes of the Web User Control this way, or by setting the attributes directly if we are working with the .ASCX files, we gain the ability to manipulate the look of our skin via these style classes. The next concept we need to be aware of is the way DotNetNuke utilizes the cascading nature of CSS styles. In our package, we created a Skin.css file but could have just as easily created an Admin.css file specifically for our page. But what would happen if we created and included both?

To answer that question, we need to examine DotNetNuke's inclusion chain. Assuming we had a Skin.css file and an Admin.css file, the hierarchy of CSS files that would be included into our page would be Default.css | Skin.css | Admin. css | Portal.css. What this means is that the first set of class definitions our page sees are contained in Default.css, the file we used to start our Skin.css in our example. The next thing that DotNetNuke will place in the chain is the generic Skin. css file if one exists followed by the page-specific CSS file named Admin.css. In this way, specific CSS files for pages supersede the generic Skin.css definitions since the styles in Admin.css are seen after those in generic CSS file and therefore are applied after those in Skins.css. The last CSS file in the chain is an important one. If we had styles we wanted to preserve throughout all of our portals in our DotNetNuke installation, then we would define them here. The file, itself, is found in the same directory as `Default.css`, but unlike `Default.css`, it is included at the very end of the chain and is therefore seen and applied last to our pages. To start out with, the `Portal.css` file is empty just like `Default.css`.

Now let us turn our attention to our container. We follow a similar process for creating the `Container.css` file associated with our `BlueHeader` container. The complete source code for the `Container.css` file is presented here.

```
.BBSHead    {
    font-family: Tahoma, Arial, Helvetica;
    font-size: 11px;
    font-weight: bold;
    color: #FFFFFF;
}
```

In both the `BlueHeader.htm` and `BlueHeader.ascx` files, we define a custom style called `BBSHead` for the formatting of the module title that will reside in our container. Alternatively, we could have defined this style within our `Skin.css` file and ommitted our `Container.css` file from our project entirely. Functionally, the end result would be the same; however, when a skin package starts to include many different custom styles, it is easier to distinguish the styles that deal with our skin from those that deal with our container if they are in separate files.

Just as in our Skin example, the CSS files associated with our container are included in a standard sequence. Let us assume we included both a generic `Container.css` file along with a specific `BlueHeader.css` file in our package. The full stylesheet sequence we would have rendered on our page, inlcuding our files from our Skin exmaple, would be `Default.css | Skins.css | Admin.css | Containers.css | BlueHeader.css | Portal.css`. This allows specific container stylesheets to supersede generic stylesheets.

Creating the Skin Package

Now we have arrived at the stage where we can bring it all together and build a package to be uploaded into our DotNetNuke portal application. Before we get to the packaging, however, we still have one last item to include in order to fully flesh-out our skin package. We will need an image to serve as a thumbnail preview for both our skin and our container. The thumbnail file is not required, but if we really want to let our users know that the skin is well made, then we probably would not want them to see a generic **Image not available** graphic when they try to choose our new skin. We associate thumbnail images to the pages and containers they represent by following a consistent naming convention. In our project, we will include two files, one in our Skins folder named `Admin.jpg`, while the other will reside in the Containers folder and be named `BlueHeader.jpg`. The `Admin.jpg` image serves as a preview of our `Admin.htm` or `Admin.ascx` file. Similarly, the `BlueHeader.jpg` image serves a preview of our `BlueHeader` container. The most common method of creating these thumbnail images is to preview the skin in a browser and grab a desktop screen capture. The thing to keep in mind as you create your thumbnail images is the fact that in the end, it will be rendered as a 150x112 image.

So, now we truly have all the pieces to our skinning puzzle complete. The following figure illustrates how both of our projects look at this point.

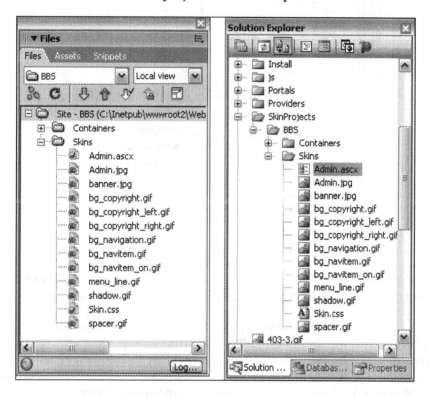

The next step is the actual physical packaging process. We begin this process by browsing our computer and navigating to the directory where our skin project is located. Once we arrive at our skin project root directory, we open up the **Skins** folder and send all of the contents to a ZIP file named `Skins`.

This step is illustrated in the following image. Pay particular attention to the fact that the files within the directory are being zipped rather than zipping the entire `Skins` folder.

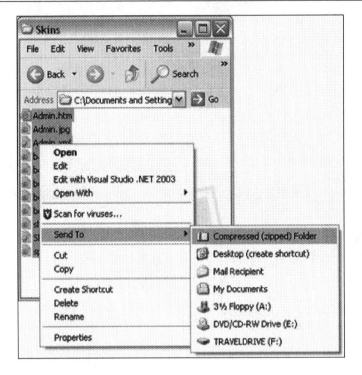

Once the new ZIP file is created, we go back and change the name to `Skins.zip`. In order to keep our project well organized we will then cut and paste this ZIP file one level higher in our folder hierarchy. This `Skins.zip` file is one of the two components that will make up our complete skin deployment package.

To create the second component of our skin deployment package, we perform a similar process with the files within our **Containers** folder. Again, we take special care to ensure that we zip the contents of the directory rather than zipping the actual folder. Once the ZIP file is created and renamed to `Containers.zip`, we cut and paste the file one level higher into the root directory of our project.

The last step we take before we are ready to deploy our skin is the creation of the complete skin package. To do this we create a new ZIP file within the root directory of our project and give it a name. This is the name that will be used to refer to our skin when users are presented with a list of skin choices to apply to the whole site or an individual page. In our example, we will call our skin package `BBS.zip`. We then drag and drop both the `Skins.zip` file and `Containers.zip` file onto our package file. While placing ZIP files within ZIP files is uncommon, the DotNetNuke skinning engine was designed to handle packages created in this way. The following illustrates how our project root directory will look at this point.

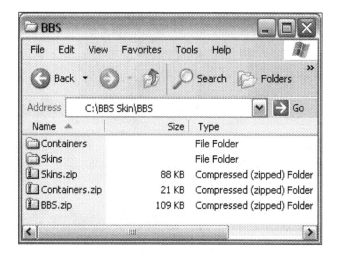

Now we have a complete skin package that is ready to be uploaded and applied to our DotNetNuke portal. We begin by hovering over the **Host** main menu selection; notice that there is an entry titled **Skins** at the very bottom of the sub-menu dropdown. Clicking on this selection brings up the following display.

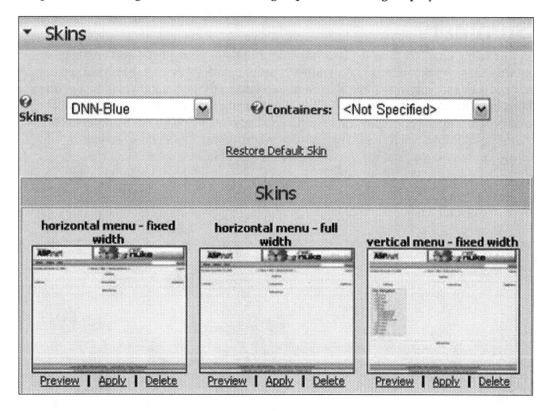

By hovering over the module action menu, we can choose **Upload Skin** from the list of available actions. This will take us to the **Upload Skin Package** display illustrated in the following image.

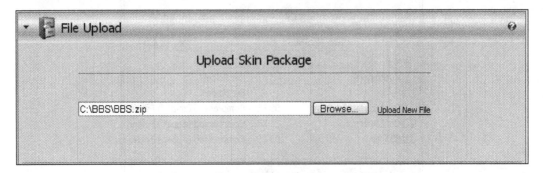

Now we can **Browse** for our skin package and **Add** it to the file list box as shown. We then click on **Upload New File** and check the status report for any errors in the upload. If all goes well, we can now return to the Skins page under our host menu and apply our skin just as we did earlier in the chapter.

Summary

In preceding chapters, you learned how to administer your portal and create custom modules. Now you not only know how to upload and apply a custom skin package to your site, but you now have also been exposed to the entire skin creation process both from the point of view of a web designer using Dreamweaver, and from that of a programmer working in the Visual Web Developer design environment. The skinning building blocks are simple and straightforward in terms of structure, but allow for an endless amount of variation in terms of how your site can look.

10
Deploying Your DNN Portal

Once your portal is looking the way you want it to, it is time to share your creation with the rest of the world. We want to transfer our site from our local computer and set it up on the World Wide Web.

When you are done with this chapter, you will know the following:

- How to obtain a domain name for your site
- What to look for in a hosting provider
- How to modify your files to prepare for moving to a host
- How to set up your database on a hosted site
- What file permissions are needed for your site to run

Acquiring a Domain Name

One of the most exciting parts of starting a website is acquiring a domain name. When selecting the perfect name, there are a few things that you need to keep in mind:

- **Keep it brief**: The more letters that a user has to type in to get to your site the more difficult it is going to be for them to remember your site. The name you select will help to brand your site. If it is catchy then people will remember it more readily.

- **Have alternative names in mind**: As time goes on, great domain names are becoming fewer and fewer. Make sure you have a few alternatives to choose from. The first domain name you had in mind may already be taken so having a backup plan will help when you decide to purchase a name.

- **Consider buying additional top-level domain names**: Say you've already bought www.DanielsDoughnuts.com. You might want to purchase www.DanielsDoughnuts.net as well to protect your name.

Once you have decided on the name you want for your domain, you will need to register it. There are dozens of different sites that allow you to register your domain name as well as search to see if it is available. Some of the better-known domain-registration sites are `Register.com` and `NetworkSolutions.com`. Both of these have been around a long time and have good reputations. You can also look into some of the discount registers like BulkRegister (`http://www.BulkRegister.com`) or Enom (`http://www.enom.com`).

After deciding on your domain name and having it registered, you will need to find a place to physically host your portal. Most registration services will also provide the ability to host your site with them but it is best to search for a provider that fits your site's needs.

Finding a Hosting Provider

When deciding on a provider to host your portal, you will need to consider a few things:

- **Cost**: This is of course one of the most important things to look at when looking for a provider. There are usually a few plans to select from. The basic plan usually allows you a certain amount of disk space for a very small price but has you share the server with numerous other websites. Most providers also offer dedicated (you get the server all to yourself) and semi-dedicated (you share with a few others). It is usually best to start with the basic plan and move up if the traffic on your site requires it.

- **Windows servers**: The provider you select needs to have Windows Server 2000/2003 running IIS (Internet Information Services). Some hosts run alternatives to Microsoft like Linux and Apache web server.

- **.NET framework**: The provider's servers need to have the .NET framework version 2.0 installed. Most hosts have installed the framework on their servers, but not all. Make sure this is available because DotNetNuke needs this to run. If they only have the 1.1 framework installed then you will need to use a 3.x version of DotNetNuke.

- **Database availability**: You will need database server availability to run DotNetNuke and Microsoft SQL Server is the preferred back end. If the hosting provider supports it, SQL Express is also an option, although it will be limited to 4GB and 1 CPU.

- **FTP access**: You will need a way to post your DotNetNuke portal files to your site and the easiest way is to use FTP. Make sure that your host provides this option.

- **Email server**: A great deal of functionality associated with the DotNetNuke portal relies on being able to send out emails to users. Make sure that you will have the availability of an email server.

- **Folder rights**: The ASPNET or NetworkService Account (depending on server) will need to have full permissions to the root and subfolders for your DotNetNuke application to run correctly. Make sure that your host either provides you with the ability to set this or is willing to set this up for you. We will discuss the exact steps later in this chapter.

The good news is that you will have plenty of hosting providers to choose from and it should not break the bank. Try to find one that fits all of your needs. There are even some hosts (`www.WebHost4life.com`) that will install DotNetNuke for you free of charge. They host many DotNetNuke sites and are familiar with the needs of the portal.

Preparing Your Local Site

Once you have your domain name and a provider to host your portal, you will need to get your local site ready to be uploaded to your remote server. This is not difficult, but make sure you cover all of the following steps for a smooth transition.

1. Modify the compilation debug setting in the `web.config` file: You will need to modify your `web.config` file to match the configuration of the server to which you will be sending your files. The first item that needs to be changed is the debug configuration. This should be set to `false`. You should also rebuild your application in release mode before uploading. This will remove the debug tokens, perform optimizations in the code, and help the site to run faster:

   ```
   <!-- set debugmode to false for running application -->
   <compilation debug="false" />
   ```

2. Modify the data-provider information in the `web.config` file: You will need to change the information for connecting to the database so that it will now point to the server on your host. There are three things to look out for in this section:

   ° First, if you are using MS SQL, make sure `SqlDataProvider` is set up as the default provider.

   ° Second, change the connection string to reflect the database server address, the database name (if *not* `DotNetNuke`), as well as the user ID and password for the database that you received from your provider. This can be found in the `<connectionStrings>` section and in the `<appSettings>` section of the `web.config` file. Make sure you change it in both places.

- ° Third, if you will be using an existing database to run the DotNetNuke portal, add an `objectQualifier`. This will append whatever you place in the quotations to the beginning of all of the tables and procedures that are created for your database.

```
<data defaultProvider="SqlDataProvider">
    <providers>
      <clear/>
        <add name = "SqlDataProvider"
          type = "DotNetNuke.Data.SqlDataProvider,
              DotNetNuke.SqlDataProvider"
          connectionStringname = "SiteSqlServer"
          providerPath =
              "~\Providers\DataProviders\SqlDataProvider\"
        objectQualifier = "DE"
        databaseOwner = "dbo"
          upgradeConnectionString = ""
          />
```

3. Modify any custom changes in the `web.config` file.

4. Add your new domain name to your portal alias: Since DotNetNuke has the ability to run multiple portals we need to tell it which domain name is associated with our current portal. To do this we need to sign on as Host (not Admin) and navigate to **Admin | Site Settings** on the main menu. If signed on as Host, you will see a **Portal Aliases** section on the bottom of the page. Click on the **Add New HTTP Alias** link:

5. Add your site alias into the **HTTP Alias** box and click on **Update** to finish:

6. Configure your application to work with the .NET framework 1.1: If you enter HTML into a textbox while using the 1.1 version of the .NET framework, you may get an error message "**A potentially dangerous Request.Form value was detected...**". To stop this from occurring, set the `validateRequest` attribute in the `web.config` file to `false`:

```
<pages enableViewStateMac="true" validateRequest="false" />
```

Now the code files for your DotNetNuke installation are ready to post to your hosted server. Before that can happen, you need to set up the database on the server.

Setting Up the Database

Many hosting services still use SQL Server 2000, so we will be using Microsoft's Enterprise Manager to accomplish this task. There are a few ways to get your database set up on the remote server. It all depends on how you want to start your site on the hosted server. If you have set up your localhost site by applying skins, adding modules, and installing forums, generally setting it up how you want to see it on the Web, you probably do not want to have to recreate this information when you post it to your hosted account. On the other hand, you may want to just get DotNetNuke up and running on the hosted server and then set it up how you want it.

We will cover both methods. We covered this when we set up our site locally, but if you set up a fresh install of DotNetNuke on the hosted server, it is important that you change the default Admin and Host passwords as soon as you have it running.

Backup and Restore Database

Since most hosting services still use SQL 2000, we will be using Microsoft's Enterprise Manager to accomplish this task. If you do not have access to these tools or if you have been using MSDE for you local server there are tools that you can use to accomplish the same tasks. You can use free tools such as DbaMgr (`http://www.asql.biz/DbaMgr.shtm`) or the command-line interface with Microsoft's osql utility (`http://msdn.microsoft.com/library/default.asp?url =/library/en-us/coprompt/cp_osql_1wxl.asp`). Either way, the basic concepts of this procedure will be the same.

If you want to keep the information and setup that is located in your local database, you will need to make a backup copy of the database. To begin, open **Enterprise Manager**, drill down on the **(local)** server, and open up the `Databases` folder. Look for `DotNetNuke` and right-click on it to bring up the menu. Select **All Tasks** and **Backup Database** to begin the back-up procedure.

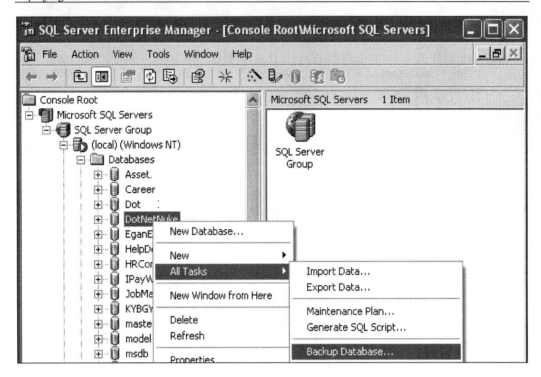

On the **General** tab, leave all the default settings and click on **Add**. In the **File Name** box, enter the location where you would like the backup saved and fill in a name for your backup. It is common to put an extension of .bak at the end of the file name, but it is not necessary. Click on the **OK** button on the **Select Backup Destination** dialog and then click on **OK** again on the **General** tab. You will receive a message when the backup completes successfully.

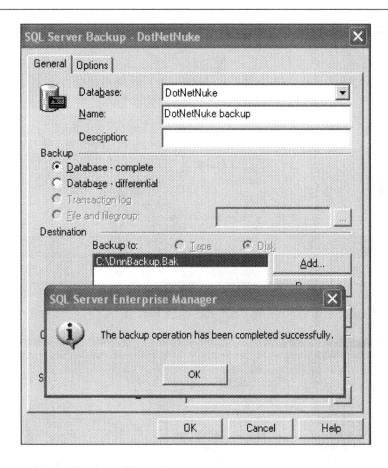

What you do with the backup file will depend on your hosting provider. Some providers give you the ability to do backup and restore operations on your own; other providers will do the restore for you. Contact your provider to find out how you can restore the database on its server.

Build New Database

If you would like to start your site from scratch on your hosted web server, you will need to manually create the database that will hold the tables and stored procedures needed to run DotNetNuke. This procedure will differ depending on your provider. Some may give you web access to your database; others will allow you to use Enterprise Manager to connect to your database server. We will be using the Enterprise Manager to accomplish this task. To get to Enterprise Manager, click on the **Start** button, go to **Programs | Microsoft SQL Server | Enterprise Manager**. Drill down on the (**local**) server by clicking on the plus (**+**) signs, right-click on Databases, and select **New Database**.

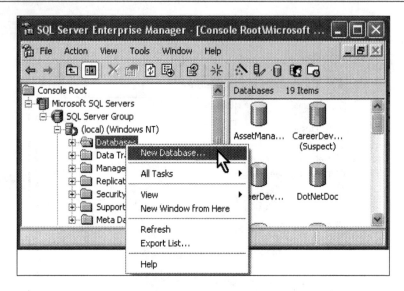

Type **DotNetNuke** into the name field and click **OK**.

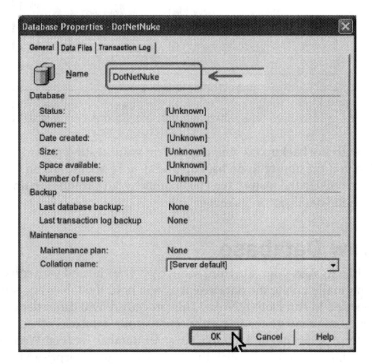

It will take a few moments for your database to be created. This will generate the system tables and stored procedures. The actual tables and procedures needed to run DotNetNuke will be created when you navigate to your portal for the first time.

> Note that the `web.config` connection strings that we
> discussed earlier will need to be set properly for this
> to work.

FTP Your Files

The easiest way to transfer your files from your local computer to the hosted server is to use File Transfer Protocol (FTP). You will need to obtain the location of your FTP account from your hosting provider. Once you have this information, you can use any number of tools to send your files. FrontPage XP and Macromedia Dreamweaver both have tools available to FTP files. You can also find free FTP programs such as FTP Commander (`http://www.vista.ru/2inter.htm`) or SmartFTP (`http://www.smartftp.com/download/`), which will also help you transfer your files. Once you have uploaded your files to the server, you need to give the appropriate file permissions for your portal to work correctly.

The file permissions needed for your portal will differ slightly depending on the type of server on which your account will be hosted.

If your portal will be hosted on a Windows 2000 server using IIS5, the **{NameOfServer}/ASPNET** user account must have read, write, and change control of the root application directory (this allows the application to create files and folders). This will be the directory that holds all of your files. Your provider will know the folder that needs permissions as it'll be setting up the virtual directory.

If your portal will be hosted on a Windows 2003 server using IIS6, the **{NameOfServer }/NetworkService** user account must have read, write, and change control of the root application directory.

Some providers give you the ability to set these permissions yourself; others will need to set the permissions for you.

Once the file permissions are set, all that is needed to complete the setup is to navigate to your site. If you are starting from scratch, your database tables and stored procedures will be created and you are ready to start adding content to your portal. As with any software installation, we have not covered all the issues that can arise. If you run into any issues during installation, make a descriptive post in the DotNetNuke forums for additional help (`http://www.asp.net/forums/showforum.aspx?forumid=90`).

Summary

In this chapter, we covered the steps necessary to take the site you created from your local machine and post it for everyone to see on the World Wide Web. The tasks needed to accomplish this are not difficult, but may require the assistance of your host provider. With our portal up and running, we will discuss how to run multiple portals from one DotNetNuke installation.

11

Creating Multiple Portals

One of the more compelling reasons to use DotNetNuke is the capability to create multiple portals off one installation of DotNetNuke. All of the portals will share one database, which makes portal backup easy. In this chapter, you will learn the following:

- Why you would want to create multiple portals
- How child portals differ from parent portals
- How to set up multiple portals
- How to create a portal template
- How to use the Site Wizard to update your site

In this chapter, you will see what different types of portals are available to you, how to use the wizard to set up your portal, and how to create templates so you never have to duplicate your work.

Multiple Portals

Before we get into how to set up multiple portals, let's understand what is meant by multiple portals and why they are important. In a typical web-hosting environment, you purchase a domain name and contact a hosting provider to host your site. In normal situations, this is a one-to-one arrangement. If you then want to host another website, you follow the process again, creating another hosting account, with additional fees, and set up your site.

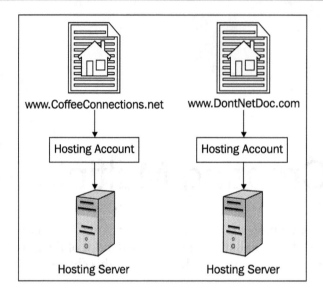

This can become time-consuming and expensive. Although this can be avoided by either spending more money to get a dedicated hosting account (you have full access to the server) or by creating sub-domains and pointing to subfolders on your site, it will take some technical knowledge on your part, and, if you use sub-domains, could get kind of messy. DotNetNuke solves this dilemma by allowing you to create multiple portals easily using a single hosting account.

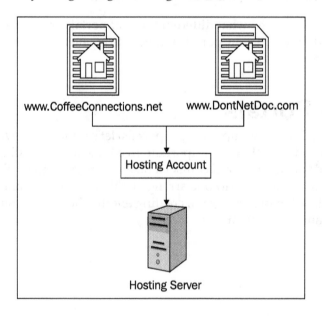

So why would you need multiple portals? Well let's say that you have your portal up and running, and then get a great idea for a second site dedicated to the "World of Chocolate". And then your spouse decides to sell hand-made crafts and needs a website to do it. Finally, during a family dinner you decide you want to put up a website dedicated to your family tree.

Normally you would need to create separate hosting accounts, build the site, design the look and feel, add the needed functionality, set up the database, and finally post your site on the Web. This could take you weeks or months to set up, and the costs would be proportional to the number of sites you needed.

When you have a DotNetNuke portal up and running, there are no additional costs to create additional portals, and with the help of wizards and templates in DotNetNuke, you could have these sites up in a matter of hours or days.

 It is important to note that when considering the costs of multiple portals, you need to take into account the amount of traffic each one will have. Most web-hosting services sell plans based on the disk usage of your site. This may require you to purchase a plan that accommodates more traffic.

Parent Portals versus Child Portals

Parent portals are sites that are defined by a unique URL (`www.CoffeeConnections.net`, `www.e-coffeehouse.com`, etc.). Parent portals allow you to run multiple sites from the same host and same DotNetNuke installation. This means that each domain name is unique but points to the same location. DotNetNuke handles how to route the requests depending on which domain name is entered.

Child portals, on the other hand, are sub-portals related to your main portal and share the domain name of their parent. A directory is created on your web server allowing the portal to be accessed through a URL address that includes a parent name and the directory name combined (say `www.CoffeeConnections.net/TestingPortal`).

Setting up a Parent Portal

The first thing that needs to be done before you attempt to set up a parent portal is to purchase a domain name. As discussed in the previous chapter, this can be done through many different providers. In working with `CoffeeConnections.net`, we have realized that the sale of coffee-unique coffee beans has grown into a nice-sized side business. To help this part of the company grow without overshadowing the original concept, we have decided to have a companion portal called e-Coffeehouse.com.

Registering Your Domain and Setting the DNS

Setting up multiple portals on a DNN site does not mean that we have to share the same name as the original portal. So, to give our new portal its own name, we need to purchase a domain name. When you purchase the domain name, you will need to tell it *which* domain name server (DNS) to point to. You will need to set up a primary and secondary DNS. The following screenshot shows an example of this when registering a domain name on the Network Solutions website.

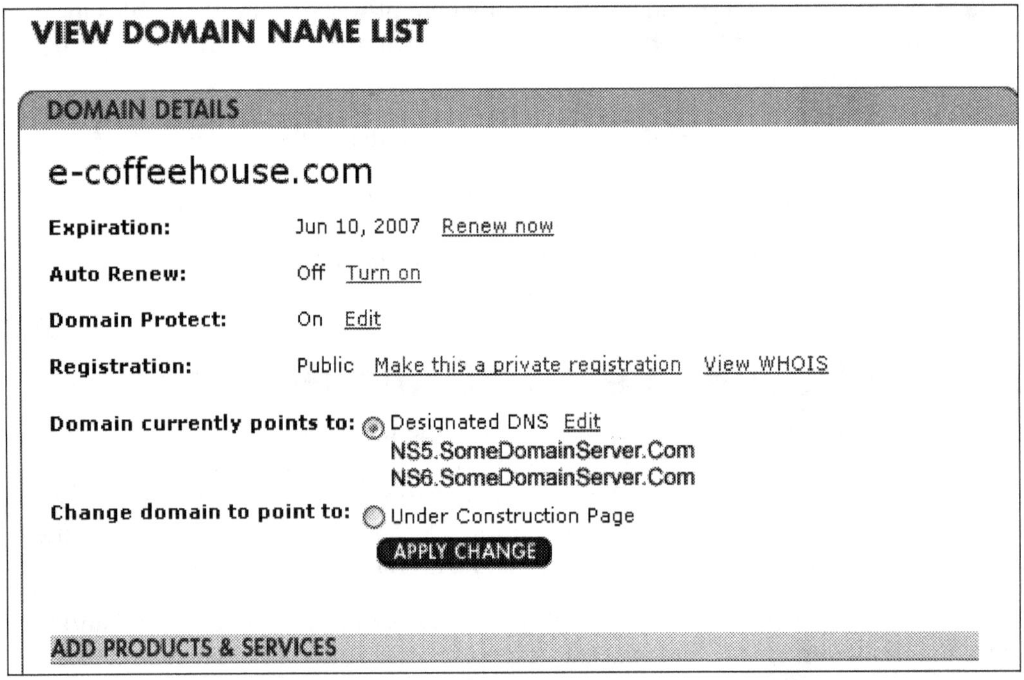

VIEW DOMAIN NAME LIST

DOMAIN DETAILS

e-coffeehouse.com

Expiration:	Jun 10, 2007 Renew now
Auto Renew:	Off Turn on
Domain Protect:	On Edit
Registration:	Public Make this a private registration View WHOIS
Domain currently points to:	⦿ Designated DNS Edit
	NS5.SomeDomainServer.Com
	NS6.SomeDomainServer.Com
Change domain to point to:	◯ Under Construction Page
	APPLY CHANGE

ADD PRODUCTS & SERVICES

To get your domain server information, you will need to contact the company that is hosting your site to find out the name of your DNS server as well as adding your new domain name to your hosting account.

Most hosting providers will have a control panel that will allow you to add your domain names and find your DNS. The next screenshot shows an example of this type of screen.

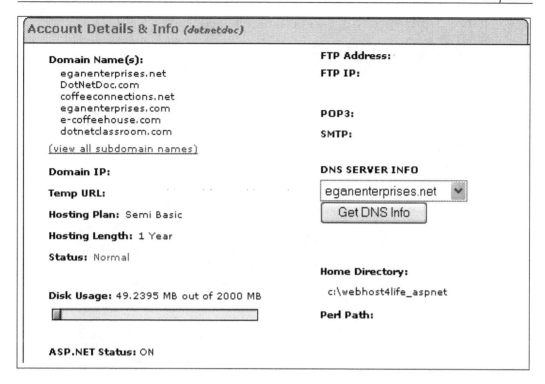

Once you set the DNS, you will need to wait a few days for it to propagate. On completing these tasks, you will be ready to set up your portal within DotNetNuke.

Creating a Parent Portal

In the previous chapter, we moved our local implementation of DotNetNuke to our hosting provider. Now we are going to create a parent portal from this installation. For this, log in as host and navigate to **Host | Portals.** This will bring up a list of the portals that have already been set up. To add another portal, access the context menu next to the **Portals** icon and select **Add New Portal.**

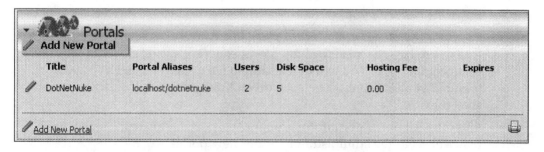

You will then be presented with the **Portal Setup** dialog box.

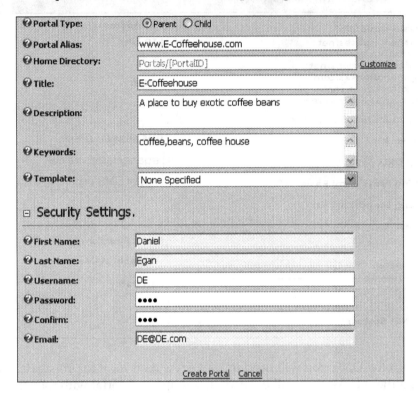

- Select the type of portal you want to create: In this instance we will, of course, be creating a **Parent** portal.

- Enter the portal alias: This is the website address of your portal (excluding the http://).

- **Home directory**: If desired, you can change the location where the framework will save portal-specific information. This includes skin and container files.

- Enter the name for your portal.

- Select a template for your portal: You can create templates for your portal so that when they are created, all the skins, containers, modules, and tabs will be created for you. You will find a sample file under the portals/default folder of your installation. Select **DotNetNuke**, which will create an empty shell for you.

- Enter the administrator information for this portal. This will create a user that will act as the administrator for this new portal.

- When finished, click on **Create Portal**.

This will create a new empty portal all ready for you to modify.

 As mentioned earlier in this chapter, in order to create a Parent Portal, you will need to make sure that a domain name has been purchased and that the DNS is pointed to the server hosting this parent portal. If this is not completed, the parent portal will not work.

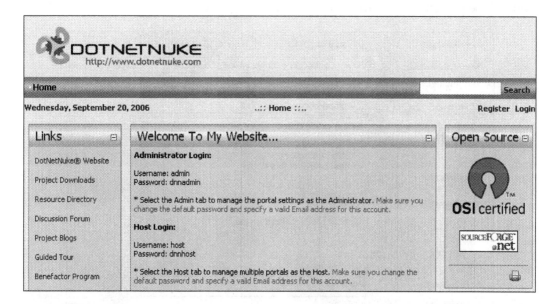

It is important to note that your new portal will use the default properties defined in the Host Settings module. Once the portal is created, these settings can be modified in the Admin Site Settings module.

Setting Up a Child Portal

Child portals, as opposed to parent portals, give you a way to create separate portals without having to set up separate domain names. For this, log in as host and navigate to **Host | Portals**. This will bring up a list of the portals that have already been set up. To add another portal, hover the cursor over the pencil icon next to the **Portals** icon and select **Add New Portal**.

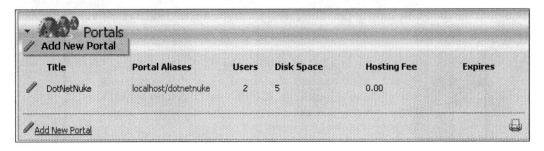

You will be presented with the **Portal Setup** dialog box:

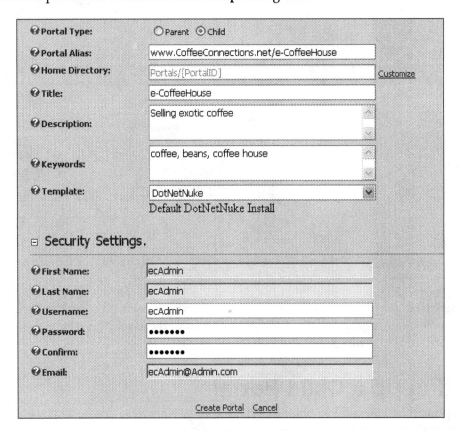

- Select the type of portal you want to create. In this instance, we will be creating a **Child** portal.

- Enter the portal alias. Since this is a child portal, it is run off a directory on you main site. When you select **Child** portal, it will fill in the name of your domain with a forward slash (/). Just add the directory name for your portal.

- Enter a title for your portal.

- Enter a description and key words for your portal.

- Select a template for your portal. You can create templates for your portals so that when they are created, all of the skins, containers, modules, and tabs will be created for you. You will find a sample file under the `portals/default` folder of your installation. Select **DotNetNuke**, which will create an empty shell for you.

- Enter the administrator information for this portal. This will create a user that will act as the administrator for this new portal.

- When finished click on **Create Portal**.

This will create a new empty portal all ready for you to modify.

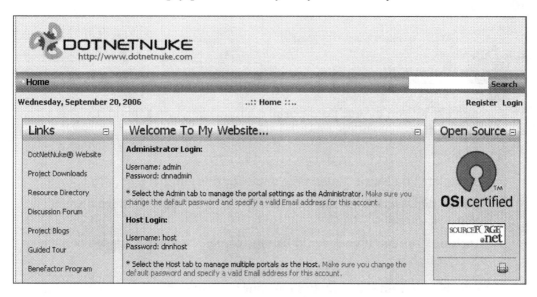

The new portal will use the default properties defined in the Host Settings module. Once the portal is created, these settings can be modified in the Admin Site Settings module.

Creating Portal Templates

In the previous examples, we created our sites using the default DotNetNuke template. While this is helpful if you want to create a site from scratch, you usually wouldn't want to have to add all of the common functionality you would like on your portal each and every time you create a new one. Fortunately, DotNetNuke makes creating a portal template easy.

When you previously created new portals by going to **Host | Portals**, you may have noticed a section called **Export Template** at the bottom.

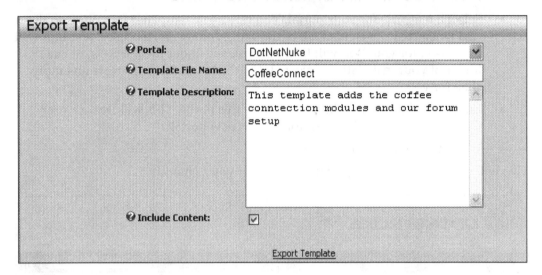

This section allows you to save your portal configuration into a template. This includes your menu navigation, modules, and module content.

- **Portal**: Just select the portal you would like to export.
- **Template File Name**: Enter a file name for this template.
- **Template Description**: Enter a description of the kind of information this template contains.
- **Include Content**: If you would like the content of the modules to be saved, check this box.

Click on the **Export Template** link to save your template.

The Portal Template Has Been Created to C:\DotNetNuke\Portals_default\CoffeeConnect.template

This will save your template into an XML-formatted file. If you would like to see the file that is created, navigate to the location presented on the screen. When setting up future portals, you can use this portal as a template.

Using the Site Wizard

The site wizard will allow you to customize your site by walking you through an easy-to-understand step-by-step process. To access this wizard, sign on as host and click on the **Wizard** icon in the top panel of the screen:

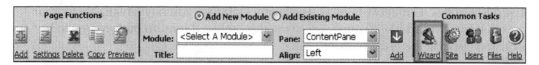

This will bring you to the first step in the site wizard. The first page asks you if you would like to apply a template to your site. If you did not do this when the site was set up, you can accomplish this now. If you already have content on your site, it will ask you how you want to deal with duplicate entries. For example, if you already have a Home page with modules and the template has a Home page with modules, how would you like to resolve this conflict? You have three choices:

- **Ignore**: This will ignore any items that already exist on your site.
- **Replace**: This will replace anything on your site with what is contained in the template.
- **Merge**: This will merge the content in the template with what is already on your site. This may produce multiple menu items or modules, but these can be deleted later.

Click on **Next** to proceed to the next screen in the wizard.

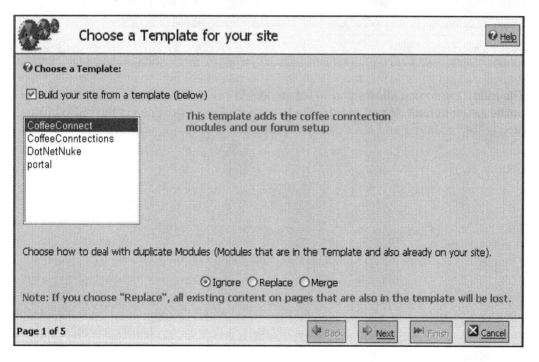

The following screen allows you to apply any skin that you have available to your portal. If you would like to apply a certain skin, select the radio button next to the skin and click on the **Next** button.

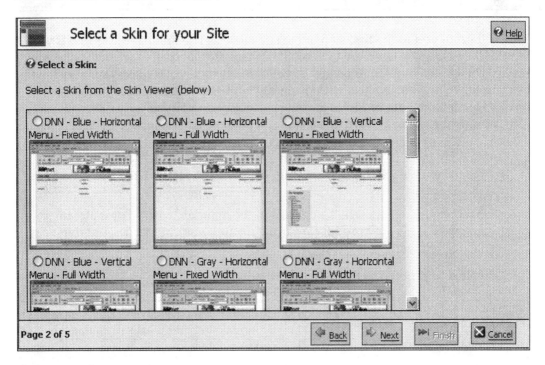

The following screen allows you to set any container that you have available to your portal as the default. If you would like to set a container skin, select the radio button next to the container and click on the **Next** button.

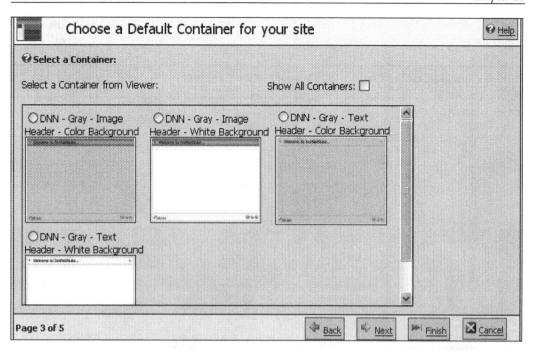

The following screen allows you to add a description and keywords for your portal. Click on the **Next** button to continue.

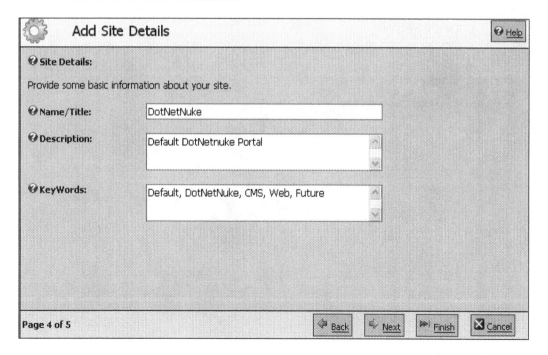

The last screen allows you to select the logo you would like to use for your site. In the default DotNetNuke skin, this would show up in the header of your portal.

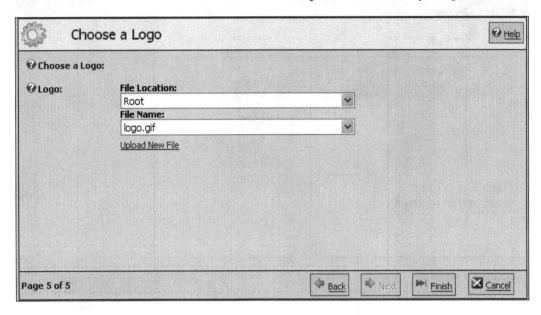

Click on the **Finish** button to save your settings.

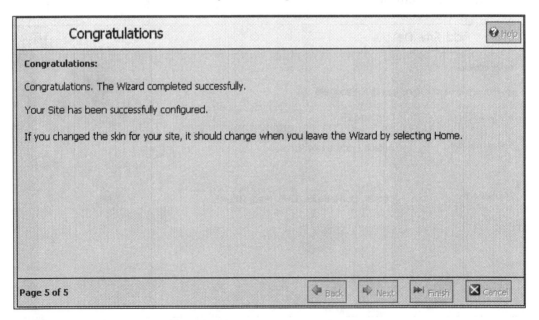

To view the changes, click on the **Home** menu item. Any changes that you made will now be reflected on your site.

Managing Multiple Portals

As the host user, you will have access to every portal you create. To manage your portals, you just need to navigate to the **Portals** page by going to **Host | Portals** from the main menu.

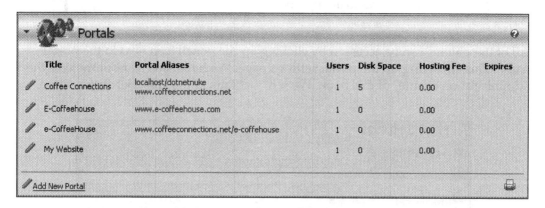

You can access each site by clicking on the **Portal Aliases** link or edit each site by clicking on the pencil icon next to the portal. You will notice that next to each portal there are columns for the following:

- **Users**: The number of users registered for the particular portal.

- **Disk Space**: Since each separate portal shares the same hosting environment, you can set the disk space allowed to each. This will limit the amount each admin will be able to upload to their particular site.

- **Hosting Fee**: If you are charging a hosting fee for each site, you can place that fee in this section.

- **Expires**: You can enforce the fees that you charge for each portal.

It is important to note that even though users of each portal are kept in the same database, they are only assigned to the portal that they registered on. In a default implementation of DotNetNuke, a user would have to register for *each* portal they would like to be a part of. If you need to manage users in a multi-portal environment, I suggest the ITSCS Manage Users PRO available on Snowcovered.com. It allows you to manage users from all portals as well as replicate user credentials to multiple portals.

All of these items can be accessed by clicking on the pencil icon next to the portal name. This will bring up the portal settings page. We have seen most of these in the administration chapter of this book. We will just look at the **Host Settings** section:

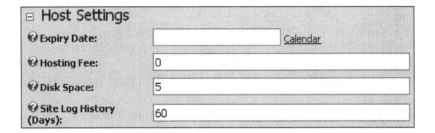

This is where you can set the information found on the Portals page. Only the superuser (Host) sign on is able to see all of the portals that have been created. The administrators of each portal will only be able to see the information related to their portal.

Summary

In this chapter, we learned how to create multiple portals that can all be hosted from one account. We have seen how to create and use templates, and how to use the **Site Wizard** to upgrade your site. We then finished this off by showing you how to manage these portals once they have been set up. Not only will this functionality allow you to create multiple portals, but since all of the information is stored in one database, backing them up is simple.

Index

Packt Open Source Project Royalties

When we sell a book written on an Open Source project, we pay a royalty directly to that project. Therefore by purchasing Building Websites with VB.NET and DotNetNuke 4, Packt will have given some of the money received to the DotNetNuke project.

In the long term, we see ourselves and you — customers and readers of our books — as part of the Open Source ecosystem, providing sustainable revenue for the projects we publish on. Our aim at Packt is to establish publishing royalties as an essential part of the service and support a business model that sustains Open Source.

If you're working with an Open Source project that you would like us to publish on, and subsequently pay royalties to, please get in touch with us.

Writing for Packt

We welcome all inquiries from people who are interested in authoring. Book proposals should be sent to authors@packtpub.com. If your book idea is still at an early stage and you would like to discuss it first before writing a formal book proposal, contact us; one of our commissioning editors will get in touch with you.

We're not just looking for published authors; if you have strong technical skills but no writing experience, our experienced editors can help you develop a writing career, or simply get some additional reward for your expertise.

About Packt Publishing

Packt, pronounced 'packed', published its first book "Mastering phpMyAdmin for Effective MySQL Management" in April 2004 and subsequently continued to specialize in publishing highly focused books on specific technologies and solutions.

Our books and publications share the experiences of your fellow IT professionals in adapting and customizing today's systems, applications, and frameworks. Our solution-based books give you the knowledge and power to customize the software and technologies you're using to get the job done. Packt books are more specific and less general than the IT books you have seen in the past. Our unique business model allows us to bring you more focused information, giving you more of what you need to know, and less of what you don't.

Packt is a modern, yet unique publishing company, which focuses on producing quality, cutting-edge books for communities of developers, administrators, and newbies alike. For more information, please visit our website: www.PacktPub.com.

GDI+ Custom Controls with Visual C# 2005

ISBN: 1-904811-60-4   Paperback: 272 pages

A fast-paced example-driven tutorial to building custom controls using Visual C# 2005 Express Edition and .NET 2.0.

1. Learn about custom controls and the GDI+

2. Walks through great examples like PieChart control

3. Customize and develop your own controls

Enhancing Microsoft Content Management Server with ASP.NET 2.0

ISBN: 1-904811-52-3   Paperback: 180 pages

Use the powerful new features of ASP.NET 2.0 with your MCMS Websites.

1. Get Microsoft Content Management Server Service Pack 2 up and running

2. Use the most exciting features of ASP.NET 2.0 in your MCMS development

Please visit **www.PacktPub.com** for information on our titles